With the Boys

With the Boys

Little League Baseball and Preadolescent Culture

89-999

Gary Alan Fine

The University of Chicago Press
Chicago and London

Gary Alan Fine, professor of sociology at the University of Minnesota, is the author of *Rumor and Gossip*, with Ralph Rosnow (1976); *Shared Fantasy: Role-Playing Games as Social Worlds* (1983); and *Talking Sociology* (1985).

The University of Chicago Press, Chicago 60637
The University of Chicago Press, Ltd., London
© 1987 by The University of Chicago
All rights reserved. Published 1987
Printed in the United States of America

96 95 94 93 92 91 90 89 88 87   5 4 3 2 1

Library of Congress Cataloging-in-Publication Data

Fine, Gary Alan.
  With the boys.

  Bibliography: p.
  Includes index.
  1. Little league baseball.   2. Baseball for
children—Social aspects.—United States.   I. Title.
GV880.5.F56   1987   796.357′62   86-16056
ISBN 0-226-24936-0
ISBN 0-226-24937-9 (pbk.)

To the boys

Contents

Contents

Preface

For three years I shared springs and summers with remarkable people: some of America's preadolescents. Their remarkableness derives, not from the fact that they are unusually insightful or articulate for their age, but from the fact that they are not. Like every group of children—all of us at one time—they constructed a social community and a common culture. This culture survived and flourished even while under the control of adults who attempted to suppress it.

This research project had a serendipitous origin. During the autumn of 1974, while a graduate student at Harvard, I prepared a proposal to the National Science Foundation for the funding of my doctoral dissertation a laboratory study of small groups. By late winter I learned the dissertation was to be funded; however, because of logistical problems the experimental groups could not be run until July.

This left four "empty" months. I felt that small-group research had been too confined to the psychological laboratory; as a result, researchers had neglected the *content* of group interaction. I believed it important to examine small groups in natural settings. At the time, the research problem I had set for myself seemed fairly well delineated: What social psychological factors influence the creation and dissemination of culture and how are these influences reflected in culture content?

The inspiration to examine Little League baseball teams seemed propitious. A Little League baseball team is a culture-producing group that has both task-oriented goals (winning baseball games, learning technical baseball skills) and socioemotional goals (having fun, making friends). In addition I enjoyed spending time with children, and the timing of the Little League season (from April until June in my first site) was perfect for this research.

I was fortunate to receive the immediate support of the president of the Beanville Little League, the first league I contacted. (All names of places and persons associated with Little League are pseudonyms.) He introduced me to the coaches and league officials, and his help contributed to the success of this year of research. Eventually the project was expanded to cover five leagues in three years, with two teams examined in each league and with the Beanville league examined during two successive years (a description of each locale is provided in appendix 3). Each year I sharpened and broadened my theoretical interests and refined my methodological skills. The five leagues and ten teams provide some basis for generalization, rare in participant-observation studies. I am aware of no other participant-observation study that has examined as many different social groups as intensively as this study.

Many people must be thanked for aiding this research. I've mentioned the help of the Beanville league president in inviting me to the league tryouts and introducing me to the adult coaches at the "draft." In each league, the league president enthusiastically supported this research, and this sponsorship was necessary, as new research bargains had to be struck each year with men and boys who had no particular reason for helping. On a day-to-day basis, coaches were vital in permitting the research to take the form that it did. Of the forty-two teams in the five leagues, only one coach refused to have his team participate in this research. Most of the other forty-one coaches were more helpful than I had the right to expect. I was always permitted to attend team meetings, sit in the dugout, ask questions, and generally make a nuisance of myself while these men were attempting the almost impossible task of teaching baseball skills, keeping order, and promoting team rapport. The requirements of confidentiality prohibit naming these gentlemen, but I do appreciate their special kindnesses. Likewise, many parents who might have treated this research with suspicion did not do so but provided insight on how the league looked from the grandstand and the home. While the focus of this research was not on parental behavior or attitudes towards Little League, this information was important for understanding the environment in which Little League games were organized.

Finally, I will always have a deep personal respect and fondness for my preadolescent friends and gratitude that they permitted me a second childhood long before it was due. Among several hundred preadolescents, some became special friends and key informants, and if this research adds to our knowledge, it is they who made it possible. Thank you, Rich, Wiley, Brad, Kip, Justin, Harry, Whitney, Hugh, Frank, Tom, Rod, and Hardy—but a few of my pseudonymous friends. Each of the players in his own way helped the research to be a success by answering questions or completing questionnaires, or just tolerating eavesdropping. As John Johnson (1975) well described, participant observation is grounded in personal relationships, and so the participant observer may feel that he is using his subjects, as I did at the time. My thank you is an inadequate apology to my friends.

Outside the social world of preadolescence and Little League baseball, I am grateful to three graduate students at the University of Minnesota—Harold Pontiff, Paul Roesti, and C. Steven West. Harry Pontiff was responsible for collecting all the data on the Maple Bluff Little League—questionnaires and field observations. His field notes are a model of clarity and richness of detail. I used his participant observation notes readily, although my own are still something of an enigma to me. Paul Roesti and Steve West conducted postseason interviews in the Sanford Heights and Bolton Park leagues in Minnesota with parents and players. Their ease of rapport was remarkable, and the data they collected provide an important complement to my own research. The data collected by Pontiff, Roesti, and West serve as a cross-check on my own observations, allowing me to correct some of the more obvious elements of my own observer bias.

Many colleagues have made important contributions to my thinking about the issues described in this book. Among these individuals are Alan Dundes, Roger Abrahams, Gregory Stone, Janet Harris, Jay Gubrium, Norman Denzin, Thomas Hood, Richard Mitchell, Harold Finestone, Pat Lauderdale, Elizabeth Tucker, Carl Couch, Steven Zeitlin, Donald Bird, Victor Marshall, Mark Granovetter, Harrison White, Ron Brieger, Ray Bradley, Joseph Galaskiewicz, Philip Nusbaum, James Leary, Barry Glassner, Jim Thomas, Michael Radelet, Lyle Hallowell, and Donna Eder. I appreciate their criticism and advice and (of course) absolve them from blame for any sound advice ignored or misapplied.

Sherryl Kleinman commented on drafts of much of this book. Her advice was often painfully accurate and has contributed immensely to the strengths of this book. I am particularly grateful to my dissertation advisor, Robert Freed Bales. It was important for me to have a dissertation advisor who willingly tolerated and encouraged the development of my ideas, even if they were somewhat distant from his own. While he steadfastly maintained his own view of social interaction and was candidly critical of my theoretical failings (*some* of which I don't consider to be failings), he encouraged me to present those conclusions that I thought to be correct, regardless of his own theoretical orientation. His concern was that I present whatever I believed (and could support) carefully, consistently, and vigorously. I value our discussions and disagreements.

My wife, Susan, somehow tolerated the fact that I was away from home six nights a week, three months a year, for three years. While she did not *always* accept this fact graciously, at least it was better than if I had been a merchant seaman. She hopes this research will make me a better father; I hope so, too.

Gloria DeWolfe typed most of this manuscript (including this paragraph), and no secretary could be better—and I would claim that even if she weren't typing this. If my writing has improved, as some friends note, it is because my "typing" has. I also thank Carol Gorski for making the diamonds described in the book sparkle.

The title of this book was the suggestion of Rich Jannelli, a Beanville player. I felt it captured the flavor of this research better than any title I could create. These are boys, developmentally and in terms of the colloquial use of "boys" to indicate male friends, particularly those interested in traditionally male activities. I take the blame for the contents of the book, but give Rich credit for the title.

Acknowledgments

Some material in this book is drawn from previously published articles, my own unless otherwise noted. Parts of the Introduction are excerpted from "Organized Baseball and Its Folk Equivalents: The Transition from Informal to Formal Control," in *Cultural Dimensions of Play, Games, and Sport*, edited by Bernard Mergen (Human Kinetics Publishers, 1986); parts of chapter 1 from "Team Sports, Seasonal Histories, Significant Events: Little League Baseball and the Creation of Collective Meaning," *Sociology of Sport Journal* 2 (1985): 219–313; parts of chapter 3 from Sherryl Kleinman and Gary Alan Fine, "Rhetorics and Action in Moral Organizations: Social Control of Little Leaguers and Ministry Students," *Urban Life* 8 (1979): 275–94, and from "Preadolescent Socialization through Organized Athletics: The Construction of Moral Meanings in Little League Baseball," in *Dimensions of Sport Sociology*, edited by March Krotee (Leisure Press, 1979); parts of chapter 5 from "The Natural History of Preadolescent Male Friendship Groups," in *Friendship and Social Relations in Children*, edited by Hugh Foot, Anthony J. Chapman, and Jean Smith (John Wiley & Sons Limited, 1980); also from "Friends, Impression Management, and Preadolescent Behavior," in *The Development of Children's Friendships*, edited by Steven R. Asher and John M. Gottman (Cambridge University Press, 1981); and also from "Rude Words: Insults and Narration in Preadolescent Talk," *Maledicta* 5 (1981): 51–68; parts of chapter 6 from "Small Groups and Culture Creation: The Idioculture of Little League Baseball Teams," *American Sociological Review* 44 (1979): 733–45; parts of chapter 7 from Gary Alan Fine and Sherryl Kleinman, "Rethinking Subculture: An Interactionist Analysis," *American Journal of Sociology* 85 (1979): 1–20; and from "Preadolescent Slang: Local, Regional, and National Speech Patterns among American Children," *Midwestern Journal of Language and Folklore* 39 (1980): 170–83; and parts of Appendix 2 from Gary Alan Fine and Barry Glessner, "Participant Observation with Children: Promises and Problems," *Urban Life* 8 (1979): 153–74; and from "Cracking Diamonds," in *Fieldwork Experience: Qualitative Approaches to Social Research*, edited by William B. Shaffir, Robert A. Stebbins, and Allan Turowetz (© 1980 by St. Martin's Press). I thank the publishers of these books and journals for permission to use the material cited.

Introduction

The tormented Earl of Gloucester moaned in *King Lear:* "As flies to wanton boys, are we to the gods; they kill us for their sport." These mordant lines may tell us more about the interests of boys than gods. Why do boys kill flies for their sport? Why, as Plutarch noted, do they throw stones at frogs; or why, as Swift depicted, do they pour salt on sparrows' tails? What are boys like, or, more to the point, what do boys do? While mountains of pages have been devoted to scientific, developmental studies of boys, very few researchers have actually spent time with them on their own turf.

My selected site was the world of sport—a male-dominated activity. For three years I spent springs and summers observing ten Little League baseball teams in five communities as they went through their seasons.[1] I observed at practice fields and in dugouts, remaining with the boys after games and arriving early to learn what their activities were like when adults were not present. As I came to know these boys better, I hung out with them outside the baseball setting, when they were "doing nothing." My specific goal is to describe and analyze how, through organized sport and through their informal activities surrounding this setting, preadolescent males learn to play, work, and generally be "men." What is the process by which rich veins of preadolescent male culture are developed? Much has been written about the development of sex roles, but these studies tend to occur in settings in which sex roles are formally supposed to be secondary (school, for example). In sport and in informal male activity, sex-role development and display is crucial—at least in the views of the participants. If we hope to understand how adult sex roles are shaped, we must observe the blossoming of these roles in childhood peer groups. Related to this concern with the developmet of the male role is an interest in the way adult males attempt to shape the development of preadolescent males. Most nonfamilial guardians of boys are women; yet, in sports, boys are taught by men, and these men (at least in Little League) see themselves as having specifically didactic roles. How do men attempt to teach values to preadolescent boys? Adults see Little League baseball as a distinctly moral endeavor, training boys to be upstanding citizens, much in the model of Boy Scouts and other adult-directed, youth-oriented programs (e.g., Macleod 1983). However, the fact that messages are transmitted doesn't mean they will be acquired in quite the way they have been taught. Thus, I examine moral socialization from the perspective of adults and of preadolescents.

While other settings—the family, the school—may weigh more heavily than leisure in preadolescent socialization, the distinctive maleness of these leisure settings and their voluntary character makes such locales particularly significant for seeing how preadolescent culture actually develops in its "rich and dirty" fullness. I make no claim to have compiled a complete ethnography of childhood. My observations are seasonal (spring and summer), deal primarily with male children,[2] and are limited to a relatively narrow range of activities. Yet, by observing their sport and leisure, I have learned a great deal about a small portion of boys' lives.

In this analysis I attempt to avoid being heavily moralistic. Some of the information presented will, properly, be distressing to many adults. Those who disdain competitive sports will surely be disturbed by some of the features of Little League baseball. Those who wish for a world of "moral" children will be concerned by the moral laxity among these "good boys." Those who hope for a nonsexist society will be dismayed by the overt sexism of these preadolescents gorwing up in the late 1970s. The issue of what to do with this culture is an issue largely left for others. Although I shall return to this concern in the conclusion, my focus is analytic, not ameliorative.

Behind these issues of preadolescent culture is another agenda: understanding the dynamics of cultural creation. By examining Little League baseball teams and preadolescents generally, it should be possible to understand part of the dynamic process by which all cultures are developed by means of small-group cultures (idiocultures, Fine 1979b, and subcultures, Fine and Kleinman 1979). My perspective is interactionist. That is, I argue that meaning is ultimately grounded in interaction and I take a social-behaviorist approach to culture. Boys have the power, within constraints, to shape the world to their choosing. The interplay between these constraints and their freedom is of particular interest. Further, cultural traditions are developed within social worlds. As a result, it is important to understand how the fact that boys are organized and organize themselves in small groups affects their behavior and culture. In this perspective, culture serves as a mediator among external forces that constrain the group, the internal resources of the group (e.g., personality and knowledge), and the specific behaviors of boys. Culture makes structural forces concrete. Further, the individual preadolescent boy is part of a vast subcultural network stretching through his community and throughout American society—a subculture coterminous with preadolescent communication channels (see Shibutani 1955). Beyond the specific claims I make for understanding the dimensions of preadolescent culture, I suggest techniques by which all cultures can be analyzed—by seeing small groups connected to each other in networks of groups, producing, through diffusion, a "culture."

Baseball: An American Symbol

Because of the game's symbolic centrality in our culture, baseball seems a particularly apt setting for examining what it means to be an American boy. Baseball, it is claimed, captures crucial apsects of the American spirit and American values as does no other sport or leisure activity. In the words of Jacques Barzun, "Whoever wants to know the heart and mind of America had better learn baseball" (quoted in Novak 1976, 63). As Tristram Coffin has recognized, "The picture of the father shoving a glove and bat into the crib of his first son is an American cliche simply because it symbolizes something typical about American hopes and fears" (1971, 3). Roger Angell calls our national pastime "rich and various in structure and aesthetics and emotion" (Angell 1972, 6). The symbolic significance of baseball to American (male) culture is well captured by Thomas Wolfe:

> Baseball . . . is . . . really a part of the whole weather of our lives, of the thing that it is our own, of the whole fabric, the million memories of America. For example, in the memory of almost everyone of us, is there anything that can evoke spring—the first fine days of April—better than the sound of the ball smacking into the pocket of the big mitt, the sound of the bat as it hits the horsehide: for me, at any rate, and I am being literal and not rhetorical—almost everything I know about spring is in it—the first leaf, the jonquil, the maple tree, the smell of grass upon your hands and knees, the coming into flower of April. And is there anything that can tell more about

an American summer than, say, the smell of the wooden bleachers in a small town baseball park, that resinous, sultry and exciting smell of old dry wood? (quoted in Guttman 1978, 101).

What there is about baseball that makes it such a central symbol of *American* experience—at least for males—is uncertain, although several explanations have been offered for its symbolic centrality. Voigt (1974b) has suggested that baseball is a symbol of nationalism, although this does no more than restate its symbolic centrality. Others point to baseball as reflecting a rural, white, Anglo-Saxon Protestant myth—"contract theory in ritual form" (Novak 1976, 59), explicate baseball's symbolism as a ritual exemplification of the Freudian primal horde scenario (Petty 1967), or describe the baseball fan's quantifiable, mathematically precise attempts to gain mastery over his world (Guttmann 1978; Angell 1972; Coover 1972). I argue that baseball's importance is not in what it "really" means, but that it provides the rhetorical basis for many critiques of American society.

The World of Little League Baseball

Although Little League baseball is the best-known and most successful youth sports program in the United States, it was not the first. In 1903, the first adult-sponsored youth sports program in America was inaugurated in New York City when the Public Schools Athletic League was formed; by 1910 some 150,000 children participated (Martens 1978, 6). Other programs followed, sponsored by both schools and communities. Such programs have always been controversial, and the development of private, community youth leagues resulted in part from negative attitudes among professional recreation directors and educators during the 1930s (Berryman 1975). These professionals believed that highly competitive sports harmed preadolescent development, and so they did not create professionally directed programs. This disapproval of preadolescent sports, coupled with a growing public interest in sports, gave rise to numerous privately run preadolescent athletic programs outside the control of educators and recreation directors.

Of these private organizations, none is larger than Little League baseball and none has received as much media attention. Little League Baseball, Inc., is both a cultural institution and a big business. In 1983 Little League Baseball, Inc., reported total assets of over $10.2 million and total expenses of $3.9 million (Little League

Baseball, Inc., 1984). The figure does *not* include the budget for each of the individual leagues. As of 1983 there were fifteen thousand chartered leagues in thirty-seven countries and more than two million children involved. In the Little League program itself, there were (in 1983) about seven thousand Little Leagues with over forty-eight thousand teams. There are well over half a million Little Leaguers. In addition to the preadolescent baseball program (ages nine through twelve), the organization also runs Senior League Baseball (for boys aged thirteen to fifteen), Big League Baseball (ages sixteen to eighteen), and a softball program.

The financial significance of Little League baseball can be seen in data from one league—the Bolton Park Arrowhead Little League. The Arrowhead League is an average-sized league (six Major League teams, fourteen Minor League teams in two age groups) located in a middle-class suburb. The league uses city-owned land on which to play and practice in exchange for keeping up the field and facilities for the community. During one season in the late seventies, the league spent nearly $5,000 on equipment, field maintenance, new uniforms, umpires' salaries ($10 for each of two umpires per game), concession-stand refreshments, and payments to the national organization for affiliation and insurance. Its income was derived from registration fees ($10–$25 per family, depending on the number of participating children), local business sponsorships, and revenues from the concession stand. If $5,000 can be accepted as a rough average, then local leagues spend somewhat over $50 million per year.

This $50 million is an attractive market for American corporations. The *Little League Baseball Catalog of Equipment and Supplies* is a forty-page, full-color brochure that includes ads from such Fortune 1,000 corporate giants as Alcoa, Burlington Industries, AMF, and Reynolds Aluminum. Local leagues also maintain connections with businesses and government agencies through team sponsorships by automobile dealers, fast-food restaurants, hardware stores, factories, and police and fire departments. Little League is often a central part of the community's organizational network, and frequently the mayor or members of the city council are present on opening day and at other important ceremonies.

Little League (like the Boy Scouts of America) operates under official federal sponsorship. It was awarded a federal charter in 1964, the only youth sports organization so honored. This charter makes all revenue to the Little League tax-exempt, since the organization is a quasi-governmental agency. The charter also requires that Little League must shape its mission to the needs of the United States government (particularly in dealing with foreign leagues), hardly a serious constraint for this moralistic and patriotic organization, and an annual financial and philosophical report must be filed with the Judiciary Committee of the House of Representatives.[3]

Despite its current size, Little League baseball grew from humble beginnings in the sleepy Pennsylvania lumbering and manufacturing town of Williamsport; the league was the brainchild of a local lumber company employee, Carl Stotz.[4] Stotz claims the original seed for Little League baseball was planted when, as a youth, he stood in the outfield while other players argued whether a runner was safe or out. During these boring interludes, Stotz promised himself that someday he would organize a baseball team with adult supervision where such bickering would be eliminated! Later, the idea reemerged when Stotz's two young nephews, Harold and Jimmy Gehron, were not allowed to play with a group of older boys. Stotz reportedly said to the boys, "How would you kids like to play on a regular team, with uniforms, a brand new ball for each game, and bats you could really swing?" (Turkin 1954, 6). The responses were enthusiastic, and Stotz began the arduous task of finding sponsors for the league: "[Stotz] spent the fall and winter seeking sponsors. In all he contacted 58 individuals and firms. The 58th contact was with Floyd A. Mutchler of Lycoming Dairy Farms who uttered the fateful words that were to start Little League on its way. I quote those words: 'We'll go along with the boys'" (Original League, Inc., n.d., 5).

Other sponsors were soon lined up, and league play began. This "organizational myth"[5] (Meyer and Rowan 1977) or "saga" (Clark 1970) provided a basis for the belief in the altruism of American business enterprise, the importance of hard work, and the power of a dream to overcome obstacles (see also Paxton 1949, 138–39). Because of organizational bitterness toward Stotz, the history has been rewritten, and this account does not appear in current Little League publications, but it was frequently cited during the late 1940s and 1950s.

After obtaining the support of local businesses, Stotz and a few friends organized three teams for the 1939 season. Slowly they began to construct a baseball diamond with fences, scoreboards, and bleachers. The goal was to allow preadolescents to play with the trappings of the adult leagues. In 1942 a permanent field was completed, and six years later enough leagues had been established so that a national tournament could be held (Lock Haven, Pennsylvania, beat St. Petersburg, Florida). In order to provide support for the 1948 tournament (later called the World Series), Stotz enlisted the aid of the United States Rubber Company. U.S. Rubber was pleased with the publicity it received and made a commitment to support the organization. Little League baseball was rapidly becoming a business, and in 1950 Little League was incorporated in New York State with $100,000 in assets from U.S. Rubber.

In retrospect, the tensions in the organization are evident. Little League had to decide whether it should remain a somewhat disorganized, romantic, altruistic venture or whether it should be run as a corporation. Was it to be a small-town crusader's dream or an efficient, streamlined business? In 1955, with almost 4,000 leagues established, the issue came to a head. Stotz, then the commissioner of Little League baseball, was "separated" from his organization.[6] At one point in the struggle, the Williamsport sheriff guarded the headquarters doors to ensure that the new corporate officers could not set up a new headquarters with the assets of the league. In legal action, the corporation, headed by Peter J. McGovern, a former publicity officer with U.S. Rubber, won, and Stotz bitterly called the organization a "Frankenstein" because of its commercialism (*Nation* May 25, 1964, 520).

The banishment of Stotz tarnished the organization's image and forced the league to rely on broadly stated moralistic principles rather than on an organizational history that had become unusable. Despite this, the league continued to grow rapidly to its current status as a multimillion-dollar organization. In my analysis, local leagues must be seen in this context, as branches of a large bureaucratic organization.

The World of Preadolescence

What are preadolescent males like?[7] Who is this creature inhabiting the twilight zone between the perils of the Oedipus complex and the *Stürm und Drang* of puberty? Developmental psychologists, though they do not agree precisely on which features distinguish preadolescence from those periods that bracket it, recognize that the period is more than a way station to puberty, more than a transition between two important stages of development.

Fritz Redl cleverly suggested that preadolescence is the period in which "the nicest children begin to behave in the most awful way" (Redl 1966, 395). This pithy description captures something basic about preadolescents—their "split personality," or, more accurately, the fact that by preadolescence a finely honed sense of presentation of self has developed (Fine 1981a). By preadolescence, the boy is part of several social worlds—same-sex groups, cross-sex interaction, school, and family life. Each of these settings requires a different standard of behavior. The "niceness" and "awful" behavior mentioned by Redl can perhaps be seen as referring to the child's behavior in front of parents and friends. Because these two social worlds are not entirely segregated, parents are all too aware of boys' awfulness. The conflct derives from the fact that the preadolescent has neither the right nor the ability to keep these two spheres of social life separate. When removed from peers, juveniles may be sweet, even considerate, and sometimes tender. Yet, placed in a social situation in which there is no need to be on one's "best behavior" and given situational constraints that militate against "proper" behavior, awfulness may be expressed through vindictiveness, aggressive sexuality, prejudice, and hostility (see Whiting and Whiting 1975). These are "good boys" engaging in "dirty play."

Friendship is particularly characteristic of this period, and these social ties may take precedence over relations of kin. The parent-peer cross-pressures frequently examined in adolescence originate in preadolescence, when preadolescents realize that peers and parents have markedly different expectations. While the outcome of peer interaction is generally concordant with adult-child interaction (Hartup 1970), in many specific activities and expressions it is not.

The informal social structure of preadolescence is based on two friendship institutions: the chum and the gang (Fine 1980c)—institutions largely outside the aegis of parents. Harry Stack Sullivan (1953, 227) emphasizes the crucial role of the single chum in development: "In the company of one's chum, one finds oneself more and more able to talk about things which one had learned, during the juvenile era, not to talk about. This relatively brief phase of preadolescence, if it is experienced, is probably rather fantastically valuable in salvaging one from the effects of unfortunate accidents up to then."

The chum is someone one can turn to in the otherwise tumultuous period of preadolescence. On the other hand, Furfey (1927) has termed preadolescence "the Gang Age," and the moniker is suitable. Puffer (1912, 7) exaggerates when he claims "the boy's reaction to his gang is neither more nor less reasonable than the reaction of a mother to her baby, the tribesman to his chief, or the lover to his sweetheart." Fully 80 percent of Crane's (1942) sample of Australian male college students recalled belonging to gangs during their primary-school days. Although other studies (e.g., Wolman 1951) report lower figures, many youths do hang out with gangs or groups.

The child must learn to trust and be sensitive to another person (the chum) and must acquire appropriate social poise in a collective setting (the gang). Chums and gangs provide supportive settings in which these aspects of socialization can be mastered and in which fear of failure is minimized.

Research Settings

The data I report on are based on participant observation in five communities. While these sites are not representative, they do reflect a range of middle-class American communities. Like the Little League program itself, the leagues studied underrepresent rural children, urban children, poor children, black children, and Hispanic children. With the exception of one league located in a neighborhood that lies within the political boundaries of St. Paul, Minnesota (but which is hard to distinguish from a suburban community), each league is located in a suburb. One league is lower-middle-class, one is somewhat more rural than the others, and two are more wealthy than average; however, each represents the broad American middle-class life-style. Further details of these settings and the data collected can be found in Appendix 3; a brief discussion is included here. Those readers not concerned with the precise settings may wish to skip this section.

Beanville

The first league studied was the Beanville Little League, located in an upper-middle-class suburb of Boston. The Beanville Little League consisted of three leagues, each with four teams of about fifteen players each. The league played three games simultaneously on Monday through Thursday evenings, beginning at 6:00 P.M.; six games were played on Sunday afternoons (three at 1:00 P.M. and three at 3:00 P.M.). Each team played all others in its league four times and the eight teams in the two other leagues once, for a total of twenty games. As in all Little Leagues, games lasted six innings. Games in Beanville were relatively casual, and winning at all costs was not emphasized.

In choosing teams in each league, I used two basic criteria: (1) that I was accepted by the coach and the players, and (2) that the teams seemed, at the beginning of the season, to provide an interesting contrast in athletic skills, coaching styles, or player personnel. In Beanville both factors led to my choice of the Rangers and the Angels in the Beanville Central League. I became friendly with both coaches during the preseason tryouts, and I quickly developed tentative friendships with some of their players.

Coaches and players predicted the Rangers would have little difficulty in winning their division because of their excellent coaching and players. Their coach, Donny Shaunessey, was the only coach in the Beanville Little League who was not a father of a player; rather, his younger brother played on the Rangers (Donny was in his early twenties).

The Angels were expected to finish last. Will Raskin, the coach of the Angels, was a novice in the league, only having coached younger children in the informal baseball program. The previous coaches of the Angels had been unsatisfactory—one had yelled at everyone within earshot, and the other reportedly attended games while drunk. Will, while admired for his decency, was considered somewhat odd in that he refused on principle to have his son (a fine ball player) on his team. Most adults felt that the twelve-year-olds on the Angels were weak ballplayers and that Will had selected inexperienced ten-year-olds to rebuild the team.

During the first half of the season, the teams performed as expected: the Rangers were well out in front, and the Angels performed poorly. During the second half of the season, the situation changed somewhat: the Rangers came in second during the second half, although they had the best season record and won the play-off with the Central League White Sox. The Angels still compiled a losing record, but came in third, ahead of the Astros.

The following year, while studying the Hopewell Little League, I returned for one or two days a week to follow these two teams in order to gain a longitudinal sense of cultural development and stability. This year the Angels, because of Raskin's drafting and training of young players the previous year, finished first; the Rangers, who had a new coach (an elderly man who was not energetic at teaching baseball skills) and who had lost most of their best players from the previous year, finished third with a losing record.

Hopewell

Hopewell is an exurban township located in the south-central part of Rhode Island outside the Providence metropolitan area. The Hopewell Little League, probably the best-organized league of those observed, consisted of eight Major League teams with thirteen players each. Each Major League team played two weekday evenings at 6:00 P.M. for seven weeks, playing every other team twice. The League was more competitive and exhibited a higher caliber of play than any other league.

The two teams examined in Hopewell—Sharpstone and Transatlantic Industries—had been very successful the previous year. That year these two teams battled each other in the playoff for the league championship, which TI eventually won. Because of its returning players, Sharpstone was considered the team to beat, although many felt that TI would be respectable competition. These two teams were chosen for observation because both were expected to be strong in the league standings; this choice allowed me to observe the effects of different personnel on team culture and the effects of specific events on the teams. Sharpstone was coached by two young physical-education majors at the local university, Peter Chadbourne and Dave Hundley, who were coaching as training for future professional appointments in children's athletics. Of all the coaches I observed, these two young men probably knew most about the mechanics of coaching, and because of their age they were able to develop an easy, joking relationship with their players off the field. They had coached Sharpstone the previous year and been the assistant coaches two years before.

The coach of TI was more conventional in that he was coaching because of his son, an eleven-year-old. Fred Turner had coached TI for several years and was generally regarded as a good coach, a belief attested to by the success of his teams. Unlike Peter and Dave, Fred did not have a close, joking relationship with those on his team, but he clearly enjoyed teaching the boys, and they responded with warmth and respect. Most players on both Sharpstone and TI considered their own coaches the best in the league.

Both Sharpstone and TI proved to be outstanding teams, and they battled for first place. At the end of the season TI (with a record of 12–2) nosed out Sharpstone (with a record of 11–3) for first place in the league. In the four-team postseason playoff, Sharpstone won, and TI was beaten in the semifinal round.

Sanford Heights

Sandford Heights is a suburb of Minneapolis, located about twenty-five miles from downtown. The suburb is largely homogeneous—primarily lower-middle-class and middle-class. Sandford Heights is the least prestigious of the five communities studied. For purposes of Little League (and other sports), Sanford Heights is divided into two districts with two separate Little League organizations. I studied the Sanford Heights Northern League, which consisted of seven teams of thirteen players each. Games were played on Monday through Saturday nights at 6:30 P.M. with another game on Saturday at 3:30 P.M. Each team played eighteen games during the season, three against every other team, with one to three games each week. As in Hopewell, the residents took Little League quite seriously, and attendance was higher than at other leagues. More emphasis was placed on wining in Sanford Heights than in the other leagues studied, with the exception of Hopewell.

The two teams selected had quite different expectations for the season. The Dodgers, second in the league and the winners of the Brooklyn Center American Classic tournament the previous season, expected to finish in first place. Many of their best players were returning, and the Dodgers had acquired an outstanding twelve-year-old when his father decided to become the assistant coach of the team. Doug Riley, the coach of the Dodgers, was one of the most respected coaches in the league and, despite a gruff exterior, was well liked and respected by his players. The Dodgers did not live up to their expectations, finishing in third place (11 – 7), but they reached the semifinals in the Richfield Invitational Tournament.

The Giants were not expected to be successful. Their coach, Paul Castor, was inexperienced and did not have much time to hold practices. Indeed, the only reason he was coaching at all was that the Giant coaches had suddenly decided not to coach. Castor was not chosen until after the tryouts, and the new players on the Giants team were selected by a league administrator. Although Castor was competent, his lack of time and experience caused dissatisfaction among the Giants, as did the fact that some players believed he played his ten-year-old son more than he should have. The Giants had a losing record, finishing the season at 8 – 10. The following year, when the league needed to decrease the number of teams from seven to six because of fewer players, the Giants were disbanded, and their returning players were distributed to other teams.

Bolton Park

The Arrowhead Little League is open to children from three St. Paul suburbs: the southern half of Bolton Park and the small suburbs of Wescott and Urban Glen (I refer to the league as Bolton Park in my notes). These communities are similar to Beanville in being upper-middle-class suburbs. The league consisted of six teams with fourteen players each. Each team played an eighteen-game schedule with two games each week. Games were scheduled at 6:30 P.M. Monday through Friday and at 9:30 A.M. on Saturday mornings. During a week, a team will play one opponent twice—once as the home team and once as "visitors." This increases team rivalries during critical weeks in which the better teams play. Despite this, the general atmosphere in the league is decidedly less competitive than in either Sanford Heights or Hopewell.

In no league was a team more certain to be unsuccessful than were the Red Sox. They had only won three games the previous year, and their returning twelve-year-olds were an inexperienced and awkward group. Their coach, though well-meaning and likable, had curious ideas about baseball strategy (sliding into first base, for example) and found it difficult to communicate even his more conventional notions to his team. His assistant coach, another nice man, was little more successful. Predictions of the Red Sox's success were accurate: the team was 2–16 for the season, only beating the two other weak teams in the league and losing one game by the embarrassing score of 36–4.

The team expected to finish first in the league was the Orioles. Like the Sanford Heights Dodgers, this was a team filled with talented twelve-year-olds, coached by a smart baseball man. Though the Orioles were successful, finishing in a tie for second (12–6), they did not show the power and consistency expected from them.

Maple Bluff

The final research site was Maple Bluff, an upper-middle-class area of St. Paul, Minnesota. Despite being located within the city limits, the area is decidedly suburban in tone. This league was studied by my graduate research assistant, Harold Pontiff. Of all the leagues, Maple Bluff was the least organized, and its rules were most at odds with the official Little League rules, particularly in regard to drafting players and the composition of teams (see Appendix 3 for details). The league limited eligibility to eleven- and twelve-year-olds. Also, players were assigned to new teams each year rather than remaining with their previous team. The league had nine teams, with each team playing all others twice. Games started at 6:30 P.M. on weekday evenings.

Because of the lack of continuity on Maple Bluff teams and the large number of new players, it was difficult to predict the performances of teams. The two teams chosen for intensive observation, the Pirates and the White Sox, were selected in part because of the coaches' different coaching styles. Phil Conklin, the coach of the Pirates, was a no-nonsense coach who had considerable experience (sixteen years) in coaching Little League baseball teams and knew how to teach players fundamental skills and discipline. While he was respected and even liked by his players, he did not attempt to maintain a relationship of equality with them. Assisting him was his teenage son Terry, who, while friendlier with the players, also was somewhat distant and strict.

The coaches of the Maple Bluff White Sox, Bruce Silverstein and Mitch Ashton (both fathers of players on their team), were much more easygoing and maintained teasing relationships with the boys. While they were not as experienced and did not require the same intensity of team spirit as did the Conklins, they were liked by their players and generally respected.

The outcome of the season was that the Pirates took first place with an impressive record (13–3); the White Sox, a team that played in spurts, finished at exactly .500 (8–8).

As can be recognized from this quick sketch of the five sites, the leagues differed in details. Despite these differences, the competitive baseball structure was much alike. Players were chosen for teams that played several times a week for two to three months. During this time the players got to know each other, met many of those they were playing against, and came in contact with numerous adults (coaches, umpires, parents) in roles of authority.

1

Little League and the Adult Organization
of Child's Play

Both critics and proponents agree that Little League baseball requires firm guidance of children. Although preadolescent sportsmen are not mere pawns strategically moved by their coaches, their behaviors are significantly constrained by adult desires. Many aspects of Little League baseball are structured by the demands and claims of adults—coaches, umpires, and parents—and this is where I start my discussion of preadolescent sport. I shall analyze the provisioning of resources, the structure of the setting, the formal rules of Little League baseball, and the position of adults in the game. Although Little League baseball is "play," it is play of a special sort—as similar to organized sport as to free-form activity.

Resources

Organized sport is not merely activity; it is situated activity. Indeed, most if not all human activity requires resources to permit it to occur properly. The more "organized" an activity, the more resources are required to bring it off. Adult-run preadolescent baseball leagues require an impressive array of provisions for all parties to be satisfied. These resources are largely gathered, organized, and dispersed by adults, with preadolescents having relatively little say in what should be done. Each league had an adult board of directors that oversaw its running and was charged with solving problems. Although these boards were composed differently in each league (some comprised all the coaches; some, committee chairs), in no league did players (or even ex-players) have a representative. No one was charged to speak for the boys. In each league it was assumed (no doubt correctly) that adults had the interests of the boys at heart, and further, it was assumed the adults and boys would have the same perspectives on what should be done, and when they didn't the adults were correct.

A key task in each league was to ensure the proper distribution of personnel. Some mechanism was needed to assign boys to teams and to see that these assignments were equal in number and relatively equal in age and ability. Since most leagues desire stable teams from year to year (except in Maple Bluff, where teams were picked anew each year), players on a team one year remained on that team until they reached age thirteen, when they were assigned to a league for older boys; this meant that some teams were likely to remain strong from year to year. Several leagues, recognizing this, used the model from professional sports in which the team with the worst record the previous year picked first in the draft. This implies a belief that teams in Little League should be relatively equal in ability. Determining the ability of players is, however, not an easy task. To this end, each league organized a tryout at which all preadolescent aspirants had to perform. At these occasions, organized and run by adults, every player had the opportunity to bat a pitched ball (thrown by either a veteran pitcher or an adult) and to catch a few balls hit or thrown toward him. As in any audition, the boy was "on stage" for a few minutes; what an adult could learn from this display was decidedly limited. Fortunately for coaches, this information could be bolstered by biographical material about the child, including reports from peers, and scouting information if the child had played on a Minor League team. Different coaches, of course, look for different attributes in making their judgments. The tryouts were designed to provide enough information so that coaches at the draft could choose boys to equalize their teams.

At the draft, coaches took turns choosing new boys for their teams. Most leagues had a rule that any team could have only a certain number of twelve-year-olds (typically eight of thirteen); this, too, was designed to ensure some measure of equity.

Of course, players were not the only resources to be provided. Each team needed at least one coach. This was by no means easy to achieve, as being a coach was perceived as demanding, both temporally and emotionally. At times, gentle pressure was required to recruit enough coaches. Then an informal system of socialization prevented these men from taking their tasks too seriously or not seriously enough. Occasionally this socialization did not work, and men were not invited back the following year—usually by their being "cooled out" rather than by being explicitly "dismissed." In addition the league had to recruit and reward umpires, grounds keepers, scorekeepers, announcers, and refreshment-stand operators. Each league handled this challenge differently, but each had to make decisions about obtaining this human capital. Since each league had a tradition on which to build, these decisions tended to be taken for granted, but this doesn't diminish the fact that decisions were necessary.

The Little League organization is tied into a network of other social institutions: schools, churches, families, governments, businesses. Although one rarely thinks of these other social institutions while boys play, they have their effects. One way in which the presence of these institutions is taken into account is through the timing of games and practices. Little League games are timed so as not to interfere with regular school or church time. With the exception of the Beanville League, leagues do not play on Sundays. The Beanville League, which schedules games on Sunday afternoons, is technically in violation of the official Little League rules. Fathers are not expected to alter their work schedules to coach their sons or to see them play. The integrity of the family is also supported by rules giving coaches the right to have their sons on their teams and (typically) keeping brothers together on the same team.

Businesses and government agencies are often approached for legitimacy, money, and other support. Many leagues invite local politicians to make an address or throw out the first ball on opening day. The warm symbolism proves to be appealing for both the politician and the league. Leagues frequently deal with local parks or recreational departments to ensure that they can use public land, either paying for it or agreeing to be involved with upkeep or improvements. On occasion, fire departments or police departments sponsor Little League teams. Likewise, local businesses are often approached to sponsor a team or to place advertisements in the league program, on the field itself, or on the back of players' uniforms. Local newspapers enthusiastically report the doings of these preadolescent sportsmen. As befits this patriotic, moralistic organization, close ties to government and business are seen as eminently justifiable. Further, they help provide subsidies so that individual parents need not spend as much on the material objects that Little Leagues need to function—bats, balls, bases, first-aid kits. Little Leagues are too large and require too much organization to permit the casual provisioning of resources found in informal games. One estimate (from Bolton Park in the late 1970s) was that it took $5,000 to run the league (and minor leagues) for a year. This suggests that the structure of the league cannot be entirely informal, no matter the implication of the rhetoric that children's sport should just be play.

Setting

The physical environment of any activity introduces both physical and social constraints. The physical constraints—such as not being able to run to catch a long fly ball through a chain-link fence—are very real (as players who have unintentionally attempted that feat can attest) but are generally sociologically uninteresting. Of more significance is the social control that the adult-selected physical setting imposes.

Little League diamonds encourage the involvement of parents and peer spectators. All five leagues had grandstands situated near the side of the field for the convenience of those observing the game.[1] Three of the leagues (Sanford Heights, Bolton Park, and Maple Bluff) maintained concession stands to cater to those in attendance. Loudspeaker systems in three leagues (Hopewell, Sanford Heights, and Maple Bluff) also indicated that the environment was structured for the benefit of the fans. These public-address systems were used during the game to inform onlookers of who was playing, as presumably the game would have been less enjoyable as a spectator sport if the players were nameless and not individuals with histories, positions, and records. This social organization of Little League is both a cause and a result of the audience being seen as almost as important as the players. Little League games are organized as *performance* rather than play.

The playing arena, although ostensibly designed for the enjoyment, safety, and skills of the players, is arranged so that spectators can watch the game in comfort. The field is a staging area for a dramatic performance—with a front state (the field), a back stage (dugouts), and seating for an audience (grandstands). While this arrangement may appear to be a miniature version of professional sports stadia, the two are not fully comparable. The Little League field is smaller and shorter than the adult diamond (sixty rather than ninety feet between bases). In addition, because of the proximity of the spectators to the action and because of the small social distance between the spectators and the participants, the impact of this setting is markedly different from that in our concrete colosseums.

In professional baseball the only sensory contact between the fan and the player is visual. A person seated in the grandstand cannot overhear the players in the field. Indeed, one can hardly decipher their emotions except when acted broadly (thus, baseball umpires are taught to use broad theatrical gestures in making judgment calls). In Little League baseball, the physical proximity of spectators to the game makes emotions visible, and the conversations of players can be heard. Spectators see players' emotions, not only because preadolescents are less constrained in their public performances, but also because they are more visually accessible.

This feature of the environment also applies to the spectators. Professional-baseball fans are an undistinguishable mass—typically not seen or heard as individuals—and as a result can get away with acting in ways that would be embarrassing if they were publicly identified. This anonymity does not exist in Little League baseball because of proximity and personal relationships—as the frequent criticism directed at parents attests.

The reality of Little League as a public spectacle means that the condition of the field is salient—it contributes to the satisfaction of the spectator. The field should duplicate the professional arena in its carefully manicured grass, straight, freshly limed foul lines, and newly turned base paths. One of the major problems with which adult officials must deal is grounds keeping. In some leagues (Bolton Park, Sanford Heights, Hopewell) adolescents receive a nominal wage to maintain the field; in others, parents or coaches "volunteer." The quality of this work is critically commented upon by the adults involved, although the condition of the field is of less significance to the players. One Sanford Heights father commented:

> He's been playing in it for three years, and it's been fine, but this year they didn't keep the field up at all. Grass wasn't cut or nothing. Very poor maintenance on the field. . . . If you go over to Brooklyn Center, to Iten Field, for example, you'll see a perfectly maintained field. . . . Really good, and over in Richfield, too. Real good, compared to ours (parents interview).

This was attributed to organizational problems, favoritism in the choice of those hired, and to a paucity of financial support by the businesses and citizens of Sanford Heights. This father's criticism was that the field was not aesthetically pleasing; it lacked the immaculately prepared aura of the grassy expanses on which professional ballplayers exhibit their skills. Contrasting the field, even as maintained, with the streets, vacant lots, backyards, and open parkland on which the children of Sanford Heights played informal games (with the tacit blessing of their parents) demonstrates that players are not in physical danger from the lack of grounds keeping. This criticism suggests that the physical background is a salient part of the Little League baseball experience. The attitudes of coaches and parents—in all leagues—consisted of a mixture of envy and determination to fix up their own fields, the grass always being greener on the other town's field.

Why should this aesthetic component matter? Like a theatrical set design, the field provides for a desired definition of the interaction (Bennett and Bennett 1970), which reveals that Little League is based closely on a structural concordance with professional leagues. Observers of professional baseball note the flawless perfection of the baseball diamond, the classic, pastoral elegance of the green, brown, and white field (Novak 1976, 57). Little League baseball, with the same emphasis on the environment, indicates that even at this age the game is to be set in a man-made Eden.

Rules and Rulings

Like the environment, the official rules of Little League baseball are given by adults—not subject to change by preadolescent negotiation. Little Leagues are supposed to follow the rules provided by the national organization, and coaches and umpires must be knowledgeable about these rules and enforce them without exception. Players, although not expected to memorize the rules, are expected to be generally aware of what they are allowed and required to do; they must follow the directions of their coaches who do know the rules.

Each year the national organization provides updated rule books to each local league. For a game as simple as preadolescent baseball, these rules are extensive, filling sixty-two pages in 1984. The rules attempt to cover every contingency that might arise in play and provide a basis from which umpires can make decisions without incurring the wrath of coaches.

The fact that rules are deemed necessary reflects the competitiveness of Little League baseball. In children's informal games, such a formal set of rules is not necessary. Piaget (1962) notes of preadolescent marble playing that older children are able to negotiate the rules of the game, and this negotiation is seen as developmentally valuable (Devereux 1976). When children play informal games, this negotiation is continually evident: What should be done when the old jacket being used as second base slides from its originally designated spot? Is it fair to pitch to ten year olds as one pitches to twelve year olds? These issues, important to the structure of the game, are collectively determined by the participants.

In Little League, negotiation by players is unthinkable. The rules are the final authority—at least they are not allowed to be contested by the preadolescents. In fact, players rarely contest the rules with the umpires. Ball players occasionally dispute the *judgment* of the umpire on a particular call, but in all such situations the umpire overrules them, and the coach supports the umpire in telling his players not to argue about calls:

> It is the final inning of a game which Furniture Mart is behind 12–3. The umpire calls a Furniture Mart player out at first base on a play in which he appeared to be safe—for the final out of the game. The players are surprised and angry at the call, and yell at the umpire. One says loudly: "You know where you can put that one"; another player yells: "You need Coke bottles" (for eyeglasses). Although their coach feels the call is a mistake, he tries to calm the team and tells them not to argue. The coach later blames the team for the loss and tells them that they should never blame the umpire (field notes, Hopewell).

Players are considered to have no "standing" to dispute but must abide by adult decisions.

However, adults have some leeway in negotiating rules. Besides the ultimate recourse of appealing to the local league or to the national organization, some give-and-take exists between coaches and umpires,[2] and some umpires change their calls after a convincing argument by a coach—a fairness that unintentionally encourages this sort of dispute. One umpire made a call permitting a double play on an infield pop fly; the coach whose team the decision had gone against protested, and the umpire, after checking the rule book, reversed his decision (field notes, Beanville). On another occasion a coach convinced the umpire that a foul tip caught by the catcher could be counted as a third and final strike—even though this rule was not enforced by other umpires in the league (field notes, Hopewell). All thirteen coaches interviewed in Bolton Park and Sanford Heights agreed that there were cases when they would "discuss" a call with the umpire during the game:

> Q: Do you think there are any circumstances where the coach should either argue or discuss a call with the umpire?
>
> A: Oh, yes. If there is other than a judgment call. If it's strictly a rule violation, and they are definitely in error, you should discuss it. I think you should discuss it in a gentlemanly manner (coach interview, Bolton Park).

Q: Are there any circumstances in which the coach should argue with an umpire?

A: Oh yeah. I think it's expected. Yeah, I think you do. If they're wrong, and you know they're wrong, you try and convince them that they're wrong, and if they don't admit to it then you protest it. I think that's part of a manager's responsibility (coach interview, Sanford Heights).

The assumption is that there exists a set of unalterable rules that take precedence over the decisions of the umpire, and these rules may be appealed to in the hope of righting a wrong.

Theoretically an adequate set of rules should provide a guide to the determination of every contingency in the game. In practice this is not the case (see Fine 1983), and sometimes the adults must negotiate an interpretation of a particularly confusing situation:

In the bottom of the sixth inning the White Sox scored five runs against the Pirates and only trailed 6–5, with the bases loaded and two outs. Hence, the next play will determine the outcome of the game. On the critical pitch, the ball came across the plate in such a way that the batter felt he had to move in order to avoid getting hit. He moved by sticking his head into the strike zone, rather than away from it. As a result, the ball hit him in the head (although it did not injure him). The White Sox thought that because the batter had been hit by the pitch he would take his base, and the team erupted in jubilant excitement as the game was tied and they stood an excellent chance of winning. The Pirates coach protested, feeling that the batter should not go to first base. Both sets of coaches demanded a decision from the umpire, Warren Dahlgren. Warren threw up his hands, saying "I don't know what it is, I've never had a kid get hit in the head like that before" and refused to make a decision. Warren walked over in the general direction of Phil Conklin, the Pirates coach, and asked his opinion. Phil asked him some questions about the sequence of events and responded formally and matter-of-factly: "There is two strikes and the batter bats." This decision would, of course, save the day for the Pirates. Bruce Silverstein, the White Sox coach, yelled at the umpire, "What did you ask him for?" (field notes, Maple Bluff).

To complicate matters, in addition to the players being angry and upset, the parents in the stands were also involved in a controversy and were yelling at the umpire. Four young adults were hanging onto the backstop and were harrassing the umpire by yelling at him. While this was happening, Terry Conklin, Phil's son and the assistant coach of the Pirates, walked over to Warren and spoke to him. As Terry walked back to the dugout, Warren yelled his new decision: "The batter's out!" which terminated all chances for the White Sox to win or tie the game. Bruce immediately yelled "What?!" and rushed over to home plate, where he was met by Phil Conklin and the umpire. They were loudly explaining that if a batter intentionally puts his head *into* the strike zone, he is automatically out. The indication was that the batter's act was intentional, since he put his head into the strike zone, rather than pulling it away.

By this time players were rushing onto the field ready for a fight. The boy leading the White Sox was told forcibly by his coach to return to the dugout. Phil Conklin also told his team to return to the dugout, and disaster was averted (field notes, Maple Bluff).

This example of rule negotiation is obviously an extreme and unique example of what can happen in the game setting, and it is not intended to suggest that Little League games regularly end in anarchy. The example does indicate that umpires can change their decisions and that coaches provide input. Rules require interpretation, and even which of several competing rules is applicable is not always clear. Indeed, one might argue that the play was a legitimate hit-by-the-pitch (runner on first base); a hit-by-the-pitch that hit the batter outside of the strike zone and which the batter did not attempt to avoid (a called ball); a hit-by-the-pitch that hit the batter while in the strike zone (a called strike); or deliberate interference by the batter (an out). The first three are covered by rule 6.08b; the fourth by 6.06c. No mention is made of a player's deliberately sticking his head in the batter's box in order to get hit by the pitch. Even a finely attuned set of rules requires interpretation, and this process of interpretation allows negotiation by the coaches.

Rule interpretations are in theory based on the rules, which serve as a court of unarguable last resort. However, such a perspective misses the implications of the rules. Like the law, Little League rules are for practical purposes too complex to be memorized in their entirety. In the drama of the game, coaches do not have time to read their rules at every juncture and, in fact, the physical rule book itself is rarely part of the argument. Rather, coaches debate the meaning of the baseball rules by referring to rules that (in their recollection) support their interpretation, they may cite precedents in which similar events occurred and the way they were resolved. The precedent argument is powerful in practice, as it means that the umpire will have to decide against the ruling of a peer if he keeps his own ruling. Unlike professional baseball, in which justice may be sacrificed to order (the umpire's first decision is almost always final, except when immediately overruled by a colleague), the emphasis in Little League that this is *only a game* in which fairness to each team is paramount paradoxically gives coaches the right to argue vehemently with umpires to ensure that fairness is maintained.

Order is necessary for keeping the game functioning. Part of the anarchy in the above example derived from the umpire's refusal to decide, leaving a definitional vacuum. Because of the structural position of the umpire, it would have been impossible to maintain the *existence* of the game if he had stuck to his original position that he would not make a decision. As chaotic as the game ending was, there could have been no end without some decision. Dahlgren by his statement officially denigrated his legitimacy for maintaining order, but he could not remove his authority. He provided a vacuum in which a struggle for definitional supremacy occurred, but he could not escape the eventual requirements of his role.

One final point is significant in regard to the rules distributed by the national organization. None of the five leagues follow them in their entirety, and in my observation of other leagues, those that follow the Little League rules to the letter are rare. Most of the variation derives, not from the rules of playing baseball, but from the Little League restrictions on local league actions. Some leagues play baseball on Sunday, most leagues have enrollment charges for players, several allow coaches to smoke during the game, and preseason and postseason games are played counter to the rules. Despite the publicly expressed adherence to the rules, each league interprets and ignores them according to its own perception of what is most appropriate for its own needs.

A second type of dispute in Little League involves "judgment calls" rather than rule interpretation. As with rule interpretations, the assumption is that some true, accurate, and fair ruling exists. In the case of the rules, the "correct" decision is written and can be referred to by coaches. In the case of judgment calls, once the play has ended, the evidence is forever out of reach. Although coaches believe that what occurred is unambiguous and definitive (he was safe or he was out), it is recognized that this cannot be proven. The umpire is needed to prevent perceptual or cognitive dissensus that often occurs in the sports arena, where game events may be given substantially different meanings as a function of perspective (Hastorf and Cantril 1954). Umpires are specially warned of this as part of their training: they are told to make quick decisions and to appear to be certain that their judgment is the only possible one (see also Askins, Carter, and Wood 1981).

Coaches recognize that they should not argue about judgment calls because their only retort can be that it didn't happen in the way the umpire thought it did (or at least didn't happen in the same order). Although the belief that coaches should not dispute judgment calls is widely cited, it does not correspond to behavior within the game context. Coaches do complain to umpires (and to each other) about egregious "errors." However, the point that coaches seem to be making when they say they do not dispute judgment calls is that they rarely *win* if they do dispute these calls, and besides, these disputes are technically illegal (Rule 9.02a). Although umpires have the right to eject a coach from a game for objecting to a call, in practice this happens so infrequently as to be only of anecdotal interest (once in the three years of research). As a result coaches (and occasionally their players) do dispute the judgment calls of umpires, but they do not expect that these expressions of disagreement and even anger will be heeded, unlike disputes about rule interpretations. While umpires alter balls to strikes, or make a runner who was out, safe, changes of judgment are rare.

Coaches as Directors

Little League baseball is a dramatic performance as well as a sport. To the extent that preadolescents are performers, they need a director to manage their roles for an audience. Coaches, aside from their educational function, serve as directors.

Like umpires, coaches are actively recruited by the league, and most leagues have difficulty finding enough men willing to donate their time in the spring and summer for what is often literally a thankless task. However, leagues do eventually recruit men to coach their teams, occasionally at the last minute. These men volunteer out of a desire to help the children in the community and/or their own son(s):

Q: Why did you first decide to become a Little League manager?

A1: Well, I guess I had been always pretty interested in the

kids, you know. . . . Not many parents volunteer to help. . . .
We had one year, the boys' second year in the minors in the
Little League farm system . . . when the parent we had
couldn't make it to all the games, so we were stuck doing it
anyway, and we wound up with about four or five guys who
would do it, which didn't help the kids any, no continuity at all.
And I knew I could adjust my schedule to make all of the
games. So I just figured I might as well (coach interview,
Bolton Park).

A2: Because I liked boys, because I liked working with
youth, I was a cub master for five years. I enjoy participating with younger lads, trying to teach them something . . .
(Q: How did you specifically become a Little League manager?)

I fell into it because the previous manager's wife died, and he
requested I take over. [This man was the assistant coach at the
time] (coach interview, Bolton Park).

These explanations reveal both the situated features of becoming a
coach—the need of the league to recruit men to operate the program—and the ideals of these men as expressed in their explanations of their interest in children.

Coaches typically express idealistic motives for coaching—they
wish to teach baseball skills and build character, allow the boys to
have fun, and simultaneously have a team with a winning season
(see chapter 3). But no matter what ideal philosophy the coach
starts out to teach, he finds himself mired in the mundane routine of
organizing his team so that the pragmatic accomplishment of playing (and winning) baseball games can be achieved. Coaches are not
only concerned with their ideal task of inculcating character and
baseball skills but also with the pragmatic task of maintaining order.
A team as a social unit is disorganized. It is not that individual
behavior is disorganized, but the behaviors are not collectively
focused. Occasions in which a collective focus exists do not last long.
Blumer's (1969) conception of joint action as involving the fitting together of individual lines of action is an apt metaphor, since it implies the central position of the coach as the organizer or director.
When the players are off the field, or on the field in routine situations, the coach has the responsibility to shape their behaviors and
focus their attention. Therefore, it is common for a coach to exhort
his team to "pay attention," "look alive," or "give your teammates a
little support." It is the coach's responsibility to ensure that his
team bats in the proper order, that nine players are on the field, and

that players are aware of the number of outs. The fact that in all leagues and on all teams players often are oblivious to these aspects of the games makes the coach's role exasperating.

Because of the structure of Little League, the coach must *control* his players and also *represent* them when disputes erupt during the game. Coaches tell their players that if there is to be any discussion of a baseball call with an umpire, it is they, the adults, who are to do it, not the players. Likewise, if changes are made in the lineup, the coach is responsible for the changes and for informing the opposing coach and scorekeeper. The coach is the filter through which the decisions of the officials are enforced and also the director who interprets and enforces the formal rules of Little League baseball.

This role is not inevitable: Little League could have been organized differently. One justification given by the Little League organization for adult involvement is to teach the fundamentals of baseball. Were this the only motivation for involvement, an adult presence could have been maintained with the preadolescents themselves organizing the game. However, this is impractical as the game is currently structured. Adults cannot stand the diffuse organization of children's games (Devereux 1976), which break off, continue, and become reorganized. Whether this is because children are not able to maintain attention or because they have different standards of organization is not at issue. A second consideration is that such an arrangement would place adults in an awkward situation (see Fine 1980a). The adults would be less powerful than the preadolescent players, requiring a role reversal for preadolescents and adults unique in contemporary American society. The final rationale for the current structure is perhaps the most significant: a crucial function of Little League is to build character, and this goal assumes that adults have moral as well as technical expertise. When adults structure play, interpret rules and umpires' decisions, and motivate their young charges to perform properly, the idea of a Little League game as a moral event can be sustained.

Despite the good intentions of coaches, difficulties arise in the coaching role as a function of appropriate role involvement. As is true for many roles (Turner 1978), the role of Little League coach is not defined as completely self-encompassing. The coach is expected to distance himself from the performance he directs but not be so distant that he seems superfluous. The coach must be actively involved in directing the team and must appear concerned about the outcome of the game.

A coach may be negatively sanctioned for being either overinvolved (underdistanced), or underinvolved (overdistanced). Before examining proper role distance, I shall describe cases in which the coach's behavior is sanctionable.

Overinvolvement

Overinvolvement occurs when the adult becomes so involved in the game that he forgets (or appears to forget) that the performance of his players is *after all* only a game, and that winning and losing do not *really* make any difference. A coach is especially likely to attract such criticism when he argues with an umpire and disrupts the game:

> It is the bottom of the third inning of a game between the two best teams in the league. An assistant coach of the Orioles walks over to the coach of the Astros to tell him of some substitutions that the Orioles made in the top half of that inning. The assistant coach returns to the Orioles bench, saying "I can't believe it. They are griping because we didn't give them the changes before they went out in the field." The opposing coach claims that this was an attempt by the Orioles to get around the rule that all boys must play two innings. He believes that if the boys would have had to bat in the top of the third, they would not have been put in. This refusal to accept the substitution by the Astros coach meant that the Oriole substitutes would have to play through the top of the fifth inning. The Oriole coach, recognizing the effects of such a ruling, comments: "Now we're in trouble." His other assistant fumes openly: "That's not baseball; that's chicken shit."
> The two head coaches argue with the home plate umpire and each other for about five minutes. Finally the parents, particularly those of the Orioles players, begin yelling at the coaches: "Come on. Let him hit." The conference ends with the Orioles having to keep their players in through the top of the fifth inning. Both coaches and their assistants remain bitter towards each other. The game, supposedly based on preadolescent skill, has become one of adult strategy (field notes, Bolton Park).

The Beanville Continental League season ended with the Rangers as the first-half champions and the White Sox as second-half champions. The tradition in Beanville was that when the first-half and the second-half champions were different, the teams played a three-game play-off series to determine the league champion. This year Al Wingate, the coach of the White Sox, vehemently objects to having his team play in a three-game series, saying that the League cannot afford the extra games—in terms of the expense of supplying balls and paying umpires. Other adults dispute Wingate's claim. The consensus of the other adults, most of whom dislike Wingate, is that he believes he has only enough pitching for one game. After heated discussion, he suddenly announces that the White Sox will not play under those conditions. He immediately begins putting away his team's equipment and tells his players of his decision. After he leaves the field, several White Sox players ask the Rangers if they can organize a championship game; however, without the coach that is impossible. The Rangers are declared the champions by default (field notes, Beanville).

These dramatic situations suggest one extreme that adults wish to avoid. In both cases coaches became so involved in the game that they did not recognize that losing the argument does not "really matter." Even if the "incorrect" decision had been made, the game would continue and the preadolescents would have as much exercise and fun, although the outcome might be altered. This concern with winning is a result of seeing the game as a performance designed for spectators. The coach assumes that the outcome matters; the outcome of the game is *on record*, of historical rather than evanescent interest, and thus he is concerned with seeing that rulings are made that are beneficial for the team. While this perspective is common, coaches generally control their involvement by reminding themselves that it looks "bad" for them to be too involved.

The tendency toward underdistancing is strong, particularly among the more competitive coaches. One coach told me privately that he felt he was a very competitive person, and it was an effort for him to prevent his personal feelings from affecting his coaching. Coaches must insulate their public performance from their emotional reactions. The examples above are extreme cases; however, possible overinvolvement occurs whenever a coach questions an umpire, visits his pitcher on the mound, or yells at his players. Since the coach's role is not well defined and the men are not trained in the role, it is a matter of local norms or personal definition whether such instances represent appropriate role involvement or over-involvement.

One problem with evaluations of Little League baseball is that there exist different philosophical standards by which the game can be judged. This situation is sometimes compounded by distorted perceptions of spectators, who may attribute more to the coach's behavior than is legitimate, leading to gossip and occasionally minor scandal:

> I had a long talk with Fred Turner, the coach of Transatlantic Industries, about an incident that he had been involved in the previous day, and which he was still angry about. Fred says that Harry Stanton (a Sharpstone player) hit a ground ball which hit his son, Frank, in the collarbone. Fred says that he came out of the dugout to see how his son was. In the meantime Frank recovered, and tagged Harry out when he tried to stretch the hit into a double. Fred says that he yelled to his son: "That's the way to get that turkey." However, spectators and even Harry's coach thought he said "That's the way to get that jerk." Fred said that Harry's older brother called and insulted him (field notes, Hopewell).

A coach must walk a thin line to avoid being perceived as overinvolved.

Underinvolvement

The second type of disorganization results from underinvolvement, or overdistancing. When coaches are overinvolved, they treat themselves as focal actors in the baseball performance rather than offstage directors. In underinvolvement, coaches withdraw from directing their teams and let the players organize themselves without a clear mandate to do so—often with chaos resulting. During one practice game a coach became so disgusted at his team that he simply walked away from them in the fourth inning and stayed in the grandstand for the rest of the game, leaving his assistant in charge (field notes, Sanford Heights). Sometimes coaches stand by the fence speaking to adult friends, only casually observing the game and paying no attention to what is occurring in their dugout unless the noise becomes riotous. Little League players are usually able to organize themselves; however, a total abrogation of the coach's role as director is inappropriate. Coaches are publicly criticized for not running their teams efficiently and for not preventing outbursts by their players. One Beanville coach was repeatedly condemned for not disciplining his players for their angry outbursts—crying, cursing, and throwing bats.

Coaches are expected to keep their players orderly and oriented to the serious performance of baseball, while displaying an emotional coolness. A coach's role involves the ordering of two classes of events. First, the coach is a stage manager, ensuring that certain actions are performed, and performed in the proper sequence. The concern here is not with whether the actions are done well, but whether they are done at all. For example, there must be a batting order, and this batting order must be followed. The team must put nine players in the field; it does not matter whether they are "good" players, but preadolescent bodies must fill positions. Likewise, the team must supply boys to coach at first and third base when the team is up to bat. It doesn't matter whether they know anything about the game, but they must be on the team, wear uniforms, and stand near the proper location on the field. In leagues that have a rule requiring that all players participate in the game for at least two innings (e.g., Hopewell and Bolton Park), coaches must juggle their personnel so that this rule is followed. Ignoring some of these structural constraints makes the game literally unplayable—for example, if a team does not have a boy assigned to pitch, or if no batter is present. Violations of other rules leave the game playable, but the team's position is liable to be undermined through the protest of an opposing coach. In informal preadolescent games, these "constraints" are casually (and satisfactorily) negotiated, although such solutions may take time, may be contrary to the "rules," and may change from occasion to occasion.

The second feature of the coach's role as organizer (in addition to that of stage manager) can be likened to that of the theatrical director. His responsibility is to teach players to perform well and skillfully. He must be concerned that his players publicly display baseball skills and character attributes in an appropriate manner.

Baseball Skills

Despite the claims of the Little League organization that the program provides preadolescents with training in leadership and character, most coaches and players see the goal as teaching members how to play baseball. Towards this end, coaches schedule practices both before and during the season to strengthen the skills of their players. A coach who does not hold these practices or who holds them but doesn't teach enough in them fails as a coach. One player criticized his coaches by saying, "They never really said nothing if we were doing something wrong" (personal interview, Bolton Park), and another player condemned the coaches on his team by explaining: "We didn't have enough practices. We always did the same thing at practice" (personal interview, Sanford Heights). This perspective was echoed by a Little League mother:

> I liked [the coaches] personally very much. I did not feel they had enough actual coaching as far as skills. It seemed it was easy to miss a practice. . . . Like when they would make an error they were really nice to the kids; they were very quick to say "That's all right. That's all right." Whereas some of us parents felt the kids should have been corrected right there. You made a mistake, next time do it this way. Because I don't feel they learned enough (parents interview, Bolton Park).

These comments refer to different teams and indicate that this is not an isolated problem. Coaches differ in the amount of time they have available to hold practices, and they also differ in their knowledge of baseball and ability to impart that knowledge. Specifically, the ability to teach bunting, stealing, sliding, and fielding differentiate coaches competent to teach baseball skills (and the most successful coaches) from men less trained.

Preadolescents can acquire fairly subtle athletic skills, and the better coaches recognize this. Some teams are known for the sophistication of their play, even with mediocre talent. The Sanford Heights Cards were known as a team that knew how to bunt; the Bolton Park Astros were particularly sophisticated in knowing which base to throw to, and the Sharpstone team in Hopewell was repeatedly drilled on base running, scoring runs because of their competence on the base paths. These coaches all had baseball experience themselves: one was a long-time Little League coach, another a former umpire, and the third a physical education major in college, training for a career in school coaching.

Character Skills

Coaches are also judged on their players' "character." Are the players concentrating on the game, or are they sulking, angry, or "goofing off"? Since Little League is a public spectacle, the impressions given off by the players redound to the credit or discredit of the coach. As a result, some parents and players compliment their coaches for teaching teamwork, while others criticize them for being either too lenient or too strict:

> Everyone would goof off in the games. . . . Everyone made fun of it. [What did you think of the coaches?] I didn't like 'em.

[Why?] He wasn't strict enough (personal interview, Sanford heights).

Q: Was there anything that would have made playing for [your team] better?
A: If the coach wasn't quite so strict and mean, and he didn't give such long lectures (personal interview, Sanford Heights).

Coaches must avoid both extremes in organizing the behavior of their charges. In chapter 3 I discuss the components of the moral socialization that adults attempt to impress upon their players; the point I wish to make here is about the technical aspects of the process. Whether or not players "actually" have been taught sportsmanship, they must *appear* to be sportsmanlike; whether or not they are playing diligently, this must *seem* to be the case. The attribution of good character must be arrived at by those watching the performance, if the coach is to be given credit for being a positive influence. When players do not behave as they are supposed to, the coach must not only distance himself from their behavior but must act to convince the audience that he takes the same moral view of the activity as they do (see Goffman 1971). Since the coach and the fans come from the same social world, such actions (pulling a boy from the game or throwing one's hands up in disgust) need not be hypocritical but derive from shared standards of acceptable behavior.

Parents as Audience

In each league, grandstands are maintained for the comfort of the spectators. These seating arrangements indicate that parents are expected to attend games: the grandstands (and toilets and refreshment stands) create a context that facilitates parental attendence. Thus, the physical surroundings are both cause and effect of the presence of an audience composed of parents (and peers).

While the performance is open to the general public, actually only children, early adolescents, and parents are expected to attend. When I attended games in several other leagues, I was asked whom I was there to watch: which boy was my son. The inquisition was friendly, but the question was asked because I was an unrecognized adult, a stranger whose presence did not "make sense" within the established community of parents. There is "no reason" for outsiders to be present, as Little League is defined as an activity that does not have sufficient intrinsic interest to warrant the attention of anyone not emotionally committed to attend. Little League is not an occasion in its own right but derives its meaning from the relationship of the audience member to the actors. Although the Little League contest resembles a performance, it is perceived by the audience as lacking what most public performances need to succeed—intrinsic interest. In this way, Little League games differ from professional contests, where a legitimate answer to why one is attending is, "I like baseball." However, even professional contests typically are attended by only those with an emotional attachment to one of the teams (Stone 1981), although not necessarily to a particular player.

One dramatic instance of the expectation that the audience should be limited to affectively committed spectators occurred in Beanville. One of the boys on the Rangers, Bud Wilensky, a preadolescent known for his hot temper, was the target of several biting comments from an elderly man in the grandstands, who attended Little League games only when the Rangers were playing. This stranger's comments, though no more tart than those of some parents, caused great concern for Mrs. Wilensky and the team's coach as they tried to figure out who he was and what his motivation might be. Eventually this man stopped attending, and the incident was forgotten, However, it reminds us that simply wishing to see baseball played is not a sufficient justification for attending Little League games; the audience member must have additional motivation that he or she must be prepared to announce. Over the course of the season, parents become friends and form a social group of sorts. As one mother commented, "We all stick together and get along well" (parents' interview, Sanford Heights), indicating the sociability that develops from sharing common emotions.

Players are happy to have their parents attend games (see Appendix 1), and none of the twenty-six parents interviewed had objections about other parents generally—although one or two parents were singled out for criticism. Criticism of parents as a group for their behavior is unfair. However, although parents *generally* conduct themselves within lines of propriety, they must be conscious of the appropriate performance of their roles. Although parents are an audience, they are not the faceless, anonymous crowd of professional sports spectators but are themselves watched and judged. Thus, the issue of appropriate role distance is as significant for them as for coaches or players.

Parents are expected to sit in the grandstands and cheer when a member of the team they are supporting makes a good play, and remain silent both when a member of their team makes a poor play and when a member of the opposing team makes a poor play. Despite the dramatic effects of errors on outcomes of Little League games, errors are not considered appropriate topics of comment. Similarly, the excellent play of an opposing team member, while frustrating, should be defined as a successful athletic play by a preadolescent rather than a play that damages one's team's chances. Plays are supposed to be seen in terms of skill and only secondarily in terms of their effect on the game—an approach sharply at variance with that of professional athletics.

Parents are not expected to be fully engrossed in the contest on the field. Few parents watch the entire game, and the last part of the game is better attended than the beginning. This feature of Little League game attendance is a function of suburban family routine. Typically, the boy walks, rides his bike, or is driven to the playing field thirty to ninety minutes before game time; this practice is rarely attended by parents. Since weekday games begin at 6:00 or 6:30, fathers have just arrived home from work. After a short rest or perhaps after dinner, families drift down to the field during the middle of the game.[3] The number of people seated in the grandstands during the top of the first, third, and fifth innings was counted in Bolton Park, Sanford Heights, and Maple Bluff. In all sites, attendance increased throughout the game, particularly between the first and third innings ($F = 23.2$, $df = 2,219$; $p = .001$) (see table 1.1). This was a result of fathers' schedules; the fact that the end of athletic contests are seen as more dramatic, exciting, and significant than the beginning; and the circumstance that if a boy is to be driven home, his parents must arrive by the end of the game.

In addition, the quality of the game may affect parental attendance. Data were compiled from the fifth innings of games in Bolton Park, which had three successful teams and three unsuccessful teams, and Sanford Heights, which had four teams with winning records and three with losing records.[4] In games between two successful teams, an average of 35.2 ($n = 15$) spectators were present in the fifth inning; in games between successful and unsuccessful teams, an average of 31.5 ($n = 31$) spectators were present; and at games between two unsuccessful teams, only 27.8 ($n = 12$) spectators were present. These differences are only marginally significant ($F = 2.04$; $df = 2,55$; $p = .14$), but they suggest that attendance may be partially related to the satisfaction involved in seeing a good game rather than merely watching one's offspring in his leisure activities.

Table 1.1 **Spectator Attendance** (Number of Fans and Number of Cases)

	First Inning	Third Inning	Fifth Inning
Maple Bluff	11.2(22)	14.4(24)	16.8(23)
Sanford Heights	17.6(31)	26.9(29)	27.5(31)
Bolton Park	20.8(27)	33.8(27)	36.9(27)

Even when present, spectators are not expected to pay full attention; many talk about extraneous subjects, knit, or read. Little League games are occasions in which side-involvement (Goffman 1971) is allowed and even expected. As Watson (1973) notes, a considerable amount of neighborhood gossip, shoptalk, and general friendly conversation occurs in these settings. However, despite this diffuse involvement, there are occasions in which the attention of parents becomes focused on the playing field. Parents do watch the games, although they have a wide range of secondary involvements.[5] Adults are positioned in such a way that attention, as primarily expressed through cheering, can be activated easily. Not surprisingly, cheering is particularly evident in close encounters and around important events in the game (strikeouts, outfield catches, and extra-base hits). This cheering is considered appropriate and desirable by both children and adults, and children comment on their pleasure when they hear their parents cheer for them.

Little League participants view this organization of parental activity—including late attendance, secondary involvements while observing, and cheering for one's team, as constituting appropriate involvement. At such times the role of the parent is not a topic of discussion. On other occasions, parental activity becomes problematic and raises the issue of the boundaries of appropriate behavior.

Overinvolvement

The most common problem with parents is their overinvolvement in the game. When parents criticize rather than cheer, do not let offspring who have lost a game forget about the defeat, or argue with the umpire, other spectators are apt to suggest these parents have overstepped the bounds of good taste.

Parents typically did not feel that other parents overemphasized winning. Parents in Bolton Park and Sanford Heights were asked: "In general would you say that on the team your son played for the parents overemphasized winning, underemphasized winning, or were just about right?" Of the twenty-six parents interviewed, twenty-one (81 percent) said that the parents on their son's team were just about right in the emphasis that they gave to winning, three said winning was *under*emphasized (12 percent), and one parent didn't know. Only one parent felt others overemphasized winning. Although these responses might have been more negative if I had asked about parents on *other* teams, it does suggest that most parents do not see overinvolvement as a major problem. However, when coaches were asked about the emphasis parents gave winning, seven of thirteen (54 percent) believed parents overemphasized winning, five (38 percent) believed winning was emphasized just right, and one (8 percent) believed parents underemphasized winning. Although one coach claimed "parental attitudes were much better than I was led to believe Little League was" (coach interview, Bolton Park), another commented,

> I have seen teams where the parents really get down on them. I saw it this year even. . . . I really heard some of the mothers really get on Doug and Endicott [coaches] when they lost. . . . Mothers were calling Endicott, and said it was his son's fault that they lost and didn't go to the tournament at Brooklyn Center (coach interview, Sanford Heights).

These parents have difficulty recognizing that Little League baseball is a spectator event in which audience involvement is sharply limited in content and volume. The rationale for attending should not be to see one's son's team *win* but to see one's son's team *play*.

Overinvolvement in game outcomes is also reflected in this parental comment: "This dang game is as much a sport for us as it is for the kids. We get more exicted than they do" (Watson 1973, 50); in the reflexive musings of a Hopewell mother: "I disliked the competitive feeling I underwent during a game—had to channel the nervousness—and learn to relax (and laugh at myself!)" (parents' interview, Hopewell); and in the sarcastic, observant comments of the players themselves: "Larry, a middle-status twelve-year-old, is up to bat with the bases loaded, and his teammates discuss the possibility of his hitting a grand-slam home run. One comments: 'His dad would jump the fence and kiss the pitcher'" (field notes, Sanford Heights). Because of the performance features of Little League games, coupled with a strong self-identification with one of the teams, spectators may actively attempt to affect game outcomes.

The most dramatic case of parental involvement, fortunately unique, involved an anti-Semitic comment by a parent in the Maple Bluff game between the White Sox and the Pirates (described above). During the dispute over whether the White Sox batter deliberately placed his head in the path of a pitched ball, the parents in the stands were involved in a dispute and were yelling at the umpire. Later, after the umpire had made his final decision:

Mrs. Ashton (the wife of the White Sox assistant coach) came running from around the back of the dugout, frantic, and shouting, "Did you hear that, Mr. Sociologist? Put this in your notes. That woman over there just said, 'those dumb Jew coaches, who do they think they are?' There's a lot of anti-Semitism around here, but I just won't stand for that." (Both the coach and the assistant coach of the White Sox are Jewish, while the coaches of the Pirates and the offending mother are Catholic.) Mrs. Ashton then yelled at her husband: "Jim, did you hear that?" She repeated the story pointing to the woman who was now behind the Pirates dugout apparently talking to Phil Conklin, the Pirates coach (field notes, Maple Bluff).

While this situation is unique, and we have only Mrs. Ashton's young son to confirm her report, it does indicate the degree of personal involvement possible. Rather than seeing the game as a contest between boys, it is seen here as a clash between religions. The game becomes a moral encounter.

Situated events that undermine the legitimacy of the definition of the situation are likely to lead to such overinvolvement, and they provide an opening in which parents may come to feel that they have a responsibility to examine publicly the moral basis of the game. This occurred in Sanford Heights one day when the regularly scheduled base umpire did not show up (all Little Leagues except Beanville used two umpires to prevent contested plays). A father whose son was on one of the teams was drafted as the base umpire. When his son's team scored crucial runs on two decisions that the opponent fans felt were "unfair," he was loudly criticized in a show of anger that was a topic of conversation for several days. Because this umpire was the father of a player, any decision that he made in favor of his son's team could be questioned. The other, "official" umpire commented that he was so disgusted with the fans that he almost forfeited the game. Parental overinvolvement results from a reaction to what is seen as "illegitimate" authority. Parents do not respond crudely in random situations but only when the umpire as the authority figure has been undermined.

Underinvolvement

Underinvolvement is less disruptive to the game, and some may even consider this a virtue, as do those who believe that parents should be banned from games. However, others object to parental apathy. One mother stated: "They [the parents on her son's team] were a very nonchalant group of people. I don't know. . . . We'd always laugh about it, because year after year another mother and I would be about the only two that would hit every game. I felt there was a real lack of interest by some of the parents. I was appalled that the parents didn't get there all season" (parents' interview, Bolton Park).

Although several parents and coaches felt that their fellow parents were insufficiently involved in the running of the league, this rarely influenced the performance of the game itself. Only rarely was the apathy of parents brought up during the game, and even here the game continued without difficulty—only its definition as a *performance* was undermined.

Although a lack of parental attendance is depressing, it does not affect play. The overinvolvement of parents poses more serious difficulties than does their underinvolvement. Overinvolvement openly disrupts the performance, while underinvolvement permits the game to be treated as a game whether or not large numbers witness it and whether or not players wish it this way.

Conclusion

As critics of Little League have long noted, this is one form of preadolescent "play" that is directed by adults ostensibly for the benefit of preadolescents. Whatever the benefits of this structure, it can hardly be denied that if adults were made to vanish from the precincts in which Little League is played, the game would look very different. Yet, the orientations of adults to Little League activity can vary. In depicting such variations, I relied on the construct of role distance and the related concepts of overdistance and underdistance (and their inverse, underinvolvement and overinvolvement). These features are applicable to all social worlds—too much attachment is negatively sanctioned, as is too little. Little League is surely play, but it is also acting—a public display. By examining how adults organize the rules and frames of this display—how it *can* be brought off and how it *must* be, I have attempted to organize diverse adult behaviors.

My goal is to treat Little League as a world in itself and not to attempt to trace its impact in the larger society or the impact of that society on this world. As this chapter implies, these impacts are real, but they are issues to be approached in ways other than ethnography. The internal richness of the setting should be evident: emotions are expressed; meanings are generated. My intent is to explore how adults nestle up to this social world, employing their various skills—which they use to greater or lesser effect. Little League could not exist as it does without several layers of adult participants—spectators, umpires, and coaches. All coexist, enmeshed in a web of meaning; yet, because this is "play," each group cannot appear *too* caught up to any of the others. These figures are further entwined by rules and settings which, while they do not imprison, at least tether the participants to a shared reality to which they must constantly pay tribute.

2

Little League as Sport and Play

Adults may structure and direct the world of Little League baseball, but it is preadolescents who are the stars. Just as Little League could not run without the presence of adults, baseball could not be played without the active participation of boys. As indicated in chapter 1, Little League is in a netherworld between pure play and pure work; it has both playlike and worklike components. These two metaphors—work and play—of course, explain athletic settings beyond Little League; they can be generically applied to the world of sport.

D. Stanley Eitzen and George Sage provide a concise, though broad, definition of sport as "any competitive physical activity that is guided by established rules" (1978, 12). By this definition and others, I distinguish Little League from "mere play." Some (e.g., Edwards 1973, 59) would go so far as to claim that sport is really a form of work. Yet, Little League is inherently enjoyable for most players and is a voluntary leisure pursuit for preadolescents. Done for its own sake it has an "autotelic" quality (Anderson and Moore 1960). Gregory Stone (1955) reflected this distinction in his article "American Sports: Play and Dis-Play." *Play* refers to the behaviors growing out of the activity itself—what Csikszentmihalyi (1975) described as "flow." *Dis-play* refers to the concept of work, reflecting how participants make their activities symbolically relevant to observers (other players and spectators). Although sport and play share an emergent quality and inherent satisfaction, sport must make public sense.

Part of the distinction between play and work as leisure is tied to the concept of rationalization of activity (as discussed by Max Weber and others). The expressive "flow" experience is contrasted with the structured patterning of activity. Flow, according to Mitchell (1983), emerges in activity: (1) that is meaningful and cathected, (2) where outcomes are determined by individual will, (3) where participation is intrinsically rewarding (autotelic activity), (4) where self-consciousness gives way to a focus on the action being done, and (5) where there is a focused stimulus field. To the extent that games (and sports) are socially constrained fields of activity, they cannot manifest the pure sense of flow that Mitchell described for mountain climbing. Flow in games and sport is eroded as these activities are organized and made efficient. Even though such organization may increase the complexity and coordination of the game, which might be linked to satisfaction, through the strategic and self-conscious management of resources, it takes away the spontaneous, joyful experience. Those who direct Little League baseball truly wish *both:* the spontaneous sense of flow (play, fun) and the rationalized, self-conscious organization. They want Little league to be both play and work. This inherent contradiction provides Little League baseball with some of the tension that leads to the internal and external criticisms of the game, to be discussed in Appendix 1, and leads to different standards of behavior that permeate the game.

Observers speak glibly of the activity at the Little League baseball field as "playing baseball," and few who have attended such social occasions would deny this is the proper name for some behaviors that occur there. However, if one defines the actual, physical movement involved in pitching a leather spheroid, catching the same, throwing or hitting, running on the manicured base paths, or actively preparing to do one of these things as "playing baseball," then little baseball playing occurs. Baseball, as both its critics and enthusiasts have noted, is a leisurely, even elegant game, in which long pauses occur between brief slices of action. Few players are actively involved in a ground ball to shortstop, a strike, or a fly ball to right field, and, of course, nearly half the participants "in the game" are not on the field at any one time.

Activities that occur within the boundaries of the game are seen as the sort of things upon which audiences can comment. Players are potentially subject to public comment for their skill (or lack of it). However, as is true in professional sport, public comment may be made about other actions as well. Two classes of action differ in their relationship to game meaning. First, game actions can be *of* the game—they are directly constitutive of baseball itself—throwing, swinging, running, catching, sliding, etc. They are part of the rule-generated structure of the game. The second type of action is not part of the game in the same sense because it does not advance the game, but it is *in* the game in that it is recognized as occurring within the game framework. For example, the player who throws down his bat after striking out is performing an observable action that participants or audience members may comment on, he is clearly a social actor, and his action is seen as baseball related. Yet, it is not part of the game in the same sense as swinging at a pitched ball. Likewise, the outfielder who picks flowers during the game is recognized as acting within the game framework, although his actions are of a different order than if he had picked up a ground ball. A third type of action surrounds the game framework comprises actions of players that are not directly related to the playing of the game itself. This category includes such activities as talking about beer can collections, eating ice cream, or engaging in a dugout shoving match.

Because Little League is performance, all three classes of action are observed and are commented on as an indication of the players' ability and moral integrity. Players are supposed to engage in behaviors of the game and only those behaviors. Players not in the game should be nonpersons, in that their actions are irrelevant to the game. Players not involved in a play should stand quietly but be ready for future action. Once a player has made an out, he should exit the stage.

In general, the closer one is to plays of the game, the more one is engaging in work—at least within the Little League setting. Surrounding actions tend to be playful and voluntary. Of course, this distinction should not be pushed too hard, as some baseball action can be joyful and represent a sense of "flow" as players are "caught up" in their actions.

Little League as Work

Part of the metaphoric qualities associated with work in the public mind relates to the belief that work is not supposed to be pleasurable. Some components of Little League baseball lend support to categorizing it as a work-related activity. Work is forced, directed, and constrained by rules and regulations. So is Little League baseball.

Behavioral Components of Work

Four elements of Little League point to its position as work. First, it is serious. Second, it is supposed to be a continuous string of goal-directed activities. Third, it is emotionally intensive with focused bursts of emotion. Four, like the work place, it is commonplace for injuries to occur, and in fact these are expected.

Seriousness. Events in a Little League game "really matter." Season records are kept, and histories develop. By contrast, in informal softball games no scores are kept and the outcome is only of peripheral interest. In Little League, coaches often use strategy to help their players win:

By the fourth inning of the opening day game it has started to get dark, and teams must complete four innings for the game to be counted. The coach of the team that is ahead believes the opposing coach is stalling, hoping to have the game cancelled. Finally the first coach tells his batters to swing at all pitches, deliberately missing them, to ensure the inning will be over quickly and the game counted. After the third out, players gather around and congratulate the boy who just struck out (field notes, Hopewell).

One coach went further and added an economic incentive:

Chuck Rymer, the coach of the Cubs, told his team that he felt that they were making too many errors and not getting enough hits. He said that as a new policy if a player made an error in a game the player would give him a dime. The coach would give the player a dime for each hit that he got. Chuck told me later that the system worked well, and that the Cubs began hitting better. However, he only enforced the policy for one game (field notes, Sanford Heights).

As a joke, another coach offered his players a dollar for every home run. These short-lived actions made the players into wage-earners temporarily and changed the Little League game into something resembling work.

Coaches are not the only ones who are serious; players are as well. One boy took the game so seriously that he talked about knocking down opposing batters when he pitched, and he did appear to "brush back" several batters. Other players deliberately slid into infielders when running the bases. One of the most frequent complaints aimed at coaches by their preadolescent charges was that they didn't call enough practices and that they were not strict enough in enforcing discipline. Players generally accept the legitimacy of the organizational structure of Little League: the mandatory batting order, the rule that compels all players to play for at least two innings, and the rule that requires all pitchers to have at least three days' rest between pitching assignments. These worklike rules are taken for granted by players and are accepted as being in their best interest—even though they remove much of the flexibility from

the Little League structure and differentiate it from informal baseball games.

Continuousness. Once a Little League game has begun, nothing
is supposed to distract the players from the goal-directed task at
hand. Players are instructed to keep their minds on the game (Coakley 1980). Many coaches and some players insist that players not run
to the refreshment stand during the game, as this is considered in-
compatible with the task of playing baseball. Food distracts from
the attention players must direct to the game:

> Dino buys some gum from a local vendor during the game, and
> his teammates gather around him asking for pieces. It looked
> like feeding time at the aquarium, with Dino tossing out gum to
> a sea of outstretched hands. The team totally ignored the game
> while the gum was being distributed (field notes, Beanville).

Continuous attention to the game characterizes some players
more than others. Certain players identify with major league players and reveal their interest in each detail of the game:

> Roger Lemon of the White Sox displays his professional orien-
> tation when he is pitching. He is careful where he places his
> foot on the pitching rubber. His preparation before the windup
> is definitely modeled after major leaguers: he holds the ball be-
> hind his back, bends down studying the batter for a few sec-
> onds, takes a full windup and delivers the ball. This contrasts
> with many pitchers in the league who simply throw the ball
> without any ritual preparation. His enthusiasm for the profes-
> sional display of the game is also demonstrated in the way he
> reacts when the pitch is called a strike. He will sometimes
> throw his hands slightly in the air and mutter a quiet "yay" to
> himself. Most of the time he is pensive and serious, and is to-
> tally wrapped up in the game (field notes, Maple Bluff).

I discuss below how attention to the game is seen as work; here I
note only that work consists in the belief that all one's actions should
be game related. Such an orientation to Little League is most evident in close games, contests with significance for the team's record,
and encounters with teams considered rivals or equals.

Emotional intensity. Little League is not always a beatific world.
Emotions are often intense. Even joy may seem like work in its formal and ritualized aspects. Most teams have an unstated (but nonetheless rigid) policy requiring players to greet any boy who hits a

home run after he crosses home plate. Although players feel a surge of genuine emotion when the home run is hit, by the time the batter crosses home plate the impact may have dissipated, and the public representation of that emotion is all that remains (Hochschild 1983). For some teams at some times, this ritual seems forced, as coaches must tell their charges to greet the returning hero. Even pleasure can be turned into a commodity. The relationship between work and emotion in Little League is more evident for "negative emotions," where a heightening of emotion is characteristic of an overly serious attitude toward the game and an underdistanced role. For example, in the tumultuous ending of the game between the Pirates and the White Sox, described in chapter 1, players of both teams rushed onto the field, ready to do battle. Other events such as the following relatively minor incidents occur every few games:

> In the fifth inning of a game between Transatlantic Industry and Hopewell Police in which Transatlantic Industry is ahead 5–1, Tom McDarrell, the TI star catcher, grounds out routinely. He becomes upset and begins sniffling. His friend, Tim Mizell, tells him to "take it easy." Tom remains upset, muttering "God damn it to hell. Shit." A teammate chides him, "Every time you make an out don't take a fit." Within a few minutes Tom has recovered, and the incident is not mentioned again (field notes, Hopewell).

> Jason Shaunessey, the leading home run hitter for the Beanville Rangers, struck out three times today. The first two times he claimed the opposing pitcher was rotten and too slow. After the second strikeout he was near tears. After his third consecutive strikeout Jason violently threw his bat against the backstop. Although Jason was criticized by his coaches (the assistant coach called him a "girl" after the second strikeout for crying), he was not removed from the game (field notes, Beanville).

Such episodes form part of the "mundane reality" of Little League baseball. While they may cause comment and concern, they do indicate that the boy is concerned with winning and is taking the game seriously. They do not significantly discredit a boy's identity with his audience, although they may suggest that his own self-image is being revised:

> Immediately after the game Vince Tozzari, the losing pitcher for the White Sox, walks into the dugout with a very hurt look

on his face and walking with a numb gait as if shell-shocked. Several players comfort him: "Don't blame yourself, Vince." However, some of the final runs were caused by Vince, including one which scored on a passed ball. Vince blames himself for the loss, sitting and sulking on the dugout bench, not emerging for the ritual handshake with the winning team (field notes, Maple Bluff).

Emotional display is taken seriously, and to the extent that Little League baseball can be likened to work, this intense emotion must be appropriately placed (Zurcher 1982).

Injuries. As in other workplaces, Little Leaguers are subject to on-the-job injuries. Players must learn to take these "accidents" in stride. Coaches' assurances to their players that there is no danger of injury should not be taken literally:

> The Sharpstone assistant coach tells one of his ten year olds, who is afraid of being hit by a pitch: "You'll never get hit." He adds under his breath: "More than once in a while" (field notes, Hopewell).

When players are injured, if the injury is not severe, they are expected and usually desire to continue to play, despite the pain. Little Leaguers with bloody scabs are common. Sometimes the injury is so severe it cannot be ignored:

> In practice today Ray Weigert, a ten year old on Sharpstone, was severely injured. He was accidently hit on the side of the head by a bat swung by Jim Pozzi, another ten-year-old. One could hear the crack of bat against head at some distance, and Ray fell down, bleeding profusely, both fascinating and scaring the other players. Ray was rushed to the hospital, fortunately located by the field. He remained conscious, required four or five stitches, and will be able to play baseball in two weeks. At the end of practice Dave Hundley told the other players that Ray will be back soon, and it was his own fault for not wearing a batting helmet. This statement might have been made to reassure Jim, who seemed upset all throughout practice, blaming himself for what had happened. After Ray was taken to the hospital, players stood and looked at the bloodstained spot where Ray's head hit. Still, the practice continued without letup. Later in the practice, another player was hurt, spraining his ankle. After assuring themselves that he was not severely injured, players ignore him (field notes, Hopewell).

The connection between participation and injuries is not unidirectional. Players implicitly agree to take the risk of injuries when they sign up for Little League. This danger is seen as inevitable and acceptable. In addition, the social context of Little League baseball teaches boys that the proper response to these injuries (at least the milder sort) should be a studied stoicism. Although no one welcomes injuries, all realize they are integral to the sport and must be overcome if boys are to be seen as "men" working in a potentially hazardous environment.

The Rhetoric of Work in Baseball

In chapters 3 and 4, I discuss the rhetorical strategies used by players and coaches; here I note that part of the rhetoric of both players and adults is that baseball should be played diligently. Although most participants emphasize that Little League baseball should be "fun," they also argue it should be done "right." The learning of sport adds to its enjoyment.

The coach of the Hopewell Sharpstone team emphasized to his players that when they stepped onto the field they owed it to themselves to be serious and to be constantly hustling. Other coaches repeated similar themes. One parent, helping to coach a team in Sanford Heights, commented: "You guys aren't working very hard. Not trying. I hope that's not any indication of the season" (field notes, Sanford Heights). A coach told his team: "I will not criticize physical errors, but I will criticize mental errors. . . . We intend to eliminate those . . . they may lead to your being taken out of the game . . . they are caused by not having your head in a game" (field notes, Sanford Heights). This emphasis on Little League as work takes the form of commenting on the need for "hustle." Hustle contrasts with a lackadaisical attitude to the game and with the belief that Little League baseball is only a side involvement unworthy of rapt attention by preadolescent sportsmen. One reason Little League rhetoric—the moral talk used by coaches and players—is so focused on the work components of the game is the assumption that if this point were not emphasized Little League would "degenerate"—that is, become pure, anarchic fun. This possibility must be guarded against through moral talk.

Part of Little League rhetoric involves the issue of control. Like production-line workers, Little Leaguers must come to recognize that they are under the control of management and that they must acquiesce in this authority structure. The coaches on the Sharpstone team provide a good example, insisting their players call them

"Coach" when on the playing field. This policy underlines their authority in the baseball setting. Several coaches appointed players as team captains, and these preadolescent leaders aided the coach in establishing control and in enforcing discipline. In doing this coaches did not relinquish their authority as disciplinarians. For example, one assistant coach said when he felt his players were granting themselves too much authority, "There are three coaches on this team, and none of them are under twelve" (field notes, Bolton Park). Although coaches do not always enforce their authority, they have it available should they choose.

Attention. Perhaps the aspect of Little League that makes the performance most like work is that the preadolescent must pay attention to the activity for an extended period of time. Preadolescent attention is notably fickle and of short duration—a fact that exasperates their coaches. Coaches insist their players must always be prepared to make a play. One Sanford Heights coach gave his team a motto (almost a Zen koan): "Beeeeee Ready!" Before each game the team would repeat these two words in unison. Another coach attempted to teach his team the same lesson:

> The coach of the Astros has two defensive rules which he constantly emphasizes to his players. First, every ball is going to be hit to them. Second, they should know what to do with the ball if it is. Before the Minnesota Tournament quarterfinal game, the coach gathers his players around him before the game and asks a twelve-year-old, "Stan, what's the rules?" After a slight pause Stan responds, "Every ball's coming to me, and know where to throw it." The repetition of these rules by the Astros became ritualistic (field notes, Bolton Park).

Getting the players to pay attention often proves challenging for the coach. Even on the field, players are not always oriented to the baseball tasks at hand—particularly when in the outfield; they are overdistanced from their roles. Players pick dandelions, do little jigs, throw pebbles, and even sit down. Part of this behavior relates to the nature of playing in the outfield, where few balls are hit. As one regular infielder commented when asked to play in the outfield: "I need more action. That right field is so boring" (field notes, Sanford Heights). Even infielders may not attend to what is happening closely enough to suit their coaches:

> Bruce Silverstein, the coach of the White Sox, notices that his third baseman, Mark Quinton, is playing too far away from the

base. This irritates Bruce, who says to his assistant coach: "He just won't listen to me, will he? He just won't listen." Bruce sits pensively for a moment, then runs onto the field calling time. Bruce calls to Dick Greenberg, his second baseman, "Dick, go to third," and in an impatient tone, "Mark, go to second." At this point he doesn't say anything to either player about why he is making the move. However, after two more hits Bruce calls time again and goes out to the field. He starts criticizing Mark. The conversation can't be heard, but his gestures make it apparent he is referring to Mark's behavior at third base (field notes, Maple Bluff).

Behavior in the dugout poses even greater challenges for coaches. As I shall indicate later, dugout activity more often than not deals with topics unrelated to the game and provides prima facie evidence the players are not paying attention. Coaches comment, "Let's hear you talk it up out there. You sound like a morgue. . . . Get your minds on the game" (field notes, Bolton Park) or "Guys, you're working tonight. . . . You came to play ball tonight. You're working tonight" (field notes, Maple Bluff). I do not imply that the exhortation to work is only raised by the coach. Players expect others to talk it up, and some players criticize their teammates for not paying attention:

> At the end of the third inning Howie Novak is preparing to pop a paper bag. As he did it, Vince Tozzari, just coming in from the field, yells at him sternly with disgust: "Cut it out. Are you trying to impress your friends?" (field notes, Maple Bluff).

> Coming in from the field in the fourth inning of a close game, Harry Stanton, one of the twelve-year-old stars on Sharpstone, is furious with Jim Pozzi, a ten-year-old utility outfielder, whom he claims was "dancing" in right field. Harry mocks Jim by effeminately imitating his dance, adding "You're a fag, you know it!" (field notes, Hopewell).

Those who wish to emphasize the work component of the game frequently use the metaphor that those who are not paying attention are asleep:

> "Come on, Jim. Be a hitter. You're not even awake up there" (field notes, Sanford Heights).

> "We played that time like we were asleep. Is anyone ready to quit and go home?" (field notes, Bolton Park).

These quotations, which could easily be duplicated, suggest the pervasiveness of such rhetoric. Certainly sleep is not the only metaphor coaches use to get their teams to be attentive—one coach told his team that they looked like a girls' softball team when he felt that they weren't working hard enough. However, the sleep metaphor effectively translates the dichotomy of work and play to work and sleep. Of course, this metaphor cannot be used at all times when the team is judged not to be paying attention. If the team is wild and unruly, clearly it makes little sense to tell them they are asleep. Yet, if the team (or players) are daydreaming or restful, the metaphor of being asleep is effective. Without active attention the sustained performance of Little League baseball cannot be maintained. While it might continue to be fun or playful, it would no longer be something for spectators to watch, and thus the component of work in Little League would be undermined.

Apathy. Closely related to the lack of attention is the problem of preadolescent apathy—those situations in which players are over-distanced from the sports reality. Often during Little League games players are neither enthusiastic nor angry. They sit in the dugout watching the game quietly or talking and joking with each other. The problem of apathy rests on a distinction between players who are *in* the game, waiting for things to happen, and those who are *at* the game but not immediately involved. In the first case apathy or inattention is a serious structural problem. For example, an outfielder may not attend completely to the game and thus may miss a play. Likewise, batters not "mentally prepared" are criticized.

Although apathetic performances are formally inappropriate, in fact they are not often corrected or condemned. However, apathy is always potentially subject to condemnation from players or coaches, even when players aren't formally involved *in* the game. Thus, it is legitimate for coaches and teammates to tell inattentive boys in the dugout to "stop horsing around," "act alive," or "make yourself hoarse." Since Little League is a team activity, all activity within the fences should, in theory, be directed toward the work of baseball.

In these pages I have argued that there are components of the playing of Little League baseball that can usefully be seen as "work," at least in a moral sense. Coaches and many players expect the participants to adhere to a Puritan work ethic, preparing themselves for adult life. When they don't, moral disparagement is seen as warranted and is judiciously applied.

Little League as Play

Although in some ways Little League is like work, this picture is incomplete. Little League is also play and fun; more than that, the game can at times become riotously uncontrolled, with the task orientation of the game placed aside for the moment.

The Rhetoric of Fun

Erving Goffman, in his appropriately titled essay "Fun in Games," comments: "Games can be fun to play, and fun alone is the approved reason for playing them. The individual, in contrast to his treatment of "serious" activity, claims a right to complain about a game that does not pay its way in immediate pleasure and whether the game is pleasurable or not, to plead a slight excuse, such as an indisposition of mood, for not participating" (Goffman 1961, 17).

Obviously this analysis applies imperfectly to Little League baseball, where players, under control of an authority, are seen as having made a moral commitment to the activity. They are expected to live up to this commitment by continuing to participate. Indeed, Goffman specifically recognizes this constraint in his rueful comment: ". . . children, mental patients, and prisoners may not have an effective option when officials declare game-time, but it is precisely in being thus constrained that these unfortunates seem something less than persons" (Goffman 1961, 17).

Goffman is perhaps too pessimistic in indicating that children have no control of their own play despite what their "officials" say. First, adults do not always ignore play rhetoric, and second, there are ways by which participants inject play into games.

Most coaches recognize that fun is one legitimate feature of Little League and that they are there to facilitate fun for their boys: "Hugh Moskowitz, the coach of the Padres, tells his players at the first practice he intends to put in all the players for at least two innings per game, but will play his twelve-year-olds for most of the game, because they have "earned" it by being in the Little League program for three years. He adds, with emphasis: 'The main thing is . . . we're gonna have fun'" (field notes, Bolton Park).

Coaches, even while discussing the fact that players are supposed to be serious, also recognize that Little League baseball is fun. Enjoyment has a more important role than does winning per se:

Q: What do you think the goals of Little League should be?
A: I think it should be more for the boys. I don't think it

should be overorganized. . . . I think it has a tendency sometimes not to be as much fun for the boys as it should be because
of the stress put on winning. . . . I think the goal of Little
League is to get out there, have the boys meet other boys,
have fun, and to compete. . . . Just have a good time out there
(coach interview, Bolton Park).

It is inaccurate to claim that winning is secondary or that the educational aspects of the game are not important; still, one wouldn't see
so many boys participating if they didn't have a rollicking good time.

Behavioral Components of Fun

How can we tell if preadolescents are enjoying themselves and are
"playing" rather than working at sport? Three themes are consistent with the idea of "playing" at Little League baseball (and,
for that matter, all sport): (1) excitement in the game, (2) not taking
the game "seriously," and (3) becoming caught up in secondary
involvements.

Game excitement. Under some circumstances Little League baseball can be an exciting, thrilling contest. It has the potential (not
always realized) for players to get "caught up" in the game. Csikszentmihalyi (1975) has termed this experience '*flow*'—an un-self-
conscious involvement in ongoing events. One totally immerses oneself in the activity, ignoring all distractions. Such total involvement
occurs in close games, particularly in games defined as important, in
rallies, and in pitching duels. Players may stand on the dugout
bench to cheer, and on occasion the noise from the cheering is deaf-
ening. These contrast with occasions in which the team "seems
dead" and the coach or team captain must generate an artificial excitement. In situations of "play," excitement emerges from the game
events themselves.

Most of the time, even on the most enthusiastic of teams, players
are not excited. However, excitement can be kindled if players are
emotionally involved in the game. When a player hits a home run,
his teammates typically run from the dugout to greet him as he
crosses home plate; they pat him on the back and shower him with
praise. While this greeting may be forced, often it is joyous. The
action of one player provides a legitimation for his teammates to express their role involvement. This kindling of emotion also occurs
when a game that has appeared hopeless is suddenly won:

After the regulation six innings Hopewell Police is tied with
Jamesville Hospital 7–7. In the top of the seventh inning play-

ers on Jamesville Hospital become very exicted after loading the bases and scoring two runs. The Hopewell Police team is quiet, depressed, and near tears. However, in their turn at bat, Police scores three runs, winning the game. Players on Hopewell Police become ecstatic, and Kip Taviss, their twelve-year-old third baseman, climbs on the backstop and screams "his head off" with excitement (field notes, Hopewell).

Cheering provides a measure of the excitement that can be infused into a Little League game. This cheering, when not created artificially, is part of the playful aspect of Little League baseball and is almost as much fun as actually being in the game (Larson 1980). Some teams in Bolton Park had special cheers that, although appropriate in the game situation, were also infused with playfulness:

The Astros have a unique manner of cheering for their teammates [subsequently adopted by two other teams]. When one of their players (e.g., Bill) comes up to bat and is waiting for a pitch, they yell out: "Come on Biiiiiiiiiiiiiiiiiiiiiiiill!" The cheer ends at the moment the pitch has been resolved as a ball, strike, or hit. Then the cheer begins again. The players on the bench are "in" the game as much as the boy who is up at bat (field notes, Bolton Park).

Teams in other leagues also respond with vigorous cheering in unison, reminding a listener of a tribal chant to propitiate the gods in preparation for war. One team in Hopewell kept up a chorus of "Dadde-eye" ("that's the eye") while their players were batting. However, this cheering does not occur at all times but only with intense involvement in the game. These are not behaviors forced on the team (although cheering sometimes is) but emerge from the excitement of the situation.

Not taking the game seriously. Although intense involvement in the game can imply seeing the game as fun, I shall now consider the opposite—not treating the game seriously, which also indicates the existence of fun. This involves undermining the work ethic implied in Little League baseball:

Sandy Foy, a ten-year-old occasional first baseman, tells me after he comes in from fielding that he pretended a ball was lost over the fence so he could continue to search for it and not play. Actually he had kicked it into the high grass near the field (field notes, Hopewell).

Preadolescents in their practice and sometimes in their play may act in ways that indicate they are more interested in the enjoyment that can be generated from their play than from the formal rules:

> Justin is practicing bunting for Sharpstone. At one pitch he turns completely around in the batter's box and then bunts. The coach tells him that will get him thrown out of a game. Justin thinks his play is a big joke and is so amused that he replays it for his teammates (field notes, Hopewell).

The player, while seemingly working within the constraints of baseball, is actually playfully undermining it. Occasionally this happens in the game itself, as when an outfielder seeing a fly ball hit out of reach throws his glove at it, transforming work into play. Throwing a glove at a batted ball is even more common in practice and provides a message to the coach that his fielders have lost interest. Similarly, stolen-base practice may become chaotic when players are more interesting in performing humorous or bizarre slides than slides that are competent in sports terms. The coach must decide how much of this silliness to permit. Obviously coaches differ on the extent to which they feel they can permit practices and games to drift out of their control. Most seem threatened when players change the definition of Little League from a competitive and learning situation to one characterized by voluntary, playful activity. Some of the most graphic examples of the playful attitude occur within the game itself:

> Bruce Smith trips over Randy Catlin's foot while coming into the dugout. Apparently Randy tripped Bruce on purpose, although Bruce obviously thought it was funny. Their coach criticizes them, implying it was malicious. He says to Randy: "How many times have I talked to you about clowning around. I can't count the number of times." Defending Randy from criticism Bruce says "it's all right," indicating that no harm was done (field notes, Maple Bluff).

> Joey O'Brien and Don Lawrence of the Cardinals often joke during games. When Joey hits a triple, Don, who is white, goes over to third base and gives Joey, also white, a big "black-style" handshake with his hand raised rather than at belt level. This ritual consists of several complicated motions and ends in a mutual bump of rear ends. Joey knew the performance of this ritual and followed Don precisely (field notes, Maple Bluff).

Although coaches can become distressed at silliness during the game, this attitude is not inevitable: some coaches occasionally permit playful antics:

> Just prior to the top of the sixth (and final) inning, Tony Denton, a high-status Pirates player who had been injured and removed from the game, went running out to shortstop and called the pitchers and infielders together in a huddle. Apparently Tony was telling the others to act in unison when he gave the signal. Occasionally the group would stand up on their toes and crouch down with their hands on their knees. As this was happening Terry Conklin, the Pirates assistant coach, looked at his father Phil, the Pirates coach, with a look of disbelief and asked: "What's going on there?" Phil replied in an amused tone: "Oh, I don't know. They're just having fun. Let 'em be. In another five years they'll be out working" (field notes, Maple Bluff).

Fortunately for the structure of Little League, playfulness, a form of overdistance, did not become so prominent that the game itself became subverted. These activities serve as temporary changes of tempo rather than constituting permanent orientations to the game structure.

Side involvements. Little League baseball is not continually exciting. When the game is interesting, players' attention focuses on what is happening; however, when the game is routine, as is more often the case, players' attention can be drawn to other activities that are more interesting at the moment. For example:

> Randy Brosky and Tom Capek of the Pirates are in the dugout playing a ball game initiated by Tom. It consists of bouncing a ball at an angle off the floor and one wall of the dugout so it lands in the upper rafters of the dugout. There is a small crack where the rafters meet the back wall, and the object of the game is to get the ball into one of these cracks. The task is sufficiently difficult that it holds Tom's attention for most of the game (field notes, Maple Bluff).

> Carey Kasky is sitting in the Orioles dugout eating a box of Red Hots (cinnamon candy drops). He begins throwing them at his teammates; the coaches (including his father) do not interfere. Soon most of the players are throwing Red Hots and are laughing wildly. Todd Caxton, one of the twelve-year-old stars on the team, throws a Red Hot which hits Carey's father

on the back of the neck. The team thinks this is hilarious. Mr. Kasky doesn't become upset at this fooling around (field notes, Bolton Park).

These incidents are but two of many side involvements: throwing dirt, playing with water balloons, chasing each other, playing soccer in the dugout with a rock, tossing hats in the air on a windy day, and many other activities, mundane or exciting. The game can be transfixed, because engrossment varies as a consequence of the immediate situation. Although one player told me "we eat and sleep Little League" (field notes, Sanford Heights), sometimes they eat and sleep during the game.

This differs from not taking the game seriously, in that it involves, not a transformation of the game itself, but rather an alternative to the game that is defined as providing greater enjoyment than what would have otherwise occurred. Preadolescent boys do what they wish, but even professionals (see Luciano and Fisher 1982; Bouton 1970) may become distracted, engaging in alternate activities that are more appealing and hence "more fun." Since Little League is voluntary, it is a challenge for adults or work-oriented children to force others to keep their attention on the task.

Two features characterize side involvements. First, their existence means players are not paying attention to the game. In other words, the game is not generating an adequate amount of fun to maintain engrossment in what is happening. This by itself does not produce "goofing off" or "fooling around." Second, there must be an alternate activity that does engross the player—even if such an activity is as mundane as throwing pebbles or splashing water. Together these two features produce an alternate world of meaning that competes with Little League baseball for the player's attention by providing "fun" in a spirit of play.

As long as this side involvement is a "secondary" involvement, the Little League game can continue unabated; if ever involvement becomes primary, the sport is threatened—as in the following instance:

Tim Mizell and Boyd Timasheff are fooling around in the dugout while their team is batting. Tim says to Boyd: "Open your mouth and close your eyes and you'll get a big surprise." At this Tim throws a pebble into Boyd's mouth, which begins to bleed. The coach becomes upset at their "horsing around." However, his knowledge of the incident comes only from its unfortunate outcome. Had Boyd not been cut, nothing would have been done to stop their kidding as they were not monitored in the dugout (field notes, Hopewell).

In every Little League game, numerous side involvements occur, but fortunately for the serious performance of Little League, they rarely become primary, and no Little League game has been called on account of "fun."

The Character of Work and Play

I have argued that there are components of Little League baseball that may be defined as being worklike and other aspects that seem playlike. The metaphors for both work and play adequately described parts of Little League baseball. Preadolescent attention and action oscillate. Rarely is any situation so engrossing that it is not subject to shifts of focus. As should be clear, it is not the playing of baseball itself that is inevitably work; such performance can be play, if treated in that way—as a voluntary, nonconstrained, nonpressured activity. Likewise, activity outside of the game framework can be mundane and in a sense worklike. The definition of work or play depends, not on whether or not the activity is baseball, but on how that activity is treated.

It is impossible and futile to define the performance of Little League baseball as either work or play. To the extent baseball is treated as task oriented and externally directed, it is a form of work; to the extent it is flexible, free, and involves choice, it is play. In fact, it is both; each metaphor contributes to our understanding.

Of course, one should remember that our notions of work and play are metaphors and should not be reified. *Work* and *play* are simply terms that outside observers and inside participants ascribe to activities, but they are not the activity itself. People act in ways that seem appropriate under the circumstances without a self-conscious consideration of what sort of action they are engaging in; they behave in ways that seem appropriate at the moment. The distinction between work and play as separable concepts is false, and nowhere is this better illustrated than in preadolescent sport—where winning and fun combine together to produce a game that is appropriate for spectators to observe and worthwhile for participants to play voluntarily.

3

Moral Socialization: Adult Concerns

Little League baseball is not only a world of action, it is also a world of talk. In the next two chapters I examine dimensions of moral socialization—divided pragmatically by their source, to explain how children come to accept the rightness of what they are expected to do on the Little League field, and implicitly in other arenas of their lives. In this chapter I explore the rules that adult males— coaches—present to their young charges. In the following chapter I discuss socialization among peers—how preadolescents believe they should play baseball. Through this talk, the boy's self and his knowledge of how to present this self to others are being developed: What is the range of appropriate behaviors and roles available, and how can one manipulate them in a variety of situations? Children are not being exposed to moral verities; rather, they are taught to use moral statements and beliefs in situations in which such morality pragmatically applies. Their use of rhetoric suggests to the world that these boys are becoming *mature*.

Adult-Child Socialization

Adult-child interaction is viewed by adults as a profoundly moral enterprise (Macleod 1983). Adults believe that they have a moral obligation to teach values and social propriety to those children with whom they regularly come into contact. These moral messages are reflections of their world view—at least the ideal or "ought" form of that moral order. Adults present moral dicta so as to deny the possibility of negotiation; however, preadolescents, examining these statements in their situational context, learn that moral dicta are only presented occasionally, they are situationally grounded, and they are rhetorical exhortations as much as absolute statements. By the time children reach preadolescence, they are skilled at manipulating moral messages to foster their chosen impressions.

In dealing with children, the adult assumes he must treat the

59

world as an ideal world, this view must be accepted by children (even though it is empirically unfounded), and the actions of children must reflect it. In other words, children are not instructed in the situational contingencies of moral decisions. Yet, moral issues are open to negotiation. Consider the dilemmas of "Beaver" Cleaver in those classic television morality plays, "Leave It to Beaver." Beaver was continually acting on the basis of situationally based morality, characteristic of preadolescence. The moral drama consisted of his adult caretakers discovering the situationally grounded character of Beaver's action and insisting he renounce those actions based on this morality, using instead absolute, conventional middle-class morality.

Adults profess "ideal" moral rules while in the presence of children. Yet, preadolescents are not so naive as to accept such transparent arguments. Children, particularly with their peers, behave more in accord with the world as they observe it than with the world as professed by adults. Preadolescents share a peer culture that is resistant to adult pressures. However, adults generally deride this facet of childhood socialization, and attempts at conversion ("socialization") are seen as desirable (see Dreitzel 1973; Speier 1973). Most children are willing to be parties to this exercise in hegemony—in part because of the rewards provided to those who conform. Successful socialization is learning when to express the moral verities proclaimed by adults, discerning which ones they "really" mean, and knowing what moral rhetoric to adopt when caught red-handed. I do not presume a cynical exploitation—rather, situations have a coercive power over absolute moral statements. Just as adults use moral statements situationally and pretend they are absolute, so do preadolescents.

Moral indoctrination is particularly prevalent in institutions that have *character-building* as an explicit goal—e.g., schools, religious groups, families, athletic teams, and Boy Scout troops (Hantover 1978; Macleod 1983). With its emphasis on competition and achievement, organized sport is a social setting in which the child acquires "character" from adults.

Most athletic proponents claim that participation in organized sports is an excellent way for children to build character, although some researchers doubt this verity (see Ogilvie and Tutko 1971; Edwards 1973, 103; Stevenson 1975). Character building is heavily emphasized in Little League rhetoric, which presumably is believed. The Official Rules of Little League Baseball proclaim that the purpose of the organization is didactic:

Little League Baseball is a program of service to youth. It is geared to provide an outlet of healthful activity and a training under good leadership in the atmosphere of wholesome community participation. The movement is dedicated to helping children become good and decent citizens. It strives to inspire them with a goal and to enrich their lives towards the day when they must take their places in the world. It establishes for them rudiments of teamwork and fair play (*Little League Baseball:* 2).

Whether Little League achieves its motto of "Character, Courage, Loyalty" has been vigorously debated; however, most coaches *try* to match this ideal. The coach is given responsibility for instructing his players in the need for hard work, cooperation, competition, sportsmanship, and good citizenship, as well as teaching them the proper techniques for playing baseball. According to a Little League official, the boy should learn from his coach how to handle his feelings. "The coach is a voice—guiding, teaching, offering opinions on the boy's progress and assessing his value as a person" (Johnson 1973, 1).

Most studies of athletic socialization treat athletic morality in general terms, with little attention to the situations in which values, norms, and behaviors are transmitted. To specify socialization I will focus on four basic themes that coaches employ to instruct their players in the moral order of sport: (1) effort, (2) sportsmanship, (3) teamwork, and (4) coping with victory and defeat. These four are central to the moral enterprise called Little League baseball and also have implications for the preadolescent's mastering of presentation of self in the adult world. Obviously these four themes are glosses for complex constellations of attitudes and behaviors; still, they reflect goals that coaches feel are important.

Depicting the Moral Order

Moral statements in sport result from attributions that coaches make about players and their motivations. The coach doesn't respond to baseball plays but to the *meanings* of these plays for him. This attribution of motivation allows the coach to develop a moral stance. Although coaches cannot be certain about players' motivations, they feel confident in their beliefs, and treat these beliefs as a basis for talk. The actual beliefs and feelings of the players are inaccessible to the coach; they are only available through talk and behavior that are taken as indicators of internal states, and through conventionalized understandings about what preadolescents "should" be feeling in such situations. The general acceptance of the coach's comments by players suggests the adequacy of social conventions and the authority of the coach's definition.

Moral evaluations are found in two types of settings. Coaches may impart these messages as "set pieces" in formal talks before and after games, or the messages may be part of the interaction between coach and player during the game. In general, comments during a game are less global than declamations that bracket the game; however, both reflect moral verities, and both are based on adult assessments of preadolescent beliefs.

The Importance of Effort

It is an American cliche that "if something is worth doing, it is worth doing well." In sports, this proverb is psychologically central. However, knowing whether an action is being "done well" is not always easy: how do we judge? The assumption is that *trying* is recognizable and is distinct from success and failure (see Iso-Ahola 1976, 43). Some Little League coaches make this distinction explicitly, claiming that they do not care about winning as long as their players do their "best":

> There are several ways to play baseball. Some people play to win. But I believe that if a game isn't fun, it isn't worth doing. Other people believe that the only reason to play baseball is to have fun, and they often fool around and play baseball only half the time. I believe that baseball is a game to learn, to learn to develop your skill, to get the most out of yourself, and if you do that, baseball will be more fun than you imagine. Your goal for the year is to be a winner. That doesn't mean winning every game. Sometimes you will be up against teams that are better than you. It does mean to give everything you've got. If you give everything that you've got, you're a winner in my book. The only one who cares is the man who made you, and He made both teams, both winners and losers. Give everything you got (field notes, Bolton Park, first practice).

> I believe in taking Little League baseball seriously. There is a time to horse around and a time to be serious. I take the Little League pledge of doing your best seriously. If we play good

ball and lose, you'll never hear a cross word from me. You will hear from me if you play bad ball and win. That's as bad as losing (field notes, Sanford Heights, first practice).

These coaches assume that players will "horse around" if given the chance, so they warn players that Little League is serious. Since most coaches believe that trying one's hardest ultimately will lead to victory, it follows that coaches may perceive a lack of effort when team records are unsatisfactory. Some coaches explicitly proclaim a connection between effort and success:

Whenever you guys are inside the fence I want to see you hustle. The name of the game is hustle. I promise you that if you hustle, you're going to win this year (field notes, Hopewell, first practice).

Only three words—hustle, pride, and class—and everything will fall into place (field notes, Maple Bluff, first practice).

Coaches treat defeat as prima facie evidence of lack of effort or "hustle." Although a coach may praise his team for good effort in a losing cause, this is rare and often occurs when a poor team almost vanquishes a superior team.

Ascription of effort to individual players. Poor efforts by individuals are often interpreted as representing an absence of hustle and not merely physical inadequacy. A lack of motivation is more easily correctable than a lack of ability.

Coach to eleven-year-old utility outfielder after he misses a catch in practice: "David, you got to want to, you know" (field notes, Hopewell).

Assistant coach to twelve year old after he is called out attempting to stretch a single to a double: "If you hadn't loafed on the way to first, you would have made it" (field notes, Sanford Heights).

These comments locate the problem in the player's motivation. To some extent this assumption is legitimate, and occasionally players admit that they should have tried harder. Effort is one component of well-executed baseball; however, this can be an explanation for failure even if it does not apply (see Ball 1976; Harris and Eitzen 1978). On other occasions a coach may praise a boy's motivation to reinforce his behavior:

Assistant coach to twelve-year-old starting pitcher, pitching well after losing his previous game: "You're pitching like you mean it" (field notes, Bolton Park).

Often coaches compliment a boy after having reason to question his motivation previously, in order to reinforce his "improved attitude." It is difficult to imagine a Little League pitcher not throwing as if he "means it," although intensity may be variable. Attributing a lack of hustle is a routine criticism, and coaches routinely do not indicate how the player should improve his skills; the implication is that the player has the necessary physical skills and needs only to activate them.

These attributions are exaggerated when coaches criticize boys for being "asleep" (see chapter 2). Such comments were directed to boys who seemed not to be paying attention, or at least who made decisions not to act (swing or throw) when coaches thought action was required. Reputation influences the coach's attribution of motivation; some boys have reputations as "hustlers" or "gutsy little ball players," while others are suspected of lacking interest ("goof-offs"). Behavior is interpreted through the coach's understanding of those "stable" traits he feels his players exhibit.[1]

Criticizing a boy for a lack of hustle is a potent weapon because it doesn't permit a response. Coaches may treat a *denial* as symptomatic of a lack of hustle; if the charges were unjustified, the highly motivated player would accept them and would attempt to do better. How many sportsmen can immodestly claim to be doing their absolute best? Also, the player has no evidence to point to in his own defense, since his motivation is internal. The cues that the coach uses as the basis of attribution do not make an adequate defense. Players rarely dispute motivational attributions, even though at times they do not accept them, whereas they *do* dispute judgments of the coach in regard to external, publicly observable events ("that pitch was way outside," "you should have backed up further to catch that"). Ironically that which the preadolescent player should know best (his feelings) is that for which he can claim least defense. From this interplay the player learns how to give criticism and accounts of behavior. One cannot adequately defend oneself from an internal accounting but can point to an external contingency that led to the event; similarly one can condemn the behavior of another by impugning his internal motivation. As a result, preadolescents defend themselves by claiming that they should not have swung at a pitch because of its location and criticize by asserting that others are lazy or not trying.

Ascription of effort to the team. Coaches make attributions not only to individual players but also to the team as a unit. In criticizing his team, a coach need not attribute a lack of motivation to all players but may see a lack of motivation among the players typically considered most motivated, coupled with the absence of high motivation among others. The criticism is a generalization rather than a description, and it represents a form of stereotyping. Again, success and desire are linked:

> Assistant coach after several errors during practice: "I'm glad I'm working nights so I won't get to see you fellows play, because I think you guys are going to get racked up. . . . Play the game like it's supposed to be played" (field notes, Hopewell).

> Coach after his team lost what he considered to be an easy game: "You didn't have any pep out there. . . . You guys didn't want it" (field notes, Sanford Heights).

Past occasions on which the coach did not criticize his team can be reinterpreted as reflecting a lack of motivation:

> Coach after his team (with a 6–3 record) loses 5–1: "You guys are sleeping out there. If you have no pride in yourself, I don't want you. . . . In other games, even in games in which you guys won, there was a lack of hustle. . . . I won't quit on you, don't you quit on me" (field notes, Sanford Heights).

Of course, coaches may retrospectively rewrite history to denigrate other teams, but this is rarer because the actions of other teams generally have less moral relevance:

> Before an important game the coach of the second-place team refers to the actions of the first-place team, which his team had beaten earlier in the week, as a model for his team to avoid. The Astros (the first-place team) had scored two runs in the top of the frst inning, and the Orioles (the second-place team) had come back to score three runs in the bottom of the first inning, eventually winning 5–4. The Orioles coach refers to the Astros' behavior in the bottom of the first inning: "There was no chatter. There was no nothing. Their heads were down like lost dogs. . . . To me, I think we're a better team than

them. . . . If we play the way we played last week, we can win"
(field notes, Bolton Park).

The coach strategically uses the behavior of the Astros to contrast with the hustling of the Orioles. Coaches employ a variety of
strategies to cope with their own frustrations at what they judge
is a team lacking in motivation, drawing from all corners of pop
psychology:

> Coach to his team before a game, after losing two consecutive
> games: "I don't know what to tell you. Just go out there and
> have fun. If you want to swing, go ahead and swing; if you
> don't want to swing, don't swing. If you want to catch the ball,
> go ahead; if you don't want to catch the ball, that's OK too. If
> you want to drop the ball behind your head, that's OK. . . .
> We've tried everything and nothing seems to work, so go
> ahead and do what you want. If you want to swing, go ahead; if
> not, go ahead. . . ." (About fifteen minutes later this talk is
> continued; players had become rowdy again after being silent
> at first): "I only ask one thing of you tonight; like I said you can
> go out and do anything you want: drop the ball, swing if you
> want, I don't care. Just do me one favor: no excuses tonight.
> None of this 'he threw it too fast'—no excuses. I'll tell you one
> thing: you're wrong. That's not the problem. It's not the um-
> pire's fault or because it's too low or too high or any of that. It's
> nobody else's fault. It's your own fault, because you're not try-
> ing" (field notes, Maple Bluff).

Although the content varies, the themes of coaches' remarks are
similar. The coach defines success as a result of effort, not external
factors, such as the umpire, the opposition, or ability. Motivation is
the only variable the coach can readily manipulate, and thus such
comments may give the coach a sense of efficacy. The athletic credo,
empirically incorrect, that "you are *only* limited by your desire" indicates the stress on this aspect of play.

This vision is conducive to blame and scapegoating, and it is not
surprising that players and coaches blame others for baseball lapses,
since their sports socialization emphasizes the intentionality of victory. Events that *in themselves* have no moral implications (victory
and defeat) are imbued with moral meaning, and players' actions are
given a moral worth that spreads to the evaluation of the player by
others. Iso-Ahola's research on players' attributions of success and
failure (1976, 1977a, 1977b; see also Roberts 1978) demonstrates that

success and failure (winning and losing) did *not* influence player's judgments of their own effort but did affect judgments of team effort. Failure tends to provoke external attributions of blame when judging one's own failure but internal attributions when evaluating the failures of others. The potential danger in competitive sports may lie less in the direct effects of competition on the self-image, than in what competition does to the evaluation of others.[2]

The reactions of players to a marginal eleven-year-old player who successfully stole second base while his team was behind 4–1 late in the game reveals this scapegoating. The boy finds himself in a maelstrom of criticism, generated as a result of the coach's questioning of the team's attention:

> After Dickie Brickman steals second base, the coach yells at the team: "Who sent him?! Who sent him?!" The twelve-year-old catcher yells at his teammate: "Dickie, knock it off!" The twelve-year-old pitcher yells: "Brickman, there are two outs, get with it!" It is never clear who, if anyone, sent him (field notes, Sanford Heights).

Dickie's teammates assume that he should have understood the situation but didn't *care* enough to know what was going on and so was blameworthy.

Team attributions need not always be negative. Teams that triumph in trying circumstances may be praised for their motivation, although more often the praise emphasizes skill. Motivation seems of particular relevance when a contrast is drawn between present effort and past indolence.

> Assistant coach after his team wins following several defeats: "See what hustle can do?" Coach: "All you did differently was hustle" (field notes, Maple Bluff).

Situations are redefined so that motivation becomes the crucial variable that produces success. This rhetoric occurs despite the competitive nature of Little League, in which it is hard to imagine teams *not* motivated to win and in which this motivation is reinforced by parents and peers.

Sportsmanship

Although sportsmanship is somewhat easier to observe than motivation, it too is situational (Allison 1981). Sportsmanship is difficult to define precisely, although it has been defined simply as the "Golden Rule applied to sports" (Jackson 1949, 13). Coaches mention it less frequently than other themes, and sportmanship is, in practice, somewhat tangential to socialization in Little League baseball, despite its emphasis in official Little League literature. The reasons for this may not be self-evident. First, Little League is oriented to success, and losing (the only time when sportmanship is perceived as problematic) is not easily handled by adult supervisors. The second explanation casts a more positive light on Little League baseball and its participants: Sportmanship is rarely mentioned because it is rarely an issue. Coaches begin the season by suggesting the importance of sportsmanship toward umpires and other teams, and preadolescents generally abide by this guideline. Most grumbling and anger is expressed within the context of team interaction and not publicly displayed (i.e., it occurs within the walls and fences of the dugout). A third explanation for the lack of general comments about sportsmanship concerns the handling of the problems that do occur. They are treated as specific cases, not as symptoms of a deeper disorder in the game; these problems are dealt with individually.

This third explanation suggests that coaches' behavior regarding sportsmanship contrasts with their behavior regarding effort. Coaches treat a lack of hustle as a potentially major problem, whereas an unmannerly act is a temporary disturbance. Coaches were unanimous in their assessment of their players as basically well mannered, whereas several coaches criticized their teams for not exerting enough effort. The coach pictures the preadolescent as a good sport except under extreme stress but as a boy who may not work hard without adult pressure.

Two major problems motivate the coach to attempt to control sportsmanship: reactions to failure and extreme rivalry.

Failure. As a result of team or personal failure, players may become visibly agitated and display behaviors that coaches consider inappropriate for their age and in the context of play. The preadolescent may forget that his presentation of self must be based upon adult conceptions of the world—a world in which hostility is inappropriate and sanctionable. Discipline may be difficult for the coach who is agitated and upset and is thinking, not about instilling sportsmanship, but about his primary goal of victory. In addition, criticizing a boy for a lack of sportsmanship when the player is already upset is not pleasant because it requires facing the boy's sour emotions and becoming a target for his anger. Finally, the boys who are most likely to engage in unsportsmanlike behaviors are those who are seen as most difficult to "reach"; that is, those who refuse to share the moral order of the adult world. When such players become visibly agitated, a coach frequently will "talk them down" but in doing this may feel that even implied criticism might make things worse. Thus, coaches regularly overlook a lack of sportsmanship or treat it as a situation that requires a maximum of personal support. Coaches differ in the techniques (support versus blame) that they find most effective:

> Assistant coach to nine-year-old who has struck out: "Don't throw your bat. Even Mickey Mantle strikes out" (field notes, Hopewell).

> Assistant coach to eleven-year-old who has struck out: "Don't throw the bat. If you're going to stand there and not swing, don't throw the bat. It's not the bat's fault" (field notes, Maple Bluff).

Little League players are generally "well behaved" in the presence of adults, and appeals to "sportsmanship" are more necessary to control parents and spectators when they fail to maintain appropriate role distance.

Rivalry. Coaches also talk about sportsmanship when players become overly aggressive toward the opposing team. Each player is expected to cheer for his team and may be charged with lacking team spirit if he is "dead" or if the dugout is "like a morgue." Simultaneously coaches must distinguish between "rattling" the opposition, which is legitimate (cf. Irace 1960) and harrassing them, which is not. Coaches distinguish between these on the basis of the importance of the game, the score, and their own attitudes toward the other team (e.g., the existence of a bitter rivalry):

> The coaches of the two best teams had a fierce rivalry over five years. In one game, which meant the championship if the team in first place won, and in which the son of the second-place team's coach was pitching, the assistant coach of the first-place team tells his players: "Get him rattled. Get him rattled." He later tells his players to ask the umpire for the count of balls and strikes: "That rattles him to think about the count" (field notes, Bolton Park).

> In a game which had to be played over because of darkness, and in which the team that was ahead thought the coach of the other team had been stalling, the assistant coach of the team which had been ahead told his players to rattle the opposing

pitcher who was pitching poorly: "Can't you see this guy's having problems? Get on him" (field notes, Hopewell).

Coach to his team in the last game of the season—a game that will not affect the standings: "Guys, you got a big lead; I don't want any monekying around out there, I want no talking to them. I want you to be good sports" (field notes, Maple Bluff).

The relevance of sportsmanship is situationally determined—and not absolute as some have suggested (Jackson 1949). Behaviors that are legitimate on one occasion are not in another, and players must learn to recognize the cues legitimizing "unsportsmanlike" behavior. It is not that sportsmanship is unimportant, but it is a rhetoric raised on occasions when it is in one's self-interest. Preadolescents become adept at sanctioning adults whom they feel are behaving undesirably, using the rubric of sportsmanship to demonstrate the moral weakness of the adult's behavior:

A twelve-year-old first baseman remarks sarcastically to his teammates about the opposing coach in a hotly contested preseason practice game: "Real sportsmanship. He goes to the catcher: "If that guy in the batter's box doesn't get out of the way [when the catcher is throwing to second base, trying to catch a base runner], I want you to take his head off" (field notes, Bolton Park).

Although it happens rarely, the preadolescent's own coach may be subject to moral evaluation, as when one twelve year old claimed his coach, who had become involved in a bitter argument with a rival "has the worst manners of any coach" (field notes, Bolton Park).

Teamwork

Adults often view preadolescents as egocentric, or as only beginning to develop a sense of others' needs and desires. Preadolescent action is considered the fulfillment of personal goals rather than group ends. Although the young child is largely self-centered, by late preadolescence this attitude is being transformed into an overriding concern with the peer group and the good opinion of others (Kohen-Raz 1971, 119).

Yet even older boys do not always display the concern with teamwork their coaches feel is appropriate. Twelve-year-olds, who are very conscious of their self-presentation, may orient themselves to a peer (or reference) group that is not identical to the team. Thus, a boy may gain more status by being a "prima donna" (a term generally used by coaches) or a "hot dog" (a term used by players) than by being a "team player."

Because coaches believe that their players often think primarily of personal glory rather than team success, they see teamwork as part of the moral order in which they must instruct their players. Coaches state this belief explicitly; one coach, when asked about the goals of Little League baseball, responded:

> You know, you got the opportunity for cooperation with other people and to try to accomplish something as a team; being a team effort is very important whether you're a good player or not. . . . This teamwork is very important. That's one of the things that life's all about, is working as a team. Little League is that opportunity (coach interview, Sanford Heights).

To be sure, there is a pragmatic aspect to this emphasis on team-work in that teamwork is believed to correlate with success but learning teamwork is a moral goal in itself. One coach commented that Little League baseball was as important for preadolescents as the army was for young men in that it taught them to work as a unit (coach interview, Sanford Heights). The Little League team may be a boy's first organization that has an overt *collective* task that is en-forced and can only be achieved with his active participation. In this, the Little League team differs from families, church groups, school classrooms, and Boy Scout troops.

The importance of teamwork is stressed at the beginning of the season and throughout the year whenever the coach ascribes a lack of cooperation:

> Expos coach to players at a preseason practice: "For the past three years we have been the big team, but this year we're the little guys. . . . This year we've got to play together as a team." Later he reminds his players: "Pull for your team. We don't have room for a bunch of individuals. Every one of us must do our best. Last year we had a lot of prima donnas, and we only came in third." One of his returning twelve-year-old players deliberately belchs, and the team laughs uproariously (field notes, Sanford Heights).

The reaction of the Expos players to the coach's remarks indicates that the charge made to them can be rejected. Whether because of different personnel or different situations, teams respond variously to coaches' comments. The belch by the Expos player symbolically indicated the lack of teamwork evident that year; the raucous laughter was the team's ratification of that lack of concern with competitive Little League baseball. Although one must be wary of explanations based on the experience of a single team, the Expos finished mired in last place, winning only three of eighteen games, well below preseason predictions. The Expos were known throughout the season for their lack of team spirit—on which their coach commented in the postseason interview:

> They weren't really problem kids; it's more with attitude. It's not that they were creating problems, but they really weren't playing the best they could together (coach interview, Sanford Heights).

Whether their last-place finish was *caused* by their lack of teamwork, it was attributed to that.

Other coaches with similar philosophies but different players found that their players did accept teamwork as a desirable goal:

> Coach to team before their first game: "On the Cardinal team everyone plays. We're not the Cardinals. We took the *I* out. We're the Cards, or you'll have to say Cardinals without the *I*, which sounds funny." Players laugh approvingly (field notes, Sanford Heights).

This team's laughter is a ratification of the coach's moral order of baseball, not an affront to it, as was the case with the Expos.

As with effort, the presence or absence of teamwork is believed to be obvious and easily defined. Again, the proof of the pudding is in the eating, as a successful team may be praised for demonstrating teamwork:

> Coach to team after victory: "I was very proud of some of you guys. It was a good team effort" (field notes, Sanford Heights).

> Coach after a come-from-behind victory: "Isn't that nice to come back and win it? It was a team effort. Everybody played well" (field notes, Bolton Park).

Contrast this to a statement made by a coach when he judges his team to be playing poorly:

> Coach to team after a preseason loss, while the entire team is angry and depressed: "Some of you guys played yourselves out of jobs. No thinking out here. No aggression is being shown on balls. Nobody wants to take charge out there. You're a team; you got to play as a team. You got to start to think. You can't

stand there with two outs and let the ball go by" (field notes, Sanford Heights).

Examining these quotations, and listening to them in context, convinces me that the coach is not responding to a clear indicator of a concrete phenomenon. Rather, he makes a situationally constructed evaluation, indicating that several players are making mistakes or that a confluence of superior plays is occurring within an athletic sequence. An exceptional throw by one boy and an exceptional catch by his teammate are together defined as an example of teamwork indicating team momentum (Adler and Adler 1978, 162). If the two actions occur in separate plays, the coach might not use the construct of "teamwork" but rather that of "hustle" to describe the behavior.

The rhetoric of teamwork and team spirit is connected with that of effort in such activities as cheering for one's teammates and avoiding fights with them. Whereas "effort" is linked to personal responsibility and group actualization, "teamwork" is considered to be a social responsibility, as exemplified in one coach's family analogy: "We are a team. We are a family. We got to pull together" (field notes, Bolton Park). This analogy explicitly places the coach in the position of father and also defines sports as a moral enterprise. As with effort and sportsmanship, mentioning teamwork is part of the adult's interpretive process—a process that creates morally significant issues from the physical movements of children.

Winning and Losing

The final moral issue incorporates the other three within its scope. One of the major aspects of Little League baseball recognized by both critics and proponents is the fact that in Little League boys learn how to win and lose. They learn how to behave in situations both of victory and of defeat, although because of team structure, ability, and coaching, some teams must learn to deal with victory more often than defeat, while others learn the reverse.

Both victory and defeat pose moral issues, although the former are considerably more pleasant to deal with. Coaches frequently begin the season by deemphasizing the importance of the win-loss record of the team as long as the other moral factors, discussed above, are met:

> The coach during the team's second practice gathers the team in front of him: "What would you say if I said you have to win all your games to satisfy me?" (Some of his players say they

can do it.) "What would you say if I said you would have to win the pennant to satisfy me?" (Some overly agreeable players, not trained in adult rhetoric, say "sure"). "You won't have to do any of those things. There are four things that you have to do to satisfy me. The four things have to do with integrity. Do you know what it has to do with?" (One player answers "honesty.") "That's basically right. It means being what you claim to be. You do the same things when we [the coaches] are looking and when our backs are turned. It also means not cheating. We want you to be an encourager. Mainly to the other guys on the team. Third is sportsmanship. That means not griping when you lose. That means not griping when the umpire makes a call against you. That means not riding the other team. That's the way some teams win, but that's not the way I want you to play. The fourth is dedication. That means playing as hard as you can, and dedication means playing as hard as you can in practice as well as in games. That's what I expect out of you. I'm not dissatisfied with last night's practice, but if you don't improve from last night, I will be dissatisfied. If you lose a game to a better team, I don't care. I don't want us to beat ourselves" (field notes, Bolton Park).

However, the issue of what constitutes a better team is problematic, particularly because most coaches expect to win many more games than they lose and expect to come in first or second. Most coaches find these expectations frustrated. And such global statements may be systematically different from the conduct of the coaches within a game, as the overarching concept of integrity takes a backseat to the pragmatic concern of *winning* baseball games. Players learn that integrity is a rhetorical strategy one should raise only in certain times and places.

The adults involved with Little League tend to be oriented toward winning, losing, and competition, and they reveal this in symptomatic behavior. The coach of the Astros arrived at the field on opening day at 8:00 A.M. (The opening day ceremony starts at 9:30 A.M.). He told me he drives around all night before opening day. Another coach told me that the year before, the Astros coach drove to Duluth, and another year to Eau Claire, Wisconsin. This other coach claims he himself gets so nervous before opening day that last year he stayed up all night and painted his team's helmets (field notes, opening day, Bolton Park). The emotions the coach discusses with his players are those he faces in himself. Several coaches indicated privately that they must make a serious and sustained effort to control their personal drive for "victory at all costs" in order to be a "proper role model" for their players.

A victory is evaluated by different moral factors than a defeat. In victory the success of the team is seen as symptomatic of some positively valued trait the team displayed that day or throughout the season. A victory reinforces team behavior. Something (obviously) has been done right. It is difficult to specify what the team did to produce victory, since at this age winning is largely due to luck and such uncontrollable factors as vacation schedules or pitching rotation. As a result, coaches are often vague and do not reinforce any particular skill; they teach the child that he is good when he wins for whatever reason:

> Coach to a poor team after a close victory: "You guys played exactly the way you're capable of playing. . . . You're back in the groove" (field notes, Bolton Park).

> Coach to team after an important victory following several defeats: "Guys, I want to tell you something—I'm proud of you guys for your game tonight. I don't care what happened the rest of the year—you guys were superb . . . and I'm talking about each and every one of you did something. You guys were superb, and I don't care if we lose another game or what happens the rest of the year; first of all, we deserve this one. You guys were super. That's what you call hustling, and that's what you call going off and getting 'em. Every single one did something; everyone did something. You guys were super. . . . You guys were unbelievable. You guys can be proud of yourselves tonight. That made up the whole season right there; one game made up the whole season" (field notes, Maple Bluff).

Coaches have difficulty identifying diffuse causes of events. Although coaches can and do refer to specific aspects of a successful performance, these events are taken as representative of the successful performance as a whole.

On other occasions the coach must explain defeat, and there are as many explanations for defeat as there are ways for preadolescents to lose baseball games. Defeat is a sign that something went wrong and that some explanation is necessary. Yet, some defeats are more galling than others, and coaches may feel their losing team played either well or poorly; if well, they may compliment the boys on a game well played but lost (see Iso-Ahola 1976). Also, the coach may feel that in defeat the team needs moral support so as not to take the loss too hard or, on the other hand, may feel the team lost because of overconfidence and thus needs to be brought "down to earth." Finally, the coach may react on the basis of his expectations—a last-place team that loses a close game may be told it played well, while a first-place team that loses an important game in the same manner may be lashed for a sloppy job. Postgame comments derive from the observable events and also from the social meanings of those events for the coach and his players.

Under favorable situations the coach may compliment his vanquished team:

> After his last-place team loses 10–5, the assistant coach comments: "You guys are right on the edge of hitting well. It's just a matter of reducing errors, and a little luck. We're jelling as a baseball team" (field notes, Bolton Park).

> Coach to average team after losing to one of the best teams in the league by one run: "Boys, you played excellent. Absolutely excellent. Charlie, that was an excellent hit in the end; Roger, you played just super. Great. You all played excellent. That's the kind of baseball I didn't mind losing by one run to them, because really if we didn't make that mistake in the first or second inning, we gave them two runs right there. That was a super game, guys. That's the way to play baseball. That's a super game" (field notes, Maple Bluff).

Losing does not *necessarily* lead to attributions of inadequacy. However, if some element of the players' motivation or behavior is seen as reflecting team troubles, negative attributions result. Coaches use several strategies to criticize a team for losing, including citing a lack of hustle or a lack of team spirit—particularly in games defined as representative of the season or in which inconsistency of team play is evident, such as games in which a team plays particularly poorly ("falls apart") in one inning. Losing is almost never attributed to a lack of ability (which cannot be controlled) but to a lack of motivation by the players. These are "moral" rather than technical problems and thus subject to conscious control:

> Coach to team after loss because of one poor inning: "We played five good innings of baseball. The first inning we didn't want to play" (field notes, Sanford Heights).

Assistant coach speaks seriously and deliberately to his depressed team after losing a postseason game by a considerable margin; this game was played in preparation for them to attend a postseason championship tournament: "I told you a while ago we're not fully committed to this tournament. I'll take the time to take you fellows down to that tournament, but only if I see some very significant improvement in attitude, in hustle, and most of all in team spirit. Save your arguments and fights for your bedroom, the wrestling, the boxing, whatever you want to compete in there; that's where that stuff belongs. That's an individual effort and you can do what you want; this isn't. One bad attitude begets another bad attitude, and I don't believe in it" (field notes, Sanford Heights).

Since adults define playing Little League baseball as a moral enterprise, the game outcome can be ascribed to the character of the players. The "just world" hypothesis suggests that people believe that those who have success—for whatever reason—are virtuous, and those who are defeated are liable to charges that they brought it on themselves. Because victims are likely to be unwilling to accept personal blame—attributing these events to situational rather than dispositional causes—they must be convinced. This is one reason why youth coaches hold postgame meetings to review the game: not only to discuss physical improvement (rarely the topic of these meetings) but to establish and enforce a moral consensus. Although one cannot determine the "true" cause of success and failure, an important ingredient of sports socialization is for players to believe there do exist such causes and to internalize the belief that they can control outcomes—a sense of efficacy. Players who are willing to accept these interpretations are praised for their maturity and spirit, while others who refrain from embracing the coach's explanations are branded as arrogant, stubborn, or poor sports. The fact that coaches consider most on their teams to be mature and spirited reflects the authority of the coach to enforce social meanings of game events. However, the player listening to these explanations may find in them an unstated message: that the game meaning is not an objective view of player's actions as physical movements but is "just" an interpretation. Thus, the player is socialized, not only to the moral order of Little League baseball as seen by his adult mentors, but also to the rhetorical devices involved in the construction of moral meanings in social situations.

Adult Socialization of Moral Order

Little League baseball is an arena in which the moral basis of behavior is brought to bear on individuals by legitimated arbiters of the social order. Although this analysis could be extended to sports participation generally, it seems particularly applicable to youth sports, such as Little League baseball, in which the program is explicitly didactic and devoted to "character building."

In baseball, coaches' comments are understood by the players in the immediate context in which they occur and are judged by the appropriateness of their moral messages and by how well they resemble the players' view of their own abilities and motivations (does the coach "know baseball" and is he "fair"?). Together, coaches and players attempt to construct an approved social identity for the preadolescent—often explicitly related to athletic situations but sometimes more general. This, in effect, means that coaches have license to criticize players because of the supposed long-range outcomes of such criticism. As one coach explained to his players: "We may yell at you more than you like. It will make you a better lad, and eventually a better man" (field notes, Sanford Heights). Another commented, "We're not hollering at you guys to be hollering at you; the object is to help you boys learn" (field notes, Sanford Heights).

It is important for these adult males that they teach their preadolescent boys to see the world from their perspective. To be sure, these men believe they have eternal core values, not recognizing how these values are selectively displayed. The mature preadolescent will express these same values in appropriate settings, indicating that he is well on his way to becoming a man. Clearly, rhetoric is something that is to be manipulated, but it must not be *recognized* that it is manipulated, for that would transform belief into cynical exploitation. In this chapter and the next, I argue that boys are willing students of their male instructors. They become as skilled at sports talk as they become at baseball.

4

Moral Socialization: Peer Concerns

Perhaps the most distinctive feature of male preadolescence as a developmental period is its emphasis on the peer group. Friends feel free to discuss all subjects of mutual interest with each other, including, of course, many subjects that are not fit topics for conversation with adults. Preadolescents typically "take seriously" the comments of their peers. Obviously isolated remarks don't necessarily produce dramatic attitude change, but taken together these comments shape the moral perspectives of preadolescents. This is not a passive process; each preadolescent is communicating, just as he is being communicated to. Through their own moral rhetoric, the boys are being socialized into a preadolescent "social world" in which moral codes are as sharp and also as brittle as those in their parents' world. Fathers' codes are reworked by sons, producing a world that both reflects and distorts adult male behaviors.

The moral evaluations of preadolescents I shall discuss in this chapter are those that relate to sport. Whereas adults focus on hustle, teamwork, sportsmanship, and winning and losing, the preadolescent transforms these concerns. Adults are trying to get the preadolescent to play properly and through this to be a good citizen and person. Preadolescents are more concerned with their self-presentation, which involves related forms of propriety. Although preadolescents use the themes of adults, more significant is the "moral" theme of behaving properly. This includes (1) the display of appropriate emotions—being tough or fearful when the situation calls for it; (2) controlling one's aggression, fears, and tears (a transformation of sportsmanship); (3) publicly displaying a desire to win (hustle); and (4) not breaking the bond of unity (teamwork) among preadolescents (akin to "rate busting" in industry or ratting to the police). These issues are similar to those of their coaches but at times they are transformed beyond recognition. Although this moral code is regularly broken, often it is transgressed at a cost to the boy.

Appropriate Emotions

It is self-evident that a boy's behavior is condemned when it is considered inappropriate. The question is, What is appropriate behavior? Unfortunately for the preadolescent who would like a concrete guide, one cannot compile such a list. Although one can cite some behaviors that will regularly be condemned, such as spitting at others, the evaluation of most behaviors depends on circumstance. Even spitting is legitimate in a playful "spitting contest."

Many condemnations or commendations of players are global—not specifying any particular fault or virtue. In the interviews in Bolton Park and Sanford Heights, I asked each player why he liked his best friends and why he disliked another preadolescent. Most answers were very general.

Best friends:
    "They're all nice. We do a lot of stuff together."
    "He's nice to be with. Funny. We like the same stuff."
    "He's nice to be around."

Disliked child:
    "He yells at everyone. He thinks too much of himself."
    "He's a brat and is mean to little kids."

While these preadolescents probably could have provided specific examples of behavior, they expressed their attitudes to others in general terms, even though their reference was specific, as in the following example.

> Terry Hayes, an eleven-year-old on the Expos, is generally scorned for what others consider his immaturity and his social awkwardness. One Expo says that Terry is "daffy." Another says, "He sucks." Bryan Nash, the Expos' twelve-year-old starting catcher, mocks Terry, saying with spastic gestures, "I've got cerebral palsy." Harvey Gregg, another eleven-year-old, says, "Hayes takes birth [control] pills" (i.e., he is a girl) (field notes, Sanford Heights).

None of the insults directed to Terry resulted from a particular behavior, but they all reflected a generalized, stereotyped impression. I do not suggest this evaluation was justified but only that it was *perceived* as based on evidence and seen by teammates as fair. Of course, such insulting might be used by low-status individuals, such as Harvey, to gain status or to reaffirm their relatively higher-status position at the expense of a child seen as even lower in prestige.

There are some behaviors preadolescents expect of each other. Players are supposed to take painful injuries seriously, particularly when they or their team are responsible for the injury of an opponent:

> In a game between the Orioles and the Padres a pitch thrown by the Orioles pitcher hits a Padres player on the head. Todd Caxton, the Orioles' twelve-year-old third baseman, laughs at this. Hugh Moskowitz, the Padres' star player, gets angry at Todd, and tells him sharply, "It's not funny." Another Padre chimes in, "What are you laughing at Caxton, your pitcher's face?" (field notes, Bolton Park).

Todd is condemned for what is perceived as an emotionally inappropriate response—one that is out of keeping with preadolescent propriety. He (and others) must learn to coordinate their facial expression with the emotional tenor of the event. I do not claim that a universal rule or norm exists that requires that when a boy is hit by a ball there must be seriousness. This is not the case. Situational and social factors, such as who is hit, who is laughing, the extent of injury, and the significance of the game all determine reactions. There are occasions on which laughter at injuries is not condemned:

> Late in the sixth [final] inning of a game between the White Sox and the Pirates, Randy Brosky, the Pirates catcher, gets hit in the shoulder with a foul ball and falls to the ground in pain. While the coaches from both teams go out to check on him, the players in the White Sox dugout joke about Randy's injury. Mark Quinton wrings his hands in a way reminiscent of the old Dracula movies, saying, "I hope he dies; I hope he dies." His teammates stand around and laugh (field notes, Maple Bluff).

Despite this example—hidden from the view of the opponents—laughter in the face of injury leaves a boy open for criticism, whether or not he is criticized. Boys learn that they must adjust their expressions to what has just happened in the game. A boy who cries when his team has won (because of a poor play made earlier) is thought "strange." A team that cheers itself after it lost is defined as "crazy." A boy who smiles after he makes an out faces attack:

> Jason Brown, a marginal twelve-year-old on the Astros, returns to the bench in the postseason tournament grinning

after hitting a hard line drive to the third baseman. Bill Carlucci, the best twelve-year-old on the team, snarls: "God, Jason, that's stupid, don't smile." Tom Matthews, the best eleven-year-old, seconds Bill's comment: "He strikes out and laughs" (field notes, Bolton Park).

Players whose "emotion work" is deemed inappropriate, even though these expressions might not reflect inner feelings, are tarred with the implications of their expressions. Learning how to "give off" as well as "give" impressions is a crucial tool for getting along with peers, as "given off" expressions are taken to be reflectors of inner states (Goffman 1959).

Adjusting emotion to a situation is not always easy—particularly for preadolescents. As suggested in chapter 3, the meanings (both individual and collective) of sports events are often ambiguous. Further, there is more than one type of behavior that may be appropriate. Consider two seemingly contradictory emotions of Little League baseball—toughness and fear. Both are legitimate in certain circumstances and inappropriate in others.

Toughness

The moral rhetoric of toughness is particularly evident in Little League baseball when players claim to be willing to injure or intimidate another player deliberately—an attitude also found among adult sportsmen (Clark 1981) and which in part is learned from them (Vaz 1982; Smith 1978). Preadolescents sometimes refer to sports injuries as making a player "pay his dues":

A player on Jamesville Lumber is hit on the knee with a pitch, but not so hard that he must leave the game. Their opponents yell, "Make them pay their dues." "Rooster [the pitcher] has broken another player's face or is that his rear end?" "That's the way to make him pay his dues" (field notes, Hopewell).

Aside from indicating that one's teammates may, in some cases, relish an injury to an opponent, these comments suggest that preadolescents see injuries as part of the game—not just in a technical sense but in a moral sense. To be a Little Leaguer you have to be willing to be hurt, and players sometimes tell others to injure opponents:

Dick Green of the Rangers had to run into the first baseman in order to reach first base. A teammate calls out, "Hey, Dickie, knock him down if he's in the way" (field notes, Beanville).

Mike Marchio yells to Harry Stanton, who is pitching for Sharpstone: "If you're gonna walk him, hit him" (i.e., so that the player will be taken out of the game) (field notes, Hopewell).

Another boy was called with some pride "a real kamikaze on the basepaths" because he specialized in "taking out" (knocking down) opposing fielders, even when this was not entirely necessary. As do professional baseball players, Little Leaguers see revenge as appropriate:

Maury Herman calls to a teammate who has just been hit by the pitch: "Do what Rod Carew [of the Minnesota Twins] did." I ask him what was that. Tommy Riley says, "When he got beaned in the back, he smacked the pitcher." Maury adds, "He smacked his head in" (field notes, Sanford Heights).

Despite this callous rhetoric, behavior usually does not mirror this verbal aggression. Little Leaguers occasionally attempt to knock down fielders on the basepaths (and are sometimes criticized for that by teammates), but it is rare for a pitcher to attempt to hit a batter, and I never heard a pitcher seriously claim that he did so.

Although their rhetoric might seem to indicate that Little Leaguers strive to win at any cost, this is not so. Preadolescents believe that they should be responsible for the outcome of the game; coaches who are seen as too manipulative (or "technical") are scorned:

Peter Chadbourne, the coach of Sharpstone, asks Fred Turner, the opposing coach, if he can pitch Harry Stanton. Fred tells him that he can't because of the "Three Day Rule" which says that a pitcher can't pitch for three full days after he last pitched. Peter goes back to the Sharpstone bench and tells his players this, saying that Turner was correct. Jay Taviss, a player on another team, who is standing near the bench, tells his friends on Sharpstone scornfully: "Turner goes by the rulebook. . . . Mr. Turner's head is like a rulebook." Dan Quimble, a Sharpstone player adds sarcastically: "He always has to go by the rules. He studies them at night" (field notes, Hopewell).

One Sharpstone player comments about another technical coach, "I know a coach who thinks Little Leagues is the pros" (field notes, Hopewell). Significantly, it is not only opposing coaches who are condemned for being too technical and for not letting the boys play their own game, but even one's own coach. One Bolton Park coach who was particularly oriented toward winning insisted in one important game that his players not swing at pitches, hoping the opposing pitcher would tire and become wild. Although he was right and his team won the game and clinched the league championship, his players were annoyed at his control. The players on this team were unhappy and were unanimous in telling me that they wanted to swing, even though they had just won the game. Not surprisingly, their opponents were bitter, claiming that the other team was not playing "real" or "fair." Little League is seen by preadolescents as a tough, physical game, and an emphasis on strategy is defined as fundamentally "improper" by the players, even though it is legitimate in terms of the rules and effective in terms of the outcome.

Fear

In the previous section I discussed the fact that players consider it a moral virtue to be "tough" and to pay their dues. There is another side to this rhetoric. Players fear paying these dues, but admitting this fear may be a source of stigma, particularly for low-status players. Players who claim that a pitcher has a "wicked fastball" or that they "could hardly see the pitch" may be told sarcastically that the pitcher is really slow, and their strikeout is their own fault. One boy is told he should not be afraid of fielding a baseball, because "it [the ball] won't bite you." Sometimes the criticism is serious and not sarcastic:

> Before the game Dan Ashton, one of the best twelve-year-olds on the White Sox, is talking sternly to Howie Novak, one of the poorest twelve-year-olds. Dan said that Howie had been striking out a lot lately because he is backing away from the ball: "You have to watch the ball and swing earlier." Roger Lemon, another good twelve-year-old, says to Dan in front of Howie: "He swings at anything over his head." As Dan leaves the dugout he comments: "Some people want to win the game, you know. Some people just come here because their parents make them." Both Dan and Roger yell to Howie as he is up to bat in the first inning: "Howie, swing at the good ones, buddy, now come on." "Howie, if it's in there just swing. What are you waiting for?" When Howie comes back to the dugout after striking out, Roger says to him: "Howie, it wasn't that hard. . . . Howie, Howie, you were scared" (field notes, Maple Bluff).

These boys ascribe fear to Howie, although nowhere does he indicate that is what he is feeling; indeed, he says very little during the criticism from his teammates. What could otherwise be viewed as a technical flaw has been transformed into a moral failing—one based on fear. However, elsewhere when there is a legitimating context a public profession of fear is more acceptable:

> Mark Quinton (an average player on the White Sox) sees Joey O'Brien, probably the fastest pitcher in the league, warming up for their opponents and says seriously to his coach, "Oh, Oh. O'Brien's warming up. . . . Mr. Silverstein, I ain't going to bat." Bruce Silverstein: "Why?" Mark: "He's a vicious kid! I'll play the field, yes. . . ." Bruce: "I can't play you until you want to play. . . . You get hit and get an easy base. You don't have to swing." Mark: "Yeah, you hear the stories from this kid and he's a killer." Harry Pontiff: "You're not scared of him?" Mark: "I am too!" (He turns to Dick Greenberg, his good friend) "Are you scared of what's his name? O'Brien." Dick nods. Mark: "See, everybody in this dugout is." He and Dick are the only players in the dugout (field notes, Maple Bluff).

> The Astros are playing a pre-season intrasquad game. Pitching for one of the teams is Sid Copeland, a tall twelve-year-old and one of the fastest and wildest pitchers in the league. Jon Carlson, a twelve-year-old on the other team, says to his teammates, "I wouldn't dare to swing." Coming up to bat against Sid, he says, "Let's get it over with." Sid says in a friendly tone of voice, "I'm pitching slow." Andy Sylvester says sarcastically but with good humor: "I wonder what your *fast* pitch is like!" Murray Zisk, a ten-year-old, says humorously: "I'm gonna get to Washington, D.C., you know, and I'm gonna pass a law. Don't let Copeland pitch. It's gonna be in the Constitution" (field notes, Sanford Heights).

Once a consensus has emerged about the target, public fear is considered legitimate and not subject to criticism, particularly if it is expressed in a good-natured, confident way. Among preadolescents, as elsewhere, meaning changes as a function of agreed-on definitions.

Self-control

Social actors are conscious, controlled beings; we are seen as "responsible" for our actions. Yet, at times emotions get the best of us. This emotionality seems even more true for preadolescents than for adults. In order to be seen as moral, boys must contain the emotional turmoil they often feel. Instead of discussing the display of emotion, here I consider its suppression and the development of a stoic acceptance of the world. I shall consider the moral components of the control of externally directed anger, inner-directed anger (tears), and the public display of pain. Such control represents the embodiment of the male sex role; the preadolescent boy is learning, through the reactions of his peers, how to channel his behavior, how to control his body, and how to look "cool," even when he may be feeling hot. Since there is no secure way of knowing what a person is feeling except through words and gestures, these outer signs become crucial as means of promoting a self-image. Children see how their public behaviors are accepted, as their peers show little compunction about criticizing them vigorously. Boys learn how to act like men.

Anger

Anger is usually thought of as aggression directed outward, stemming from the frustration of some action or goal. As with any activity in which people care about the outcome, sports failure can be very frustrating, and this frustration may express itself in anger and aggression. Yet, much as it might be regretted, anger is part of Little League baseball (see chapter 2). Boys do throw bats and helmets, and also boys attack others, particularly those who interfere with their angry performance, saying things like: "Get the hell away from me," "Just leave me alone," and "Shut up, you faggot."

Players see this anger as a social problem but one they often respond to with consideration, depending, of course, on the actor and the circumstance. Players are generally sympathetic to each other's anger, and the angry player is not scorned, although he is told that others see that behavior as inappropriate. Long public arguments are rare in the preadolescent community because the consensus is that such arguments are wrong and reveal moral defects of the participants. Likewise, loud cursing is seen as undesirable, and preadolescents try to convince their peers that they should calm down:

> Tom McDarrel, one of the best twelve-year-olds on Transatlantic Industries, grounds out in an important game in which TI is losing. His twelve-year-old teammate Tim Mizell, another of the best players on the team, tells him to take it easy. Tom, almost quaking with anger, mutters: "Damn it. God damn it to hell. Shit." John Cole, an eleven-year-old, tells Tom sharply, but not hostilely, "Every time you make an out, don't take a fit" (field notes, Hopewell).

Even the angry player himself later may feel that his behavior was deserving of public criticism:

> Henry Sims confided in me that he got kicked out of the game that evening because of "my hot temper." He had told Kip Taviss (an opposing player) to "shut up." Interestingly, he thought that because of his outburst he *should* have been taken out of the game (field notes, Hopewell).

Anger is recognized as a difficult problem to correct in that it emerges from the events of the game. However, preadolescents also recognize that some players get angrier than others, and they may be singled out for personal criticism when they get angry—as John criticizes Tom in the example above. Control of one's anger, while not always possible, should be practiced on most occasions. The adult's notions of grace under pressure and of sportsmanship are reflected in the preadolescent's attempts to control his anger except when under great stress.

Crying and Moping

In a sense, crying and moping are the inverse of anger, in that these behaviors are directed inward, even though they too are public behaviors. Paradoxically the same boys who become angry easily are also the boys who cry and mope a lot. Generally these are preadolescents whose public presentation of self clearly reflects their feelings. Crying and moping are common in Little League games, partly because of the importance of competition. Despite the frequency of these behaviors, and despite the fact that in some circumstances whole teams briefly display them, they are not considered proper. Like anger, crying indicates a loss of self-control.

Of course, the evaluation of crying depends on the crier. Players who aren't much liked and players on rival teams are scorned:

> Rod Shockstein, a twelve-year-old (whom I have seen crying), says scornfully about Barry Martin, a low-status eleven-year-old on a different team, that Barry "started bawling" after he struck out (field notes, Sanford Heights).

Players on one's own team are more likely to be supported when they cry, particularly if the crying does not occur too frequently and the boy is liked:

> Graham Salter, a twelve-year-old on the White Sox, is crying loudly and visibly. I asked Vince Tozzari (another White Sox

twelve-year-old) why Graham is crying. Vince says, "Oh, he missed a ball at third base." It sounded as if Vince didn't want to make a big thing of it for Graham's sake. Many of the players came by to comfort him, saying: "Don't worry, everyone makes mistakes"; "Everything will be all right." One player comes over and puts his arms around Graham (field notes, Maple Bluff).

Although crying can be reacted to sympathetically, it is wrong, even when the players recognize it as something they all do:

A number of the twelve-year-olds on the Dodgers are conversing. Maury says that Roy cried after making an error in the game against the Giants. Roy objects, saying: "Oh, bull roar." Maury then says he saw Stew crying. Stew doesn't deny it but says "So has Harmon; so has Frank." Maury and Frank both admit crying. By the end of the conversation crying is not defined as "sissy" (field notes, Sanford Heights).

Crying indicates players are taking the game more seriously than they should and have forgotten about impression management—it represents the boy's "true feelings." In this way, we may differentiate boys from girls. While some might question the sincerity of a girl's tears but not their sex-role appropriateness, a boy's tears would not be questioned for their sincerity but only for their sex-role appropriateness. In fact, big boys do cry, but turning this into a moral message depends on the circumstances and who is judging whom.

Pain

Part of the male stereotype is that one should be stoic in the face of pain. Preadolescents occasionally must play baseball in pain when injured (see chapter 2). Although there are individual differences in reaction to pain, most players wish to continue playing if possible:

Tony Denton, the best twelve-year-old on the Pirates, is sitting on the bench when his team is at bat, his arm bleeding. The Pirates' coach, Phil Conklin, insists he go to the concession stand to get his arm treated. Tony hesitates several times, saying, "Naw, it'll be all right," but Phil keeps pressuring him and eventually he has it treated. When the Pirates go out to the field, Tony is still pitching, but it is obvious his arm is hurting him. Randy Brosky, the catcher, at one point yells to his coach "Mr. Conklin, there's something wrong with Tony."

Phil talks with Tony, but he is left in to pitch (field notes, Maple Bluff).

Pain is not as directly moral as some other issues: extreme pain is recognized as so debilitating that loud complaints and even a request to be removed from the game can be legitimate. Since pain is only known through internal neural impulses, it is impossible for anyone other than the person hurt to know how much pain he feels. Even the injured player can only compare his pain with the memory of other pains he has had and not with the range of all human pains. Despite this internal evaluation of pain, others do attempt to judge the magnitude and severity of pain from a variety of clues, including what caused that pain and how the pained individual looks. This evaluation, shaped through the public comments of one's teammates, influences what one is supposed to do, but, like the judgment of hustle, the community's evaluation of pain is based on ambiguous and opaque signals. Despite this, the judgment may have considerable force in causing the player to control a public announcement of pain.

Desire to Win

Preadolescents want to win the games in which they are involved—at least on most teams, most times. A player or coach is resented and condemned if others feel he is not contributing to that goal (see Vaz 1982). The drive for victory is emphasized in preadolescent rhetoric:

> The Orioles are ahead of the Royals, and Chip Doyle, a twelve-year-old on the Orioles, says to his teammates: "Let's just wipe these guys out. Let's kill them." Another Oriole player adds, "Let's waste them" (field notes, Bolton Park).

Even when a team has a wide lead (in some cases twenty-plus runs), the batters still wish to score as many runs as they can. Although they don't want to win through adult technicalities, most players are not opposed to winning through forfeits:

> In Maple Bluff, teams are able to draft players from the minor league for a game when they don't have enough players because of absences or vacations. However, the rules require that they must have at least seven of their own players. Today the Mets were scheduled to play the Pirates but had only six players. At first the Pirates' coach said they would play but

later decided to leave it up to his players. He told the players: "We are now nine and two; if we don't play we will be ten and two. We are tied for first place. If we play and we lose, that's the game. I've just told the ump to come back in ten or fifteen minutes while we make a decision. . . . It's in your hands."

Tony Denton (their star player) argued forcefully that the only sensible thing to do was to accept the win and bolster their record. Most of the other good players agreed with Tony. Carl Wrightsman, one of the poorer players, argued briefly that the Pirates so outclassed the Mets that they were sure to win but after more persuasion he changed his mind. The only dissenters were Doug Johnson and Greg Petit. Both argued they were supposed to be playing for fun. Tony responded to Doug, a utility player, by saying, "You just want to play because you'll get to play the whole game." (The Pirates themselves had only nine players.) When it came time for the vote, Tony asked: "How many want to win?" Aside from Doug and Greg, all of the players voted to take the forfeit (field notes, Maple Bluff).

Winning is important to these players, particularly to those on the better teams. It is hard to know what players on other teams would have done, but I suspect that most teams would have done the same.

No team likes to lose, and players are supposed to try as hard as they reasonably can (a somewhat ambiguous measure of effort). Players are expected to be present for all the team's games, but they recognize that some absences are unavoidable, and most players miss at least one game during the season. Sicknesses, injuries, and family commitments are considered legitimate excuses, but staying away from the team too long or during important games can provoke rebuke, since such absence is defined as indicating a lack of desire:

Russ Ward, the eleven-year-old starting first baseman on the Orioles, has missed two weeks because he was at his parents' summer cabin. During this time resentment toward him increases, and some players talk of kicking him off the team. Before the first game of the third week, Jerry Goslin, an eleven-year-old, says authoritatively, "I think that Ward quit." Carey Kasky, one of the best twelve-year-olds on the team, adds, "Good, he sucks anyway." Russ then arrives and denies he ever thought of quitting (field notes, Bolton Park).

Tim Roncalio, an eleven year old on the Dodgers, is absent for the semifinal tournament game. One of the players reports (correctly) that Tim had gone fishing rather than come to the game, and this leaves the Dodgers with only nine players for this important game. Frank and Roy call Tim "a dink" for not showing up. Frank is particularly bitter: "We might as well kick him off the team, the fucking puss. . . . If we have to forfeit [because of a lack of players], I'm gonna kill Roncalio." Paul adds, "Roncalio's so stupid; he went fishing" (field notes, Sanford Heights).

Little League, despite its status as leisure, is not morally voluntary. As I noted in chapter 2, players (and coaches) see Little League, including scheduled practices, as a firm commitment. Yet the cause of disgrace is not absence per se but illegitimate absence.

Being present doesn't ensure that a boy will avoid criticism. If a boy is judged not to be paying attention (and thus not hustling), he may become the target of criticism tinged with sarcasm. A teammate who felt one player wasn't paying attention accused him of starting a tick collection in the outfield (field notes, Hopewell). When a boy behaves inappropriately, he potentially commits a moral infraction, indicating he is not "with it."

Players are not equally likely to be criticized. Those players who are defined as the very best will not be much criticized even when they make an error for which a poorer player would have been condemned. The player's entire baseball biography (his reputation) is taken into account in making judgments. So, the one or two best players on a team are relatively immune from criticism for lack of effort; likewise most of the younger players on a team will not be criticized. It is rare for a nine-year-old player to receive the criticism that is reserved for older boys. Criticism is ultimately *moral*— it is *deserved* because these players should have done better but "chose" not to. A third characteristic of players is that they be "teasable"—very shy boys are rarely criticized. As I shall discuss, "show-offs" or braggarts are particularly likely to be criticized.

Sarcastic criticism is most evident in situations that are not in themselves of great significance, whereas angry criticism (You suck!"; "I hate that kid!") is more common on important occasions. Both sarcastic and angry comments are moral, but in the first instance they imply an overt concern with effort and ability and in the second they involve a derogation of the boy's core self.

Just as coaches judge internal motivation from physical behaviors, so do preadolescents, although they emphasize different issues. Preadolescents focus on ignorance, incompetence, and fear, while coaches are more concerned with effort. However, both assume that the player could play well if he wanted to. This message is at the core of rhetoric throughout the sports world in slogans and other social messages (Snyder 1972).

Looking Professional

As Stone (1962) has recognized, appearance is important as an announcement of self. Little League players wish to look like those ballplayers with whom they identify (see Caughey 1984). The boy must announce to the world that he is appropriately dressed and, hence, that he takes his identity seriously. Boys who come to games with mismatched socks or with dirty uniforms are teased. One boy who wore regular black socks to a game was taunted by a peer: "Where did you get those socks, the Salvation Army?" (field notes, Beanville). Another boy who wore his cap with an oil stain on it was told: "That's your nigger lipstick" (field notes, Sanford Heights). On some teams, players make a point to look as professional as possible:

> Roger Lemon shows up at the game today with charcoal rubbed under his eyes. This seems to be part of the "professional athlete" look, which the better players on the White Sox are adopting. It involves the cultivation of the appearance of the professional athlete and evidently reflects anticipatory socialization. Besides the charcoal, players wear cleats, batting gloves, and wrist bands and make a conscious effort to make sure their socks are pulled up properly (field notes, Maple Bluff).

Later in the season, members of other teams teased Roger about the charcoal under his eyes, claiming he was using eyeline shadow and looked like a "cover girl" (field notes, Maple Bluff). These comments remind us that the evaluation of appearance is not objective but is based on local (and team) standards. Thus appearance can be transformed into a moral issue—the basis for an insult:

> Most of the older players on the Dodgers have worn shorts to practice today. When they see the Phils practicing in long pants, Frank comments, "Look at them scuzzies; they're wearing long pants." When the Dodgers' coach comments that they can't practice sliding in shorts, several of the Dodgers assure

him *they* don't mind sliding in shorts (field notes, Sanford Heights).

Rather than emphasizing that they look like baseball players, the Dodgers imply that by sliding in shorts, they are like professional ballplayers because they are tough. The Phils, defined as afraid of being hurt when sliding, are "scuzzies," a derogatory term for those who are not tough, masculine, or mature. Clothing communicates a message about who one wants to be on the baseball diamond, and so it is used in the moral construction of selves.

Preadolescent Social Unity

Like any social group, preadolescents seek to maintain in-group unity, a dramaturgical loyalty. Generally speaking, it is improper for a preadolescent to "rat" or "tattle" on a peer to an adult. Loyalty also assumes that no preadolescent should present himself as better (or worse) than another. As a result, we find the paradox that it is legitimate to blame (or praise) a peer, but it is not proper to praise (or blame) oneself. One's self is typically not a fit subject for discussion.

Dramaturgical loyalty is evident when players tell their teammates to "talk it up" or to "make yourself hoarse." Although some players privately object to the conventional belief that "talking helps," most cheer so as not to be thought disloyal. Anyone giving aid to an opponent, for whatever reason, is suspect. During a practice game between the Phils and the Dodgers, Dickie Brickman of the Dodgers plays for the Phils, who don't have enough players:

> Dickie hits a triple for the Phils against the Dodgers. Larry Niro calls to him, half-joking: "I hate you. Don't come back." Harmon comments, "Dickie, I'm gonna flatten your nose." Maury adds, humorously but in a mock menacing tone, "Dickie, you made a bad mistake!" Throughout the game, every good play Dickie makes is described by his teammates as traitorous; every error is seen as a deliberate attempt to help the Dodgers (field notes, Sanford Heights).

The team is a powerful group that has the authority to define situations, even informal ones. Teams administer their own justice:

> In an informal game run by the Astros' players themselves, Bill Carlucci, a twelve-year-old star player, is called out at

first. Bill claims he is safe and stays on first base. None of the Astros tries to make him leave, but one player calls out to his teammates, "Don't even play on him, 'cause he's already out." None of the Astros tries to throw Bill out, and when he crosses home plate, Peter Fletcher, an eleven-year-old, jokes: "He never came in. He's a figure of your imagination." However, Bill is allowed to bat in his regular position, and afterward is treated like anyone else (field notes, Bolton Park).

Despite some individual variation, preadolescents believe that loyalty to their team and its judgments is important.

Being Hot and Cool

As noted above, an unstated moral prescription is that players shouldn't make themselves out to be better than their peers. Enforcement takes several forms, including stigmatizing players who see themselves as "hot" or "cool":

Tim Mizell, a twelve-year-old on Transatlantic Industries, says sarcastically about Lenny Steel, another TI twelve year old, after Steel strikes out, "Steel thinks he's so hot" (field notes, Hopewell).

Maury says about Frank, his former best friend: "He thinks he's the strongest kid around, but he ain't. He thinks he's cool" (field notes, Sanford Heights).

Other boys are criticized for being "prima donnas," "hot-dogs," or "braggarts." These boys are defined as having made an identity claim of which others feel they are not worthy; by this claim they seem to be putting themselves above their peers. While others can say these things, the boy himself cannot:

After Cliff Alsop, a nine-year-old on Sharpstone, makes an error, Ray Coleman, the other nine-year-old on the team, comments, "I would've had that." Jim Pozzi, his ten-year-old teammate, comments nastily, "How do you know that?" (field notes, Hopewell).

Greg Petit, a nonathletic twelve year old on the Pirates, watches Lane Gervais at third base, looking for a chance to steal home. Greg says to Chris Conklin, who had just criticized Lane: "God! I would have been stealing by now." Chris turns to Greg and says in a voice dripping with acid: "Yeah. You would have been out too" (field notes, Maple Bluff).

Greg's problem (and Ray's as well) is that the criticism is couched in terms that he could do better than another player, particularly one of equal or higher status, and this must be rejected. As one Little League player commented in criticizing several younger players, "They're trying to act bigger than they are." He adds that older kids don't like younger ones who are "big talkers" (field notes, Sanford Heights).

Particularly resented are players whose fathers coach, *if* others believe they receive special treatment:

Chip Doyle of the Orioles criticizes Ted Beezley, the eleven-year-old son of the coach of the Astros: "He thinks he's so hot; he'd still be on the minor league team if it wasn't for his dad" (field notes, Bolton Park).

This moral evaluation may have little to do with Ted's actual behavior, but the resentment is real. Only a boy who is exceptionally good or exceptionally diffident can escape the scorn of his peers when his father coaches.

The resentment players show to peers can also extend to the fathers of these peers, if these fathers are perceived as publicly overvaluing the ability of their sons:

Dan Holmberg, a good twelve-year-old on the Astros, hits a long fly ball at the tournament field, which is caught. Bill Carlucci whispers to his teammates that Mr. Holmberg, an assistant coach for the Astros, is "gonna start bragging." Mr. Holmberg does indeed say that his son got a great hit, as the team starts giggling. Bill whispers: "He's always bragging. . . . Shut up, it makes me sick." Bill says sarcastically that Mr. Holmberg will say it would have been a home run in Bolton Park (which is probably true), and Mr. Holmberg says exactly that (field notes, Bolton Park).

The moral issue here is that players (and their parents) must know their place in the preadolescent hierarchy. No absolute rule exists for what one can legitimately say and what one will be criticized for saying. Obviously the immediate situation contributes to the reaction a player will receive. Players are less likely to be criticized in games in which their team is substantially ahead or when the loss doesn't really matter, but even so there is a moral structure for appropriate comments. An unstated ability gradient exists, and boys should know where on this gradient they stand. Learning this is part of the socialization that comes through the process of social comparison and allows boys to align themselves to a social community—a process of understanding one's looking-glass self and the attitudes of the generalized other.

Like their coaches, preadolescents share criteria for making moral evaluations. Actions in sports are not simply technical issues but are moral. For boys as for men, the moral implications of behavior are not self-evident; rather, they must make sense of behavior—in other words, they must construct the meaning of a situation. From these examples, it is evident that these children are skilled rhetors in their ability to manipulate symbols. Even though the issues that are important to them are not always identical to the issues that are important to their adult guardians, the centrality of moral concerns remains.

Players Judging Coaches

Just as adults socialize children through their critiques, so may preadolescents judge their guardians—sometimes directly, often through private talk venting frustrations. The Little League player believes that his goal is to play baseball and to win, and with this in mind he expects and desires to have rigorous practices to acquire the fundamentals of baseball. Most preadolescents actually prefer a strict coach:

> The following dialogue between two members of the Dodgers takes the form of a mock sports interview:
> *Frank:* Now how about the coach, Mr. Riley? We've heard rumors that he is very mean in the dugout after games. What do you have to say about that?
> *Maury:* Well, he ain't really that mean; in practice he's mean, but you know he's supposed to be mean. He's a little rough on us, and he's a good coach. . . . How do you think the coaches been treating you lately?
> *Frank:* Well, they've been really a little too good. I think they should get a little rougher on us when we make an error in practice (taped transcript, Sanford Heights).

Players are impressed by a coach who takes the playing of baseball seriously and, through his seriousness, forces them to take the game seriously:

> Most players on the Cards seem generally pleased with their coach, Bernie Cashmore, who is considered to be particularly

strict. Rob Constantine comments about Bernie: "He's cool. He's strict and that's good. He should make us do more work." Dan Gregory says that by being strict Mr. Cashmore keeps their minds from wandering off the game (field notes, Sanford Heights).

Coaches who are not strict, who do not teach enough baseball, or who do not hold enough practices are often criticized as "too easy." Most of the coaches who were not liked, were condemned because "they should have us work hard enough," "they allowed us to goof off in practice," "they lacked discipline," or simply they "weren't strict enough." Coaches who attempt to be nice guys—and *only* to be nice guys—are found wanting. What might otherwise be considered a technical problem of teaching them how to play baseball has been transformed into the moral issue of insufficient strictness.

To indicate how players' expectations of their adult leaders develop and are channeled, I shall describe the experiences of one team, the Sanford Heights Giants, that resented and generally did not respect its coach. This man, Paul Castor, was a last-minute recruit who signed on after the league tryouts, when the league discovered that the young men who had agreed to coach the team would not do so. Castor was promised that his ten-year-old son (Colin) would make the team if he agreed to coach.

Paul Castor was an easygoing man, genuinely concerned about his children and his community responsibilities. Although he had little baseball experience, he was a good athlete and tried to be fair to his players. His main concern, expressed when he agreed to coach, was about the amount of time it would take; his job prevented him from being at the diamond before 6:00 P.M. (games started at 6:30 P.M.) and from holding many practices. In addition, unlike most coaches, Castor had no adult assistant to help him run his team.

Although Paul publicly told me that he believed in being the boss, he started out preseason by downplaying his authority, telling the team he had never coached baseball before, and he generally ran an informal practice. He commented in the postseason interview:

A lot of the time [in practice] they just wanted to horse around. So the question is, Is the coach gonna be a good guy, or is he gonna be a strict by the rule [coach]? For the first twenty minutes we're gonna do nothing but take infield practice and for the next twenty minutes we're gonna do this and this. . . . I find it hard in ten-, eleven- and twelve-year-old boys to keep their interest that long. . . . In practices I would let the boys pitch to me. They seemed to enjoy that. Try to strike me out or whatever, and I tried to be kinda a pal to them, like one of the guys, rather than being a coach or a disciplinarian, and we seemed to get along quite well then. But then the practices are almost meaningless to a certain extent when you do that (coach interview, Sanford Heights).

Paul tried to be an equal with the boys. Those occasions when he attempted to have the team do relatively unpleasant activities did not last long. For example, Paul made the team do calisthenics (jumping jacks and touching their toes) at their first practice; however, after the second practice, at which players seemed bored by the exercises, the subject of calisthenics was not raised again. This lack of discipline and control was also evident after games:

> While the coach of the Phils insists that his players clean up the dugout area before they get their free treats at the refreshment stand, Paul lets his players get treats, telling them that some of them (not naming anyone in particular) should return to clean up the dugout. None return, and when it is obvious that they will not return, Paul and I clean up the mess (field notes, Sanford Heights).

In part because of the lack of baseball training, the Giants, although finishing the season with an 8–10 record, had the lowest median team batting average (.157; the next lowest was .166); had fewer players who hit above .250 than any other team (two as opposed to four for the last-place team); and the most players who hit under .050 (three as opposed to one for two other teams).

At the beginning of the season, the Giants had a strongly defined hierarchy. Castor quickly recognized this, and from the first practice he treated his best player, Rod Shockstein, like an assistant coach; the two developed a joking relationship, rare in coach-player relations:

> Castor is pitching batting practice, and Rod is catching. After one pitch Rod asks him: "Is that a knuckle curve?" Castor answers cheerfully: "You bet." Rod says to the rest of the team, "I call him [the coach] the junk machine." Everyone laughs. "Junk" is a baseball term referring to off-speed pitches such as the curve, slider, and knuckleball. Rod's comment is made in a friendly tone of voice. Later Castor is pitching batting practice to Rod, and Rod tells him: "You bean me, I'm gonna repay.

Right up the middle" [i.e., hit the ball so it hits Castor in the crotch] (field notes, Sanford Heights).

In addition to this joking relationship that characterized the beginning of the season, Castor gave Rod extensive responsibility for directing the team—as an assistant in Castor's presence and as the team leader in his absence.

The rest of the players, sensing a lack of adult leadership, joked and generally did not take the game seriously. By the third practice, the Giants were behaving this way:

> Within an hour the outfielders were lying down in the grass and only running for an occasional fly ball. Whenever a poor player batted, all the outfielders moved into the infield, and later when the last player was batting (another poor player), all of the fielders left the field. During this, Paul said nothing (field notes, Sanford Heights).

At one practice, late in the season, only three Giants even attended. Ironically in light of this lackadaisical attitude—in part condoned by the coach—several players (particularly Rod) complained bitterly about the lack of practices and their poor quality. Paul was not entirely to blame for these problems, but the role and responsibility of the coach was a central focus for the players' dissatisfaction.

During the first half of the season, the Giants had a disappointing record of 3–6; the Giants reacted to their early defeats by blaming the coach for not holding enough practices and not arriving at the field much before the 6:30 P.M. game, while other teams would begin practice at 5:00 P.M. The belief that Paul always arrived late for games seems to have first occurred before the third game of the season when the Giants had a record of 1–1. Rod had brought the Giants baseball equipment early, and the players, led by Rod, began practicing informally without the coach. At about 6:00 P.M. Rod decided they should move to the field itself for their formal pregame warmup. Although Paul arrived shortly after, and no negative comments were made toward him, this occasion gave rise to the group belief that he would always be late to their games and couldn't even be trusted to attend. He didn't live up to the expectations boys have of their coaches. The existence of this belief was evident at the next game when Paul arrived early (5:45 P.M.) and Rod commented sarcastically to some teammates, "Coach is early for once." Later in the season one player commented, when the coach has not arrived by 6:00: "Our coach never comes on time. You gotta take that for granted." On another occasion, Rod explained that Paul usually arrived at 6:29, and Rich added: "Our coach has his head up his ass." On several occasions when Paul had not arrived by 6:00, players asked me if I would be willing to coach them if Paul did not show up. Despite this, Paul never failed to arrive by 6:30.

This expectation about Paul's lateness was a consequence of the players' acceptance of the adult rhetoric that practice is necessary for team success. One means of explaining their losses and mediocre play (and the threat to their self-confidence) was to attribute the failure to the coach. For a coach not to attend games is to abrogate his most fundamental responsibility.

To cope with their disappointment at their poor first half, players also regularly criticized their own team. Once when the Giants were losing, I commented that their opponents "look strong," to which Rich Toland, a twelve-year-old, retorted, "Not as strong as we look weak." These low expectations were reflected in the fact that players expected their teammates, even the better ones, to make outs. Thus, with one out, Hal Brattle, a twelve-year-old, said that he would not get up to bat that inning because the next two batters (the third- and fifth-best batters on the team) would make outs. Hal might have been correct in terms of the odds, but it is rare for a player to expect his teammates to fail, and in fact he *was* wrong. This lack of spirit was also reflected in the fact that no one on the team wished to purchase a team picture (during the middle of the season), in contrast to other teams. Although teams often adopt the mannerisms of professional baseball players in such things as wearing batting gloves, applying charcoal under their eyes, or batting in particular ways, the Giants only adopted one professional trait. By the middle of the season, players started to spit.

Unlike many coaches who insist the team pay attention to what was happening in the game, Paul did not attempt to discipline the team consistently. Most coaches refused to allow players to buy refreshments during play. Paul disapproved, but he did nothing:

> Denny is eating a lollypop and hands it to Paul to hold while he is warming up the pitcher. Paul comments, "You guys are here to play baseball or to eat?" Players ignore his remark and continue to eat. Paul doesn't do anything but holds Denny's lollypop (field notes, Sanford Heights).

This same laxness was evident in other areas. In Sanford Heights, teams must stay within the dugout while their players are batting; more often than not, the Giants were outside the dugout, watching the game or wandering about. Similarly, Paul allowed boys not on the Giants to walk into the dugout; girlfriends entered to flirt with their swains. Paul occasionally chased away these intruders, but they never stayed away long; the Giants more than any other team in the league had outsiders in their dugout. Paul's relaxed style— not setting or enforcing many rules—suggested to players that "anything goes." Even when he threatened to bench players for criticizing their teammates and for complaining, the abuse continued:

> The Giants have just allowed the Phils to score five runs in the bottom of the third to lead 8–0, and the team is angry and bickering with each other. Hal Brattle throws down his glove in disgust, and Rod holds his head in his hands, possibly in tears. Paul tries to reassert his moral authority by saying: "I'll do the bellyaching, not the players. You're a team. You got about as much spirit as a dead horse. Let's quit complaining." However, by this point late in the season, Paul has almost no credibility, and after Paul finishes his talk, Rod whispers, "Fuck you" and gives him "the finger" to his back. Rich sneers, "Bite my bag." Bill Anders adds sarcastically, "Let's put this game in the Hall of Fame," and he refuses to coach the bases (field notes, Sanford Heights).

Because of the scorn for the coach's baseball abilities and the lack of respect for his decisions, such a reaction makes sense. Further, it is specifically legitimated by Rod, who exercises moral control on the team. Paul never used the disciplinary options at his disposal. In contrast to other teams, players on the Giants were never benched for their behavior, and the preadolescent boys took advantage of this leniency.

This example reflects part of the paradox that confronts adult men in dealing with preadolescent boys: boys push for freedom but are dissatisfied if the adults allow them "to do what they want." The actuality of adult control is an important feature of this period. Little League is supposed to have some measure of control and discipline associated with it. A coach like Paul who lets players have a good time often finds that players are not having a good time and are blaming it on him. To a considerable degree, preadolescents accept the adult rhetoric, discussed in the previous chapter, and they expect their guardians to live up to it as well.

This doesn't mean that players desire the stereotypical Little league coach, who is nasty to his players and berates them after a game. Players resent such coaches. One former player commented about the players of such a coach after their team lost: "They [the players] look like they're walking to the rope where they're gonna get hung" (field notes, Sanford Heights). Players (particularly the better ones) want their coaches to work them hard and to keep them (and especially their less-talented colleagues) from "goofing off." However, players resent coaches who give long postgame lectures—which are seen as being pointless. A coach who impugns the character of his team is resented, and this "strictness and meanness" is considered out of bounds, whereas the "strictness and meanness" required to force a team to practice hard—even making errant players run laps—is considered moral and desirable.

Peer Socialization

In examining preadolescent behavior, one is struck with the degree to which preadolescents wish to adopt the adult male sex role; they are attempting—somewhat hesitantly to be sure—to adopt the values of their male leaders. This, of course, doesn't mean that preadolescents are mini-adults; adult values are transformed. They are the values of adults with rough edges still attached; the legacy of childhood behavior and the lack of sophistication of preadolescent behavior shape what preadolescents do and what they think is right. Yet, the standards they set for themselves and for their adult guardians reflect imperfectly those values set for them by their adults. By the time of preadolescence, boys recognize that being "men" is an important task for them, and it is a task they accept.

In the remaining chapters I will move my primary focus of attention from the playing of baseball as such to other aspects of the developing preadolescent male sex role—first by examining how preadolescent cultural themes spring up in the larger preadolescent society and then by tracing the development of these themes in the context of the small group (the Little League baseball team) and subculture. Wherever we look, we see that the preadolescent male culture represents a transformation of those messages that boys receive from their adult guardians—including messages that adult males don't know they are giving off and in some instances sincerely wish they hadn't.

5

Sexual and Aggressive Themes of
Preadolescent Boys

All people have an ethos or world view (Dundes 1971; Jones 1972)—an image of their environment and related ideas of what constitute proper and legitimate actions given this environment. Further, people share "folk ideas": "traditional notions that a group of people have about the nature of man, of the world, and of man's life in the world" (Dundes 1971, 95). These global concepts are not divorced from interaction, nor are they "static"; they can be manipulated, used, or ignored, depending on current needs. Folk ideas are internalizations of others' expectations for proper behavior and attitudes. As a result, they filter potential behaviors.

Crucial to the creation of a child's (in this case, a boy's) world view and folk ideas are patterns of human development. Whether or not we conceive development in terms of stages, a child's abilities do change over time; these changes are relatively invariant and predictable, and they both cause and reflect changes in the child's social environment. These biological and social factors provide internal and external constraints on a child's behavior and on his or her expectations and assumptions of legitimate behavior. These factors constitute the child's *imperatives of development.*

Important features of preadolescence shaped by development include cognitive skills which approach those of adults, rapidly increasing knowledge of a wide variety of behavior preserves, a heightened level of activity, and the perceived importance of friendship ties. Along with these changes comes a new orientation by adults to their offspring. During preadolescence, children are expected to develop social lives outside of situations dominated by adults (especially parents and teachers).

Erik Erikson defines the central issue in the "latency" stage (essentially preadolescence) as the relationship between industry and inferiority (Erikson 1963, 258–61), with competence as the basic value. Competence includes both the technological ethos of the society (Erikson 1963, 260) and the ability to develop meaningful relationships with others (Sullivan 1953). The developmental impera-

103

tives of this stage involve the manipulation of tools and of other human beings; the boy increasingly acts out his view of his adult masters. Obviously this view is subjective—based on the child's observations of adults, slightly older acquaintances, and the mass media—rather than an objective portrayal of how adults "really" act. "Folk ideas" of the period influence behavior at least as much as the adult-sanctioned "reality" does.

The salience of friendships and impression management is particularly central. During preadolescence the child finds himself or herself in several different social worlds, which require different sets of appropriate behavior. The popular and socially integrated preadolescent is not the one who behaves consistently but the one who has mastered techniques of impression management to present himself or herself through flexible role performances (see Elkins 1958) and to altercast others (Weinstein and Deutschberger 1963; Weinstein 1969)—that is, shape them—into supportive roles. Neither friendship nor presentation of self originates during preadolescence but, because children are expected to develop their own peer social world at this time, their importance grows. Further, the imperatives of development are played out in friendships. Friendship is (1) a staging area in which activities improper elsewhere can be tested in a supportive environment, (2) a cultural institution in which behavioral routines can be learned without embarrassment, and (3) a crucible in which the child's social self is developed (Fine 1981a).

Themes of Preadolescence

I shall focus on two major areas of preadolescent male behavior: sex and aggression. Determining what constitutes a major theme is a matter of judgment; other important issues might have been named: educational achievement, athletics, adult work-related issues. However, pragmatic and theoretical considerations led me to choose sex and aggression. First, the way in which preadolescent boys deal with these two issues has not been discussed in detail;[1] as a result, this discussion contributes to an understanding of childhood. Second, these issues reflect deviant behavior by preadolescents that is grounded in the preadolescent peer environment and not shared with adults. Schoolwork, sports, and adult work, while discussed among peers, are also discussed with adults. Thus, they are not imperatives of development to the same extent in that they are not entirely grounded in peer interaction. Third, because these activities represent deviant behavior—albeit "normal" deviance—preadolescents attempt to shield them from parents and their agents; because of their sensitivity these topics cleave to concerns of presentation of self. Fourth, these themes proved to be quite striking to me as an observer. Obviously I recognized these as concerns prior to the research, but they emerged dramatically in the course of observation. While sex and aggression may not be the only imperatives of development, they are especially characteristic of peer interaction and the achievement of peer competence in preadolescence.

Sexual Themes in Male Preadolescence

In "hanging around" with preadolescent boys (particularly those eleven and twelve years old) I was impressed by the time devoted to talk about sex and members of the opposite sex (see Martinson 1981).[2] Males maturing in our sexualized society quickly recognize that sexual prowess is a mark of maturity. One must convince others that one is sexually mature, active, and knowledgeable. Boys must try to be men. Although the techniques change, males throughout the life course are subject to the same demanding requirements.

Often evaluations occur while teasing a boy about his taste in members of the opposite sex. When boys see another's girlfriend, they often playfully remark how unattractive she is:

Frank is joking about Stew's girlfriend in Stew's presence: "She's about this tall [he extends his arm far over his head to indicate her height] and weighs ten pounds." Part of the humor is that Stew is short and somewhat stocky. Stew admits that he knows this girl but claims he doesn't like her (although from his tone I gather he does) (field notes, Sanford Heights).

Justin, Whitney, Harry, and Ray are talking about girls.
Justin (talking about Kip Taviss's girlfriend): I think Nancy's a jerk.
Ray: Tell Taviss that.
Justin (laughing): I will.
Harry: If anyone acts doofy, Laurel acts doofy. [Laurel is Whitney's girlfriend] (field notes, Hopewell).

Rich Toland has a crush on his new girlfriend, Erica. He tells his friends: "I've got the best girlfriend I've ever had. She's the cutest girl my age [twelve] I've ever seen. We made out today." Because Erica lives on the other side of town, none of

Rich's friends know her. Rich proudly invites Tom Jordan to come with him the next time he visits Erica. When Tom returns, he satirizes Erica's looks: "She was the ugliest girl I've ever seen. She has no teeth." (Tom then describes her teeth—he says "she has several very short teeth and one really long one, and a big nose.") Tom adds: "She isn't really, really bad, but she isn't great. She's the ugliest I've ever seen that anyone *liked*." After this Rich stops talking about Erica and soon stops seeing her (field notes, Sanford Heights).

Only the very few high-status preadolescents-of-the-world, such as Justin or Tom, can get away with having a girlfriend without being ridiculed by their peers. Few could say what Tom told his friend Rich: "I love Sharon so god darn much, you fucking won't believe it. I'd make out every night with her if I could" (tape transcript, Sanford Heights). In one discussion of girls who attended the Hiawatha school, the consensus of the boys present was that Tom's girlfriend Sharon was the prettiest girl in school. While some objective standards of evaluation may be involved—even at this age some girls *are* considered more attractive than others, despite their beaus—these evaluations serve social control functions within the male group. First, they indicate that a "just world" is operating in terms of heterosexual relationships. A boy should not have a girlfriend of more status than he, even if his girlfriend has to be insulted. Further, these evaluations are a means by which the preadolescent leaders can underline their positions as opinion leaders by establishing the "correct" evaluation of girlfriends, as apparently happened in Tom's comments about Erica. Finally, this system warns males of the danger of becoming too affectionate toward females, as "objective" ratings are subject to change. Although boys desire to have girlfriends who are "cute" or "sexy" or "ball-breakers," comments about a girl's charms are social constructions designed to typify her swain and prevent too much psychological intimacy.

Overinvolvement. Related to the evaluation of girls is joking talk that prevents boys from becoming too involved in their cross-sex relationships. On the surface this may seem paradoxical; if involvement with girls is mature, why is not more involvement more mature? The problem is that such a deep relationship implies an equality in power and commitment between the sexes, contrary to the male sex role. The only players who were able to sustain such relationships were those boys, like Justin and Tom, who had recognized sexual skills and high status—enough idiosyncrasy credits (Hollander 1958)—to manage such a deviant relationship. Before examining these cases, it is necessary to see how the cautions against overinvolvement operate. One technique of warning against overinvolvement is to imply humorously that the "couple" will be married:

> Larry tells everyone on the Dodgers that Roy Blivins's girlfriend is Janie Holman, "or should I say Janie Blivins" (field notes, Sanford Heights).

Or that the boy has adopted feminine behavior:

> Whitney's girlfriend Laurel left Rhode Island to spend the summer in Missouri. Whitney commented to his friends who were teasing him about how much he missed her: "We [he and Justin] think we heard her plane go by." Justin added sarcastically, "Whit was crying" (field notes, Hopewell).

Or that the boy's activities are curtailed because of his girlfriend:

> Stew must leave baseball practice early. Roy calls out to him as he is riding away on his bicycle, "Hey, Stew, Cathy is waiting for you" (field notes, Sanford Heights).

Boys must never let girls replace other boys as the focus of their attention. Only boys with high status in their peer social network are relatively immune from such criticism. When Tom's girlfriend Sharon was on vacation he mentioned publicly that he had written her a letter and that he was looking forward to her return. Justin purchased an expensive ring for his girlfriend Vicki without other boys teasing him for his sentiment.

Preadolescent boys reside in a sexualized world in which both they and their girlfriends must maintain reputations that others may attempt to alter. It is impossible to sketch the "ideal reputation" in advance because such a social image is dependent on the particular norms and expectations of the boy's immediate peer group and his own personality. However, boys generally wish to be seen as sexually potent, whereas girls lose status by having the same reputation—the double standard is very much in existence in preadolescence.

Reputations. To have a reputation is to engage in a dangerous game. Reputations may be grounded indirectly in behavior but they are given expression in talk. This applies to boys considered asexual as well as those considered "Casanovas."

Rich sees John Danville talking to some girls, and comments to those around him: "There's John-John over by the girls. What else is new?" (field notes, Sanford Heights).

Justin asks a friend: "I haven't seen you in a long time, Abs. Where have you been? Locked in your room with a girl?" (field notes, Hopewell).

While four boys are being driven to an ice cream parlor, they began talking about girls. In particular they insult Davey Massey, who is not present. One boy said that Davey "goes out" with his mother; another boy said that he went out with his younger sister (field notes, Beanville).

Boys must ensure that those girls with whom they have "relationships" are suitable partners. One sixth-grader in Sanford Heights was criticized for liking a ninth-grade girl, described as a "zit-face" and "a fucking whore." It matters little whether there was any legitimacy to these charges; what is significant is that the boy dropped her, and a friend of his defended him by saying, "He doesn't like that slut" (field notes, Sanford Heights). The evaluations that boys have of girls are closely connected to their reputations, and they must use preadolescent techniques of persuasion to keep their own reputations intact:

> Phil Osage has found out something about Jason Fowell that Jason doesn't want him to tell. It turns out that Phil learned that Jason was kissing ("making out with") a girl he doesn't like any more. In other words, Jason doesn't want his friends to learn that he was kissing a girl he considers a "dog." Jason threatens to beat up Phil if he tells (field notes, Sanford Heights).

Reputations are connected to the publicity of deeds, although the deed and the reputation may be quite different. A boy's reputation affects the evaluation and interpretation of his deeds, just as his deeds will influence his reputation. With the developmental imperative for preadolescent males to prove themselves to be sexually agile, they are pressured to reveal that they or their friends have consummated those actions that will impress others as reflecting a sexualized self:

> John-John Danville tells his friends that he got a "tanker sore" from "making out" with a girl other than his regular girlfriend (field notes, Sanford Heights).

I asked a group of boys what they did when they went out with girls. One twelve-year-old said: "Make out. Squeeze their tits" (field notes, Beanville).

One of Harry's friends says that Harry and his girlfriend sit in the back of the movies and give each other "mouth-to-mouth resuscitation" (field notes, Hopewell).

On some occasions an account will be dramatic and may be the topic of discussion for several days:[3]

There was a lot of oblique sexual talk about the fact that Dan Gregory, a high-status twelve-year-old boy with a reputation as a "ladies' man," was going to see his girlfriend, Annie. One boy said that Dan was going to pay Annie $.10 for each "base" she allowed him to reach. The following day Stew said that Dan "almost got to third." Hardy said that Dan got to first base "and was halfway to second" when Gordy, an eleven year old, called him to find out how he was doing, but Hardy said that he didn't think Dan would have gotten any further. A few days later I overheard Dan telling friends that he had gotten "halfway to second," and that he would have gone further, except for Gordy's phone call. Hardy says of Gordy, "What a gay one!" Dan adds: "The kid's weird." Dan's reputation is preserved at the expense of Gordy's (field notes, Sanford Heights).

Although Dan did not meet his objectives, his reputation increased through the talk (including the exaggerations of friends like Stew), whereas Gordy, a younger boy, was roundly condemned. Significantly, Annie's reputation was also affected, as players started calling her a "prostie," and Dan stopped considering her his girlfriend. Aside from Dan and Annie, no one knew the truth about what happened between the two of them; yet, it is not private actions but public talk that is ultimately significant. The double standard lives.

Talk about sexual behaviors. Despite what boys (and journalists) sometimes claim, not much sexual behavior actually occurs—at least it did not in these suburban communities in the late 1970s. Getting beyond "second base" is rare. Preadolescents may not be able to display their sexual sophistication by describing their own actions; however, they shape the perceptions that others have of them through their talk. Boys sometimes adopt a sexually swaggering stance in their conversations, as in this account of how to "French kiss":

Tom: First of all, you gotta make sure you don't get no more "Ahhhk!" burps in your mouth (Hardy and Frank both laugh).

It would be very crude to burp. I mean you make sure you don't have a cold, cause greenies [mucus] going through there (Tom laughs), going through her mouth would taste awful horseshit. (All laugh.)

Frank: And one thing, don't spit while frenching.

Tom: And make sure . . . make sure you don't breathe out of your mouth (all laugh) unless you're doing mouth-to-mouth resuscitation. After all that frenching, you just gotta do mouth-to-mouth to keep your air up. OK, now you take a squirt of your favorite after-shave. You rub it on your hair, and you rub it all around you. And you (Tom giggles hysterically), and you rub it all around. It sure feels good (more giggling). . . . Well, anyway, I get to my second lesson. First, you walk in, you see a sexy girl in the telephone booth. You don't know who she is, just see the back of her. Gotta make sure she doesn't have a big butt, you know. . . . You just walk into the telephone booth, put your arm around her and say "Hi." And she goes "Uhhh! Ohhh, hi" [tone sounds surprised at first, then "feminine" and "willing"]. With her tongue around, wrapped around, wrapped around the microphone, her teeth, her teeth are chattering from so much shock. You just take your pants . . . no . . . well.

Hardy: You take her pants.

Tom: Well, you just stick out your tongue, and you say [Tom sings in a mock romantic fashion], "Want to, oh baby, you mean it, you get me under your skin" (taped transcript, Sanford Heights).

This conversation is not much different from those of other "precocious" preadolescents. Through the content of these conversations, boys learn what is expected of them by their peers. The significance of this talk does not derive from the acquisition of sophisticated techniques of French kissing (although some content learning does occur[4]); rather, boys are presenting themselves to male peers as "males." This conversation fantasy dramatically suggests that males expect each other to be sexually aggressive and that females await their attempts with undisguised arousal. This short dialogue offers a world view that is consistent with male domination and female submission. By this talk, preadolescents acquire verbal skills that allow them to handle themselves within the context of similar lines of talk and prepare them to act like "males."

Acting with Girls

The sexual themes of (male) preadolescence are, of course, not only revealed through talk among boys about girls, but in boys' behavior and talk with girls. To measure this "sexual activity," boys in Bolton Park and Sanford Heights were asked in the final questionnaire:
1. Do you currently have a girlfriend?
2. How many girlfriends have you had?
While obviously the responses to these questions do not represent "the truth" and may be systematically biased, they provide insight into male-female contact as long as we recognize that these are uncorroborated self-report data.

Of the 167 boys who responded, 57 (34 percent) claimed to have a girlfriend. Boys with girlfriends reported that they had had an average of 3.9 girlfriends. Not surprisingly, the percentage of boys who claimed to have had a girlfriend increased with age (ten- and eleven-year-olds: 30 percent; twelve-year-olds: 38 percent), although these results reflect a narrower gap than I expect empirically. Boys with girlfriends may be more popular among their male peers. Controlling for age, there are significant or nearly significant correlations between having a girlfriend and several measures of peer status: (1) the number of nominations by fellow players as one of their three best friends in the world ($r = .11$, $n = 164$, $p = .08$); (2) the number of nominations by fellow players as one of their three best friends in the league ($r = .13$, $n = 164$, $p = .04$); (3) the number of nominations by teammates as one of their three best friends on the team ($r = .13$, $n = 164$, $p = .05$); and (4) the number of teammates who describe the player as one of the three best players on the team ($r = .11$, $n = 164$, $p = .09$). These data, speculative as they are, suggest a connection among statuses in all areas of a preadolescent's social world.

Behavior between boys and girls, of course, goes far deeper than claims of the existence of a relationship. When boys and girls begin to recognize in each other a potential sexual being and a desirable person with whom to be seen they lack a repertoire of sexual behavior. Boys have seen older boys talk with girls, and they are exposed to the mass media, but at this age their experience is largely vicarious. Real interaction with girls poses problems for the inexperienced preadolescent male. Much male-female interaction at this age occurs in a group, among friends. The friendship bond, in permitting a wide latitude of behavior, provides a setting in which the boy can explore modes of sexualized action; even if the boy is not successful in his quest, he typically will be supported by his friends. Broderick (1966) found that at ages twelve and thirteen, 56 percent of the boys and 76 percent of the girls in his sample preferred double or group dating to single dating. One group of twelve-year-old boys in Hopewell even went so far as to form a "club," the "Hell's Angels," that had the major function of supporting each other in their dealings with girls. The club members could communicate messages to and from girlfriends without the emotional involvement of the smitten boy. Social failures could be handled more diplomatically. This form of social activity is also evident in private parties of preadolescents (Martinson 1973). These parties, in which boys are supported by their male friends and the girls are in the company of their friends, are staging areas for quasi-sexual and quasi-aggressive behavior. Boys in Sanford Heights informed me that "making out" occurred at these events. However, roughhousing may be more common, because boys are ignorant of adolescent social norms of chivalrous behavior to girls or ashamed of showing tenderness to girls.

During preadolescence boys and girls are generally circumspect in admitting affection—in part to prevent losing face. Among boys this is shown either in overly aggressive posturing or embarrassed silence. Some of the immature affection may seen naively charming to adults:

> The girlfriends of Justin and Whitney attend their team's game. Apparently Justin had written a note to his friend Kip expressing "tender feelings" for his girlfriend Vicki. Kip threw the note away, and the girls found it. When Kip announced that Vicki had found it, Justin seemed partially annoyed but also pleased. Trading notes is one way of communicating one's feelings without vocalizing them (field notes, Hopewell).

A girl also expresses her feelings by watching the boy play baseball. A boy never speaks to his girlfriend on such occasions but may secretly enjoy her attention. It is less common for a boy to show up at a girl's softball game, although Tom attended several games in which his girlfriend Sharon played. Occasionally a boy and girl visit an ice cream parlor or attend the movies unchaperoned, but this is rare and represents behavior of youths who are more mature and more oriented to adolescent cross-sex behavioral norms than are most of their peers. More commonly, preadolescents attempt to be noticed by acting silly (by adult standards):

The Cardinals have a large number of girls sitting behind their dugout, watching them play. Their attention is directed to Joey O'Brien, one of the best players in the league. Don Lawrence, the Cardinals' catcher, shows off to get their attention by fooling around with Joey. For example, after Joey hits a triple, Don runs to third base and gives him an exaggerated handshake (field notes, Maple Bluff).

At a later age, some of these behaviors, such as throwing grass at girls or passing notes, will be considered immature (or "uncool"). However, they fit in preadolescence. The fact that preadolescent boys and girls are interacting in a continuing and organized fashion is taken as a sign of maturity by the boys; others, somewhat older or more mature, see the behavior as childish. If the boy's audiences (girls, his male peers) support him, then the behaviors represent successful impression management.

This point needs to be emphasized in regard to those behaviors adults would describe as "aggressive" and have been taken as indicating hostility between boys and girls during latency:

A group of boys come across a preadolescent girls' softball team from a different area of town, sitting around a park picnic table. The boys begin teasing them with sexual taunts: "Hey, suck me where the sun never shines," "Pluck my hairs," and "You're innocent like my butthole." The girls are not outraged and actually seem to enjoy it—at one point singing to attract the boys' attention. After whispered discussion about what to do, the boys steal the girls' Thermos and pour out the water— at which the girls squeal but don't get seriously upset. Later the boys return to the picnic table and throw beer cans at the girls, who giggle and scream. Finally as the boys are leaving, a girl calls out to one of them, "Bye, honey!" (field notes, Sanford Heights).

Attention rather than tenderness often motivates boy-girl encounters. Girls dream of popular and athletic boyfriends, who add to their prestige, just as boys look for attractive girls with whom they can say they have "made out." Children have learned images of male-female encounters from the media and from those older, and these images filter through the lens of their expectations.

Just as boys use physical aggression to "attack" girls, girls may employ public affection to humiliate boys:

Barb Richards comes up to Rich Toland and says flirtatiously: "Hi, pretty blue eyes." Rich looks extremely embarrassed, averts his eyes, and doesn't say anything to her. Later Barb takes Allen Tabor's comb, sticks it in chalk (used to mark the base paths) and combs his hair with it. When Allen finally realizes what Barb has done, he says to his male friends, with considerable exasperation (but not real hostility), "She's a devil!" (field notes, Sanford Heights).

The relationships among boys and girls are balanced, despite my emphasis on male activities. While it may be chauvinistic to claim that the girls have "feminine wiles," each sex develops techniques of impression management that allow them to cope with the other sex. Those who are adept at these skills, those who can define what the proper relationship between boys and girls should be, and those whom others define as having these skills gain prestige among peers from their public "sexuality."

Talk about Homosexuality

In addition to talking about heterosexual themes and acting "properly" in heterosexual situations, boys also attempt to define their sexualized selves by addressing that facet of sexuality defined as opposite to sexual maturity: homosexuality. To be sure, most of these boys have not met anyone whom they believe "really" is a homosexual, and most of these boys do not know how to define homosexuals, other than to say they are boys who "like other boys," or "a guy who wants to marry another guy." Despite this, homosexuality is a central theme in preadolescent male talk. In each league, boys used expressions like "You're a faggot," "God, he's gay," "He is the biggest fag in the world," "He sucks," "What a queer," or "Kiss my ass."

Obviously being "gay" has little to do with homosexual behavior; when used in informal interaction the label stigmatizes by suggesting the target is "immature." Indeed, some "homosexual behavior" (e.g., mutual masturbation) occurs among boys who would never be labeled "gay." The concept of homosexuality is related to two other concepts that boys sometimes use to denigrate others: being a "baby" and a "girl." Each insult means that the target has not lived up to expectations of appropriate male behavior, and is being sanctioned. For example, "goody-goody" boys or teacher's pets are considered "queers." Homosexual rhetoric has an additional benefit for the speaker in that its usage suggests that the speaker is mature himself. As one boy tells his friend, "In fifth grade, we were faggots. We used to wrestle [each other]" (field notes, Hopewell). Minor-league players are sometimes called "little fems" (field notes, Sanford Heights).

Like many rhetorical images, "homosexuality" is sufficiently ambiguous that preadolescents can use it without necessarily agreeing completely on its referent (Kleinman 1984). Its meaning is grounded in the situation, as it can be used to refer to any type of negatively valued behavior—from a boy who always gets into fights to one who doesn't like to participate in sports, or to a boy who has an unusual pitching style. The rhetoric of homosexuality is among the most flexible and abusive language that the preadolescent has at his disposal:

> Harmon is furious at Eugene, a boy who is generally scorned and considered to be "gay" and one who "acts like a girl." According to Harmon, Eugene gave him "the finger" in front of a teacher. Harmon slapped him, and Harmon got punished by the teacher instead of Eugene. Harmon tells his friends, "We wasted up on him the last day of school. His parents called the police." Apparently Eugene refused to tell the police who beat him up, and Harmon claimed they would have beat him up worse if he had. Harmon adds: "He just watches us going to the bathroom. He sits there and stares like he's a hungry animal" (field notes, Sanford Heights).

Despite the fact that poor Eugene was masculine enough to give Harmon the finger and then not "squeal" on his peers to the "pigs," he is condemned through the rhetoric of homosexuality.

Homosexual rhetoric does not necessarily imply hostility in the relation; friends sometimes call each other "faggots" or "gay boys," and through an understanding of their relationship, the specific performance circumstance, and a recognition of paravocal cues, no offense is taken. One boy said of two friends: "Here comes 'suck me Jay' and 'bite me Bob'"; neither Jay nor Bob took offense (field notes, Sanford Heights). Yet, even here there are constraints on what types of talk are permissable:

> Whitney calls to his friend Harry, "Hey, cocksucker." Harry responds evenly, "Watch it, Whit" (field notes, Hopewell).

Meaning is negotiable to a point, but some meanings are so fixed that they cannot be transformed easily into banter.

This body of rhetoric, together with the talk and behavior about heterosexual behavior, reveals thematic outlines of male preadolescence. Preadolescents wish to indicate to themselves and their peers that they are mature. However, like "hustle," "maturity" is not a quality that can be seen "objectively"; rather, it must be displayed so that others will attribute it to the displayer. Sexualized talk and action is an attempt by these boys to reveal that they possess "maturity" even though neither they nor anyone else can point to it, but can only point to its public representations. The preadolescent's duty is to master image-making skills and rhetorical devices that lead others to attribute to them those characteristics they wish to know they possess.

Aggressive Themes in Preadolescence

Closely related to sexual talk and behavior is the perceived need of preadolescent males to demonstrate they are men by being daring and bold. Like sexual maturity, these maturity-related qualities have no objective measures, and so preadolescents must perform actions and talk that are seen as indicative of these traits. When Redl (1966) refers to preadolescence as the period in which the nicest children behave in the most awful ways, he is referring to the aggression and "cruelty" of children. Yet, for the "normal" child, aggression is not random but is patterned within a social context that encourages it. To examine how preadolescent males use aggression, I focus on two forms of it: that directed to members of their social network (often through sexual insults) and that aimed at anonymous others. While adults may find both discouraging, and peers may find both indicate "maturity," they are different in cause and form.

Insulting Peers

Preadolescents do not hesitate to insult their peers. In their concern with establishing social ranking, preadolescents do not differ from those younger or older. However, the content of their insults reflects the developmental imperatives of the period. The insults represent a gain of status for the preadolescent who is the insulter and a loss of status for the boy insulted; in addition they teach the boy *how* to engage in informal talk.

Consider one ten-year-old boy in Sanford Heights who is criticized by several older boys. The ten-year-old, Tommy, is the coach's son. In one practice in preparation for the statewide tournament, Tommy and Harmon trade angry insults. Harmon's temper had caused problems all season, and this episode proved to be the final straw, as the coach simply walked away from the practice. After his anger subsided he returned, but Harmon's father, the team's assistant coach, felt it wise for Harmon to leave the team. The following week some of Harmon's friends met Tommy on a school bus:

> Hardy sees Tommy and a friend enter the bus and announces loudly: "Tommy sucks." Rod adds: "Tommy's a wuss." [A wuss is defined as a cross between a woman and a pussy.] In unison Jerry and Rod tell Tommy as he approaches, "You suck." Rod particularly is angry at Tommy, "Harmon can't play because of you. What a fag!" Tommy doesn't respond to the abuse from his older tormentors but looks dejected and near tears. The insults build in anger as Hardy calls Tommy a "woman," and Rod says, "Give him the faggot award." Finally Jerry takes the baseball cap of Tommy's friend and tosses it out the window of the moving bus (field notes, Sanford Heights).

First, children consider the social context of the insult. They can be distressingly cruel to each other, but this cruelty is rarely expressed without an audience. The purpose of these insults may be less to hurt the target than to indicate publicly one's own feelings to one's friends. The target of these insults typically is a peer whose unacceptability has been agreed on—at least while the insulting is continuing. Rarely does another boy defend the target, although in other situations the target might not be disliked. Second, preadolescents attempt to test the boundaries of legitimate behavior through these insults. The case described above is representative in that the insult crescendo (in this case reflecting homosexuality) continues until the target becomes upset or withdraws, or until one of the perpetrators does something that is outside the range of legitimate behavior. In this instance, tossing the baseball cap out of the bus window ends the insults. Jerry's action was outside the realm of legitimate behavior. Although he was not sanctioned by his friends, he apologized to the victim, claiming that he didn't really mean to get rid of the hat. When the target is not present, there is also a crescendo of insults, but the cruel creativity expires once the parties to the insulting get bored:

> A number of boys are hanging around talking into my tape recorded about a disliked peer who is not present.
> *Rich:* Malkis sucks. Yeah. Yeah. Yeah.
> *Jerry:* He licks my ass.
> *Rich:* Go play with zit-face [Denny Malkis's girlfriend].
> *Tom:* Go screw zit-face.

Rich: Yeah, go screw zit-face, and Malkis I wish you'd stop hanging around me, because you look so ugly, and I wish you'd go to hell. . . . Hey, Malkis, Malkis, go to hell. I saw you fucking the hell out of your sister last night. How come you hang around with your sister? Tell me, huh? How come you like that ninth grader who beat the fucking hell out of a teacher, and how come she's a zit-face?

Tom: A fucking whore.

Rich: You're [Zit-face] so fat and you're slutty, and you stink (Tape transcript, Sanford Heights).

While this conversation is atypical in that it is directed to an absent peer through the tape recorder, the increasing vehemence is typical of insult sessions. The increasing attack does not mean that players are becoming more angry at the target but only that they are trying to impress each other with their verbal skills (see Bronner 1978a, 1978b).[5]

The third significant feature of these insults is their content. Insults, however crude or "immature" by adult standards, communicate to peers that the insulter has mastered the language of maturity. Rich's claim that Denny was "fucking the hell out of [his own] sister" is one of the most intense insults a boy can direct to another, and expresses Rich's antipathy to Denny. Simultaneously it announces something about Rich himself: he can use the rhetoric of incest convincingly.

Not everyone can "get away with" insults. Interaction is constrained by perceptions of social structure. Insults can be directed down or across the status hierarchy, but it is rarer for them to be directed upward—at least if the target is present. Low-status boys who criticize someone of higher status may find themselves the target of a volley of insults:

In an important game Tim, a ten-year-old utility outfielder on the Rangers, calls out to the opposing catcher, a twelve-year-old: "There's a monkey behind the plate." One of his teammates shoots back "He's a better player than you!" Later in the game several of the older Rangers verbally attack Bruce, a low-status eleven-year-old, for criticizing their opponents (field notes, Beanville).

Tim and Bruce have ignored the social proprieties of insulting.

Despite aggressive talk, "serious" aggression among peers is rare. Glassner (1976) demonstrates that children have a system of

jurisprudence that enforces social control. Although boys sometimes strike or push each other, serious fights rarely develop, and
physically aggressive boys are often scorned. The boys with the
most prestige in the five leagues were not those who were the most
physically aggressive or who got into fights, and they had not become leaders because they had bested other boys. The rough and
tumble of preadolescence is not so rough and doesn't involve many
tumbles. Boys who regularly engage in physical aggression are de-
rided as "mental" ("mentally ill"—referring, for instance, to one
boy who reportedly beat a girl with a bicycle chain) or "faggots."
Boys do talk about beating up others, but these remarks mostly reflect the depths of a boy's feelings and are not genuine threats of
physical violence:

> In a Little League game, Frank Satsburg, pitching for the
> Dodgers, is hit in the knee with a bat that Sid Copeland, the
> best hitter on the Astros, releases by accident. Frank writhes
> on the ground in pain, apparently seriously hurt, but gets up
> and continues to play. Sid stands around with a silly, embar-
> rassed smile on his face. Maury Herman, the Dodger third
> baseman, yells at Sid: "Copeland, you jerk. . . . It's not funny."
> Turning to his teammates, Maury adds: "Look at him laugh.
> I'll beat his face in." Paul Mundy, another Dodger twelve-year-
> old, says to Maury: "Hit him with a rock." Neither of them
> does anything, and after the game the incident has been for-
> gotten (field notes, Sanford Heights).

When boys angrily threaten to fight each other, other boys step
in to cool their friends off or to change the focus. Although Glassner
speaks of a distinct preadolescent type—the "compromiser"—who
prevents fights, I did not find this role type; rather, most boys are
concerned with preventing disruption of their orderly interaction.
Often, in the aftermath of a fight all boys will be constrained in their
behavior by adults—an undesirable outcome. "Cutting words" or
"malicious pranks" rather than fisticuffs reflect the child's presentation of himself as a "mature" actor—at least in these suburbs.

Aggression against Others

Although preadolescents do not generally resort to aggressive behavior with each other, this does not mean they never explore the
boundaries of propriety. Preadolescents place a premium on "daring" behavior, which is expressed through pranks, or, as preadolescents term it, "mischief." Preadolescents known for their daring are

renowned. However, if they are too "daring" or deviant (that is, outside the range of behavior that most preadolescents feel *they* would wish to do if they had the nerve), these boys are labelled "mental," "rowdies," or "burn-outs," and are scorned (although even they have a circle of friends). Rejected behaviors include the regular use of cigarettes, alcohol, or drugs and actions that are defined as "criminal." This latter poses an interesting issue in that certain of the pranks of "normal" preadolescents might be defined as illegal by others, including their adult guardians, and might be severely punished if done by lower-class preadolescents (see Chambliss 1973). "Deviance" is not based on formal laws but on the recognition of boundaries. Of course, differences in where these boundaries are drawn are a consequence of one's social circle—some boys are more daring and choose to behave in ways that other boys would define as indicating moral turpitude.[6] Further, actions are evaluated differently becuase of the performer (and the performer's ascribed motivation). For example, some boys in Sanford Heights took pride in throwing another boy's bicycle into a creek, but these same preadolescents were furious later when some "rowdies" had punctured a tire on one of their bicycles.

Boys saw certain pranks in each community as legitimate, although "daring." This deviance was fun (Riemer 1981). Not all boys performed these pranks; however, the boys who participated in such activities were not scorned but respected for being willing to take such chances. Of course, the doing of these pranks was infrequent, although they quickly became legendary in the boys' talk. Perhaps as a function of tradition, the main pranks in each of the communities differed. In Beanville most talk was about "mooning"—that is, pulling down one's trousers while facing away from passing traffic (see Licht 1974); in Hopewell "egging" (throwing eggs at) houses or cars was common; in both Sanford Heights and Bolton Park, ringing a doorbell and running away before the homeowner could answer was the most frequently discussed prank. To give an idea of participation of boys in these pranks, forty-eight of the fifty twelve-year-olds in the Sanford Heights Little League were asked in the postseason interview if they had performed each of four aggressive pranks: (1) egging a house; (2) making a "funny phone call" (see Dresser 1973; Harris 1978; Knapp and Knapp 1976, 100–104); (3) playing the Polish Rope Trick—a prank in which two boys hold an imaginary rope across a roadway at dusk, hoping to trick cars into stopping; and (4) playing Ding Dong Ditch[7]—ringing a doorbell and running away (see Opie and Opie 1959, 378–82). The proportion of the sample who had ever performed each of these pranks were 40 percent, 52 percent, 19 percent, and 56 percent respectively. From these figures it is evident that such aggressive pranks, typically aimed at adults, are relatively common.

During the interview, players were asked *with whom* they performed these pranks. Combining all pranks for this analysis, seventy partners who played Little league baseball were named (counting a boy only once for each player asked, even if they performed several pranks together). Each player was also asked whether every other twelve-year-old Little Leaguer was one of the boy's five best friends in the league, a close friend, a friend, disliked, or neither disliked nor a friend. Of the seventy prank partners, 60 percent were among the namer's five best friends in the league, an additional 29 percent were close friends of the namer but not among the five closest friends, and 9 percent more were friends. Only one boy was not a friend, and another partner was disliked. These two cases were from the same boy who changed friends in the middle of the season, and these were *former* friends. These figures compare with 10 percent who can be named as one of a boy's five best friends in the league (assuming these twelve-year-old boys limit their choices to other twelve-year-olds; if they are not limited, the expected percentage falls to 5 percent). In the sample, 18 percent are named as close friends, another 31 percent are considered friends, 2 percent are disliked, and 49 percent are neither friends nor disliked. Friendship is the staging area in which aggressive behavior to outsiders occurs (Fine 1981a). One purpose of these pranks is to show other friends that one is willing to take chances—that one is mature, given the positive value of tricking others. The presence of friends promotes aggressive pranks in defining the action as legitimate, providing status for the boy if he succeeds, and goading him if his fear of adult condemnation or sense of guilt threatens to prevent his action.

The impression-management function of these aggressive pranks is evident in the talk of players. Some notable pranks are referred to with awe by players. For example, one boy in Bolton Park regaled his friends about the variation of Ding Dong Ditch he and some other friends performed. They took some "dog dirt," wrapped it in newspaper, lit the newspaper on fire, rang the doorbell, and ran to a safe vantage point. When the victim came to the door, he stomped on the flaming package. Then another boy rang the back doorbell, at which point the man, not thinking straight through his anger, rushed through the house, tracking it with the dog excrement (field notes, Bolton Park.[8] Whatever the factual basis of the story, it was accepted as true, caused much laughter, and made the teller the center of attention. Boys love to describe instances in which they were chased by victims of their pranks and *almost* caught.

Rather than defining pranks as expressions of an "aggressive instinct" directed at those who control them (an approach that places emphasis on internal, psychiatric effects) (see Yohe 1950), I see pranks as social actions designed to shape one's public identity (Jorgenson 1984). This identity shaping occurs in those arenas considered characteristic of those older and of higher status, and must be adventures in which not everyone within the peer network engages. Pranks are "heroic" and reveal positive qualities of self. If the internal-aggression hypothesis were adequate, these aggressive acts should occur when a boy is alone; however, they are always performed with one or several others. I do not deny that preadolescents can value aggression; obviously they do when the aggression takes culturally sanctioned forms, but this is an incomplete answer to explaining preadolescent behavior.

The Social Nature of Developmental Imperatives

In this chapter I have examined two major themes of preadolescence: sex and aggression. I do not suggest that preadolescents only talk and act on these two themes. Such a view provides a distorted picture of preadolescent life, and for many readers would tar preadolescents with these unsavory behaviors—part of the "dark side" of preadolescence. Sexuality and aggression are important behavioral components of the period, not because of their frequency, but because of the intensity of interest in these topics when they arise. Both topics represent a dramatic change from earlier years, and both swiftly change during preadolescence (most of my data in this chapter are from eleven- and twelve-year-olds). Since both topics involve imitation of adolescents and adults (although in a transformed manner), they represent the preadolescent's attempt to alter his public self in ways he feels are positively valued by his peers. One may "go too far" or "not go far enough," and both types of boys are negatively valued (as "rowdies" or "faggots"). The boy must walk a fine line in showing himself off.

Developmental imperatives are "imperatives" in that if they are not met successfully the child will be left behind or tormented for an inadequate social self, a stigma with potentially grave social-psychological effects. At every age, developmental imperatives imply social community, but it is particularly at preadolescence, with its heavy-handed emphasis on peer affiliation (the "Gang Age"), that these social elements become recognizable to the preadolescent, who now makes a great show of valuing his friends (Fine 1980c). Fortunately the preadolescent need not meet these challenges alone. Because of our cohort-based education system, the child has a set of peers who are simultaneously meeting similar imperatives.[9] While the child attempts to impress others with his maturity, his peers attempt to do the same with him; each uses the other as an audience. The friendship relation is particularly significant in that, because of its positive value and relative stability, even if inappropriate behavior does occur, this need not necessarily imply derogation of the actor; the disapproved action is not seen as part of the actor's identity. Friends typically have sufficient "idiosyncracy credits" to permit a wide range of technically inappropriate behavior. The actions of a friend are much less likely to be defined as inappropriate than are identical behaviors of others; thus, friendship cushions blows to the self.

6

Small Groups and Preadolescent Culture

Those who examine culture must do more than simply map the content and usage of that culture; they must describe the process by which culture is created and spread. In this chapter and the next, I turn to this concern. How and where is preadolescent culture generated, and how do other preadolescents learn about it? These questions raise issues about the structure of preadolescent society and the integration of cultural content. In this chapter I examine the position of culture within small groups (preadolescent baseball teams), and in chapter 7 I analyze the preadolescent subsociety and its related subculture.

The anthropological literature on culture is a rough and thorny patch, containing literally hundreds, if not thousands, of definitions of this concept. I shall avoid the question of what *culture* "really" means, satisfying myself with a pragmatically useful definition. Since my intent is to discuss the dynamics by which culture is produced, I define culture as the sum of "cultural items." In the words of Melville Herskovits (1948, 625), culture is "the things people have, the things they do, and what they think." Culture includes the meaningful traditions and artifacts of a group: ideas, behaviors, verbalizations, and material objects. These cultural traditions have meaning to the members of a group and are aspects of group life that members can and do refer to in their interaction. Specifically I choose to ignore two other broad traditions in the anthropological study of culture: (1) culture as comprising the whole of society, and (2) culture as an ideational system (an approach taken by cognitive anthropologists, structuralists, and symbolic anthropologists). The second, currently popular perspective poses particular problems in that it tends to make culture the endpoint of analysis and not the data with which one begins. For these approaches symbols do not "exist" in either a physical or behavioral sense; rather, they are concepts that must be abstracted from behavior.

My approach, focusing on cultural items, derives from a social-psychological perspective. Culture in this view consists of behavioral products, ideas that emerge through interaction, material objects made by humans or given meaning by them, and behaviors seen as meaningful by actors and observers. This approach can broadly be labeled "behavioral," as contrasted to those other approaches (cognitive, symbolic, or structural) that attempt to provide a totalistic reading of actions and artifacts, sometimes without concern for the meanings they have for participants. My analysis, grounded in symbolic interactionism, emphasizes that cultural elements must be situated in their social context.

Little League Baseball Teams as Idiocultures

While culture may be studied on several analytic levels (the society, subsociety, small group), I choose to begin the analysis at the most "micro" level—the group. If meaning derives from interaction (Blumer 1969), then culture, a set of shared understandings, is clearly implicated by this premise. By focusing on the small group, social scientists can avoid much of the difficulty of determining of what the culture of a particular structure consists. (Of what, after all, does American culture consist?). By specifying culture by its behavioral locus—seeing it as part of an activity system—the term can be meaningfully dissected. As folklorist Alan Dundes (1977) has argued, "lore" is a characteristic of all groups of any size that share at least one trait.

Every group has its own lore or culture, which I term its *idioculture*[1] (see Fine 1979b, 1982). Idioculture consists of a system of knowledge, beliefs, behaviors, and customs shared by members of an interacting group to which members can refer and that serve as the basis of further interaction.[2] Members recognize that they share experiences, and these experiences can be referred to with the expectation they will be understood by other members, thus being used to construct a social reality for the participants. This approach stresses the localized nature of culture, implying that it need not be a part of a demographically distinct subgroup but rather can be a particularistic development of any group, such as Little League baseball teams. As August Hollingshead suggests, "Persons in more or less continuous association evolve behavior traits and cultural mechanisms which are unique to the group and differ in some way from those of other groups and from the larger socio-cultural complex. That is, every continuing social group develops a variant culture and a body of social relations peculiar and common to its members" (Hollingshead 1939, 816).

In previous research, social scientists have suggested three approaches to defining *group culture*,—one reason for a new term. One view states that a group's culture is equivalent to its emotional tone, style, or modus operandi (Thelen 1954; Bion 1961; Rossel 1976). A second approach suggests that group culture refers to the habitual behaviors of group members (Roberts 1951; McFeat 1974). The third, adopted here—a micro-ethnology of small groups—focuses on the content of the shared knowledge and behavior within the group (e.g., Roy 1959–60; Giallombardo 1974; Shibutani 1978). Specifically I have argued that the concept of idioculture has five particular social-scientific virtues: (1) it permits us to specify cultures, (2) it permits a comparative analysis of groups, (3) it permits us to recognize groups as cultural units, (4) it provides for an understanding of the way in which culture serves as a mediator between environment and action, and (5) it provides insight into cultural creation and diffusion in societies and subsocieties (for discussion of these issues see Fine 1979b, 735–37).

Content of Idioculture

An idioculture consists of particular examples of behavior or communication that have symbolic meaning and significance for members of a group. Although the list is not exhaustive, phenomena classifiable as idioculture include nicknames, jokes, insults, beliefs, rules of conduct, clothing styles, songs, narratives, gestures, and recurrent fantasies. An idioculture, although not comparable to the larger culture in scope, may be extensive in certain groups, such as families or fraternities, and even on Little League baseball teams a substantial amount of culture is created and repeated during a season.

Obviously some elements have more significance than others, and these items comprise the core of an idioculture. Important items are those that are repeated on many occasions, or, alternatively, those that, although perhaps not often mentioned, have a considerable impact. The repetition of a cultural element indicates its *salience*, while its impact indicates its *centrality*. The name of a group (e.g., the Hell's Angels for a group of Hopewell preadolescents) may be highly salient, although not central (Short and Strodtbeck 1965), while certain tabooed subjects, such as traditions regarding sexual activity, may be of high centrality but low salience. Often these two factors are correlated; yet, they need not be.

Although the idioculture of a group consists of beliefs, values, attitudes, and behaviors, not every element of a group's interaction will be part of its idioculture. Idioculture is augmented if an experience occurs or information is transmitted within the group (i.e., in the presence of more than one group member) and is perceived as something that can legitimately and meaningfully be referred to (see Garfinkel 1967, 38–41)–i.e., the occurrence is *noteworthy*. In other words, the assignment of meaning to an event is the criterion that gives it idiocultural significance. For example, the behavior of major league baseball players is not in and of itself part of a Little League team's idioculture—until it is discussed within the group, at which time the group's reactions and beliefs about it will be incorporated into the idioculture. In Hopewell the players on the Sharpstone team were very interested in a fight between players on their beloved Boston Red Sox and the hated New York Yankees, and many references were made to this fight, even citing parallels to it in their own aggressive play. In Little League, a routine hit or catch usually does not have an impact on a team's culture, being "taken for granted" but it may become notable if the situation gives the event a significance beyond its expected lack of impact (e.g., a catch by a poor outfielder in a crucial point in a game—an event that did produce a nickname in one Little League scenario).

Idioculture as a Criterion of Group Membership

At the inception of any group, an idioculture does not exist; however, the formation of a culture may occur from the opening moments of group interaction. When individuals meet, they begin to construct a culture by asking for names and other biographical points that can be referred to later (Davis 1973). It is common for these early pieces of information ("first impressions") to have considerable significance in typifying members, and they are often crucial for determining the future directions of the idioculture. Finding out that one boy moved from Chicago, some players on his team began calling him "Deep-Dish" after the Chicago-style pizza (field notes, Bolton Park). On a more mundane level, simply learning a boy's name opens up many possibilities for nicknames based on linguistic variations (see Morgan, O'Neill, and Harré 1978). The fact that children have acquaintances in common (such as teachers or other coaches) leads to a presumption of common interest and a basis from which culture can grow. Eventually idioculture becomes self-generating, and direct solicitation and reciprocal inquisition are no longer necessary for social solidarity. Over time, rules are established, opinions expressed, information exchanged, and members experience events together (Sherif and Sherif 1953, 236–37). This culture can be imposed by the arbitrary fiat of an authority, by the group, or through a combination of the two. Group structure affects group culture. One must add, of course, that the converse is also true: the group culture provides a charter for or an undermining of the structure of the group.

From the first practice of a Little League baseball team, a team culture is being developed, and a new player arriving at the second practice finds that he must learn a set of information and rules of behavior in order to function as a full and equal member of the team. As the culture develops, it increasingly serves as a focus for group reference and action, and a member who attempts to enter a group that has been functioning for a considerable period of time must remain in the background until a substantial portion of the group's culture has been mastered (see Nash and Wolfe 1957). In fact, some boys who join a team during the middle of the season are never accepted, and in one case in Sanford Heights the boy felt compelled to drop out of Little League only ten days after he had joined, confirming his erstwhile teammates' negative impressions of him. Part of the problem for this youngster was that he never acquired enough of the team's traditions and gossip to be considered a teammate, and as an outsider he was shunned.

From these observations, I suggest the following proposition: *Knowledge and acceptance of a group's idioculture is a necessary and sufficient condition for distinguishing members of a group from nonmembers.*

Robert Freed Bales (1970, 153–54) has noted: "Most small groups develop a subculture that is protective for their members, and is allergic, in some respects, to the culture as a whole. . . . They [the members] draw a boundary around themselves and resist intrusion." The extent to which the culture of a group serves a boundary-maintenance function (Dunphy 1969) depends on the goals of the group, the services the group provides to its members, the extent to which the idioculture differs from the societal culture (i.e., whether it is a contracultue), and the nature of the intruder. In the case of Little League teams, because of their voluntaristic nature and non-deviant traditions, their cultures are less dogmatically used as a boundary than is true for some other groups.

A readily understood example of how idioculture operates as a means of differentiating group members from outsiders is that of joking and kidding. An outsider often finds it difficult to comprehend the situational humor of a group, since frequently it is based on unstated assumptions of members. Joking regularly refers to previous interactional episodes, and a "key" to that interaction is necessary for a comprehending, mirthful response and for continuing the joking.

Groups are characterized by information shared by members; certain groups, such as fraternal lodges, have severe penalties for revealing what to outsiders seems like trivial information. To reveal the information is thought to alter both the substance of the social ties between members and their sense of community.

A corollary of the above axiom is based upon this informational secrecy: *The greater the perceived difference between the public image implicated by an item in a group's idioculture and the group's desired public image, the more the group will attempt to shield that information from its public.*

This corollary explains the hostile reaction to tattletales, stoolies, informers, those who "kiss-and-tell," and those who threaten the group's public "face." Because the culture created by Little League teams is rather mild, there is not much secretive action. Baseball signals need to be kept secret for pragmatic reasons, and preadolescents not on the team are asked to leave the dugout area when signals are being discussed. In preadolescent informal groups, one finds a heavier veil of secrecy because certain topics discussed have a more sensitive content, including aggressive or sexual activities (such as mooning, mutual masturbation, or egging cars). Of course, there are no objective standards that allow us to predict what can be revealed or in what circumstances that revelation will occur. The criterion for secrecy is based upon the group's *desired* public image, not the image that would produce support by the general public.

Revealing "private" information indicates a lack of commitment to group regulations and thus a lack of commitment to the group. The breakdown in secrecy is seen as potentially destroying the group's very existence. For example, former pitcher Jim Bouton's (1970) exposé, *Ball Four*, was sharply criticized by the major league baseball community, which felt that because of Bouton's rather innocuous revelations they would experience difficulty in maintaining their desired public image. Umpire Hank Soar might have been speaking for many groups in stating "If we all wrote about what we know about other people, they'd be no baseball" (Bouton 1971; see Simmel 1950, 330–76). During the three years I observed Little League, a portable toilet was burned, a refreshment stand was broken into, outfield fences were destroyed, and excrement was placed in a dugout. The perpetrators of these actions were never identified publicly or to adults, but in some of these cases I learned that players had been involved, and this involvement was hidden.

Often when information is released without the group's approval, members collectively deny the allegations and/or punish the member who has betrayed the trust of the group (for example, Little League teammates will lie to protect a fellow player who has been fingered by a tattler). The effectiveness of these expectations of secrecy is evident in that these violations of group trust are rare—at least in the Little League setting.

A second corollary relates to the eventual acceptance of potential new members: *A group becomes significantly less open when a non-member is present. Groups attempt to hide their idioculture until it is believed that the newcomer can be trusted not to reveal the secrets of the group.*

This secrecy corollary is exemplified by the traditional difficulty of participant observers in the early stages of their research (Janes 1961). Only after several weeks of active participant observation and provisional friendship was I trusted sufficiently for preadolescents to reveal their secrets, dirty jokes, and escapades. Typically when preadolescents tell obscene jokes they watch for adults, and when one comes within earshot, they awkwardly change the subject. Privacy and secrecy are important for many groups, but it is privacy and secrecy of *something*, i.e., the group's idioculture.

For a new member to obtain access to a group, particularly a group in which common interests or beliefs are the criteria for membership, he must demonstrate a parallel between his own background interests (latent culture—Becker and Geer 1960) and group members' idioculture. Full acceptance occurs when the new member has (1) mastered significant portions of the idioculture and (2) behaved in accord with the group precepts, indicating that the culture of the group has been internalized. A boy new to a neighborhood frequently requires a good friend or peer sponsor to facilitate acceptance into a group by teaching and vouching for him; thus, early friendships in a new locale are important for channeling a boy's social network.

The Creation and Continuation of Little League Idioculture

The specific content of an idioculture is not created at random but shaped through regular social processes. Five factors help to explain the presence of an item in a group's idioculture—that the item be *known* (*K*), *usable* (*U*), *functional* (*F*), *appropriate* (*A*) in terms of the group's status hierarchy, and *triggered* (*T*) by some experienced event. These five factors can be schematized in an ordered relationship by a Venn diagram according to the number of *potential* items that cumulatively meet each criterion: $K>U>F>A>T$. I do not suggest that external forces determine which items are chosen, but rather they provide limits for the choices and negotiations of social actors. They provide constraints within which free will operates.

Known Culture

The first criterion for whether a potential culture element will become part of the group idioculture is that the item or components of the item be previously known by at least one member of the group. This pool of background information I term the *known culture* of the group.

This perspective is congruent with Becker and Geer's (1960) argument that the manifest culture of a group is derived from the latent culture of participants. Although culture emerges from group interaction, prior knowledge and past experiences affect the form these cultural items take, although not the specific content. Since members know other idiocultures (or latent cultures) through previous or concurrent memberships, the range of potentially known information may be extensive.

In Sanford Heights, a ball hit foul over the backstop is known as a "Polish Home Run." Such a cultural item would have been meaningless had it not been for latent cultural items—what a home run is, and the symbolic opposition of hitting a ball straight over the outfield fence and hitting it over the backstop. In other words, hitting the ball over either *end* of the field is a "home run" (and this was not said of balls that curved outside a foul line). This item also required a knowledge of social stereotypes—that "Polish" is an ethnic slur implying "backward" or "incompetent." Without this cultural knowledge the identification of such a foul ball as a Polish Home Run could not have become a part of the culture of these preadolescents. Likewise, referring to players on the basis of their uniform color as a "green bean" or "chiquita," as was done in Hopewell, suggests that cultural elements are dependent on prior knowledge.

Creativity poses no particular problems since creativity is not *de novo*—rather it reflects novel combinations of previously familiar elements (e.g., Hebb, 1974). These recombinations may be given different meanings from that of their constitutive elements by group members. Players on the Maple Bluff White Sox developed a dress code loosely modeled on observation of major leaguers, although not identical to it. Before one Dodgers practice in Sanford Heights, several players were hanging on the backstop at the practice field while one of their teammates shook the fence as hard as possible, an activity he termed the "Chinese pain shake," a phrase apparently created spontaneously. While the term may never have been uttered before, its antecedents exist in the speaker's latent culture—notably the association of Chinese with torture (e.g., the Chinese water torture) and the earthquakes that had affected China during this period, to which this activity was similar. Thus, the creation of this cultural item, although seemingly an idiosyncratic construction, can be interpreted in terms of previous knowledge. The term for that behavior "makes sense" in our culture.

Usable Culture

The second criterion for inclusion in a group's idioculture is that a potential item be part of the members' *usable culture*—that is, mentionable in the context of group interaction. Some elements of the latent or known culture, although common to all members of a group, may not be publicly shared because of sacred or taboo implications.

The usability of a cultural element is not a result of absolute criteria but of the social meanings supplied by the group. Members' personalities, religion, political ideology, or morality may influence the situational viability of a cultural item. For example, in Bolton Park one star player objected strongly to another player's reference to the "fucking umps"; another player on that same team chastised a teammate for uttering the epithet "Jesus Christ," taking the Lord's name in vain. On other teams, however, such talk is legitimate. Teams have different "moral" standards for propriety, and this is due to their adult and child personnel and to the extent to which these individuals are willing to express their beliefs to shape public behavior.

In Beanville, the Angels placed a heavier emphasis on religion that did the Rangers, although both teams were largely Catholic. Members of the Angels inquired of each other why they missed church. The Rangers never publicly mentioned church but on several occasions players did joke about abortions. While only a weak inference exists that similar jokes could not have occurred among the Angels, knowing the players I suspect that such jokes would be unlikely and inappropriate. Dirty or sexual jokes were only spread among groups of Rangers (outside the earshot of their coach) and not among the Angels.

Tied to usability is situational appropriateness. Norms for prescribed and proscribed behavior often are contextually bounded. An item of culture may be appropriate only in certain circumstances, such as when the coach is absent. When group members are in the presence of outsiders, the expressible elements of the team's idioculture may be curtailed. This is evident with regard to preadolescents who refrain from telling dirty jokes in the presence of adults or strangers. Jokes among the Beanville Rangers comparing aborted babies to ripe, red tomatoes were limited to situations in which adults (other than the author) were not present. Likewise, one boy on the Sanford Heights Dodgers was called "Mousey" by his affectionate mother. This nickname was used by peers only in his absence, since he was a high-status team member and it was a nickname he particularly disliked. This dislike made the nickname more notable for his teammates.

Functional Culture

A third factor influencing the likelihood of an item's being incorporated into a group's idioculture is its congruence with the goals and needs of some or all group members, and whether it facilitates the survival and successful operation of the group (Pellegrin 1953). Items that are consistent with these ends constitute the *functional culture* of the group. Potential cultural elements that are known and usable may not become part of the group's idioculture if not supportive of the needs of the group or its members.

Some interactionists argue that culture is a response to shared problems (Becker and Geer 1960; Hughes, Becker, and Geer 1968; Spector 1973), claiming group culture is functional and much culture production is directly related to group problem solving. This proposition is also supported by an examination of group culture in a laboratory setting that indicates those problem-solving strategies continuing across time are those that have been most effective (Weick and Gilfillan 1971).

Among Little League baseball teams, the rules and restrictions that team members enforce indicate the functional properties of group culture. The Beanville Rangers originated and enforced an operating procedure that the team would take batting practice (a desirable activity for the players) in the order the players arrived. This procedure encouraged promptness, and on occasion the entire

Ranger team arrived before any members of the opposing team. The Rangers were particularly characterized by team spirit and friendships, as players knew each other informally through this pregame activity, and the rule served as a mechanism for minimizing arguments about the batting-practice order. The preadolescents rather than the coaches ordered the team's behavior, and this procedure strengthened the position of the team's preadolescent leader, who lived a block from the field and always arrived early. Prior to the establishment of this procedure, batting order was determined haphazardly—mostly by whomever was most insistent rather than by a systematic ordering procedure by the coach. Because the ordering of batting practice had been problematic for the Rangers such a rule was functional as a problem-solving mechanism.

A Hopewell team prohibited chewing gum on the playing field because one of their players had almost choked on a piece of gum after he ran into another outfielder when attempting to catch an unexpected fly ball. Other teams in the league did not have a similar rule because the issue had never been salient. For an item of culture to be overtly functional to a group, the group must define itself, either implicitly or explicitly, as having a problem, and then the cultural item may be proposed as a solution to the problem.

Some cultural items do not directly address problems in a group but still may be said to be functional in that they achieve group goals such as entertainment or social solidarity. Although they may not be proposed in response to interactional difficulties, these idiocultural items facilitate group functioning. The creation of cultural prescriptions and proscriptions is directly tied to their functional character. The origins of nonovertly functional cultural items may not be related to the functional prerequisites of the group, but their continued usage is.

Appropriate Culture

Some potential items of a group's culture do not occur or continue despite being functional for satisfying group goals or personal needs; they undermine the group's structure in not supporting the interpersonal network and power relations in the group. Cultural elements that are consistent with patterns of interaction in a group are the *appropriate culture* of the group. A cultural item that expresses hostility toward a well-liked or legitimately powerful individual may be known, usable, and even functional (in that hostility may need to be expressed), yet may be inappropriate unless the group structure is altered.

This process is clear in the case of nicknames. Many nicknames are evaluative, and a nickname must fit the target's status in the group. During the first year of observation of the Beanville Rangers, one team member, Tom Mayne, acquired the nickname "Maniac," based upon a linguistic play on his last name and on his physical awkwardness on the baseball diamond. That year he was an eleven-year-old substitute outfielder. When team members were asked to name their three best friends on the team during the middle of the season, Tom was only named by one of the twelve other boys. According to sociometric ranking and formal status, Tom had low status. The following year, Tom started most of the Rangers' games at third base, was one of the best batters on the team, and was located in the middle of the team's status hierarchy. In sociometric ratings at both the beginning and the end of the season, Tom was named by four of the fourteen other players as one of their three best friends on the team. His previous nickname, "Maniac," was no longer in circulation, although Tom and other team members recalled its presence during the previous year. Tom's new nickname was "Main Eye," again a play on his last name, but with dramatically different connotations.

A similar example occurred in Sanford Heights. One of the eleven-year-olds on the Giants was known as a particularly poor baseball player, having gone hitless in his previous year in the major leagues. Because of his weak baseball skills and his somewhat isolated position on the team, he was called "Smell-ton," again a play on a surname. During the first week of the season, much to everyone's surprise—his own included—he hit a grand slam home run for his first Little League hit. His nickname of Smell-ton was forgotten and, for the rest of the season, his teammates called him Jim. Status is one determinant of nicknames, although nicknames label a boy and solidify his status as well.

Nicknames are not the only cultural items subject to status considerations; pranks and practical jokes are performed on low-status members, and rules are constructed so that they support the prerogatives of the older, better players—for example, by determining who should coach on the bases (high-status boys) or who should go to the refreshment stand for water (isolates).

Not only is content affected by status, but acceptance of a cultural item may be contingent on its sponsor. Potential cultural items are more likely to be accepted into a group's idioculture when proposed by a high-status member (Sherif and Sherif 1953, 252). For example, when the coach proposes some cultural element, its acceptance by his preadolescent charges is not guaranteed but is highly likely. In Hopewell, one set of coaches suggested that before a game, their players should form a circle, place their hands in the middle, and, when the coach said "Let's go," buoyantly raise their arms in unison. A coach in Maple Bluff ritually asked his team what three things they needed to win, and they vigorously responded, "Hustle, pride, and class"; a coach in Beanville would refer to a weak hit as something his grandmother could hit better than, and so the comic image of this middle-aged man's grandmother entered the team's culture.

High-status players, like coaches, find their personal status facilitates the traditions they wish to establish. Several members of the Beanville Rangers got wiffles (short haircuts) after Wiley, the second-most-popular boy on the team, got one and was proud of it. This fad continued (with one or two boys newly shaved each day) until Rich, the most popular boy on the team, publicly claimed that he though the haircut looked stupid, although he deliberately excluded Wiley from this evaluation. After Rich's announcement, only one low-status boy had his hair cut in that fashion, and the team was highly critical of his tonsorial style, saying it looked horrible and, further, it wasn't a *real* wiffle. Similar sociometric processes affected clothing conformity, such as wearing wristbands or sneakers at games and wearing shorts or removing one's shirt at practice.

Triggering Event

The range of *potential* cultural items that qualify as known, usable, functional, and appropriate is extensive, and some social mechanism is necessary to account for which items enter the group's cultural repertoire. I postulate the concept of a *triggering event* as an explanatory device to determine selection. Some bit of interaction provides a "spark" producing the specific content of the idioculture. This event can consist of any action or statement that produces a response in the group, similar to Smelser's (1962) concept of a precipitating factor for collective behavior. A member's new haircut may be sufficient to spawn a new nickname ("Kojak," "Buzz Conroy," "Peach Fuzz"). A miscue may provide the impetus for a joking sequence that remains part of group lore. A threat to the group may produce a legend, a new norm, or a prescription for group action.

Theoretically any triggering event may produce idioculture. However, some events recur and, in those cases, items of idioculture are particularly likely to be spawned, and, once spawned, will more likely remain relevant to the group as they are repeatedly functional and appropriate. The superior batting of one Beanville youngster led to his being called "Superstar," and the opposite talent of a boy in Bolton Park produced his nickname: "Strikeout King." These nicknames are both sociometrically appropriate and frequently triggered because of the athletic achievements of these two boys.

In addition, triggers that are notable or unusual are especially likely to produce idioculture.[3] Gmelch (1971), examining professional baseball superstitions, discovered that rituals emanated from particularly good performances, while behavioral taboos resulted from notably poor performances. One Bolton Park coach's old Impala began to be called a Cadillac after a foul ball nearly hit it in practice and he jokingly told them not to hit his "Cadillac." The term caught on, and the Orioles called the rusty car a "Cadillac" from then on. Notable events also affect taboos. The Sharpstone coaches brought their team red, white, and blue wristbands on opening day in order to give the team a sense of unity and specialness. When the team lost by a lopsided score, the wristbands were never worn again (see below).

Summary

Five elements—the known culture, the usable culture, the functional culture, the appropriate culture, and the triggering event together produce the specific content of a team's idioculture. Different configurations of these five factors suggest how groups come to differ in their culture and why specific forms appear and remain in particular groups. To indicate the effect of all five determinants I shall describe the creation and usage of a single cultural item considering all factors.

During the middle of the season, the Beanville Rangers created and enforced a rule that players could not eat ice cream while sitting on the bench during a game. This rule was triggered by a combination of circumstances: it occurred during a game in which the Rangers, by that time accustomed to victory, were being beaten. On the bench, one of the nonplaying, low-status players was eating an ice cream cone. This *triggered* the decision by the high-status, older players[4] (not the coach) that ice cream could not be eaten on the bench (although gum could be chewed). The rule was *known* in that it was compatible with the policy and perspectives of professional sports teams. It was *usable* in that it did not deal with any tabooed or sacred areas of children's culture, and it is comparable to the rules that children frequently make in interaction with each other (Piaget 1962, orig. 1932; Cooley 1964, orig. 1902). The rule was *functional* in relieving the frustration that the older players felt during that game and in directing the attention of the younger boys to the game. Further, the existence of a set of rules or rituals may create group cohesion (Cartwright and Zander 1953) and satisfaction (Borgatta and Bales 1953). Finally, it was *appropriate* since it was propounded by the high-status members to control the low-status members. Later in the season an older, high-status player did eat ice cream on the bench and was not criticized by other team members, although the rule remained in force for other team members.

Contrasting Idiocultures

One virtue of the idioculture construct is its ability to contrast groups that appear structurally very similar. That is, the concept of idioculture permits the comparative analysis of groups—the process that J. L. Fischer (1968) has termed *microethnography*. A series of anthropological comparisons of small communities (e.g., Rogers and Gardner 1969; Vogt and O'Dea 1953; DuWors 1952; Zimmerman 1938) has demonstrated that culture (particularly values) has a powerful effect on the structure of apparently similar communities. Yet because these communities were relatively large "groups," it is not clear to what extent these values characterized the whole community. The emphasis on values also disguised some behavioral differences among communities, although of course the values are known primarily through their behavioral representations.

By comparing two Little League teams in the same league, I suggest that the traditional distinction between idiographic (particular) and nomothetic (normative) explanations needs to be reformulated. Although team culture is not predictable in its specific content, this does not mean that the cultural traditions of a group are random. Here I specify some of the constraints on the known, usable, functional, and appropriate culture on two outwardly similar preadolescent teams that manifested markedly different cultural traditions and behavioral styles.

The Teams

The two teams played in the Hopewell Little League, and both were highly successful the year I observed them, finishing first and second in the league standings. Transatlantic Industries (nicknamed TI) and Sharpstone Auto had been the best teams the previous year, and both were expected to do well. Overall, the teams were considered roughly equal in ability—with Sharpstone given a slight edge. By choosing teams with approximately equal absolute levels of success and approximately equal baseball talent, I can examine how different personnel and cultural configurations affected group interaction.

Sharpstone Auto

Sharpstone was known for the quality of its coaching. Unlike most other teams, coached by fathers or young men who had once been Little Leaguers, Sharpstone was coached by two young men, Peter Chadbourne and Dave Hundley, who were physical education majors at the local university and who intended to coach children as a career. I was impressed by their knowledge of coaching techniques, baseball skills, and first aid. In addition, both young men were fine athletes and demonstrated skills that many older coaches could only describe. These abilities affected Sharpstone: players learned more about baseball fundamentals than did other teams. Unlike most others, players on Sharpstone learned how to bunt, steal, and run bases. The skills of the coaches created high confidence, even arrogance, among the players. That these two young men were the best and most athletically sophisticated coaches was recognized by other coaches, players, and parents in Hopewell.

Although I won't describe each player, several should be introduced:

Justin Kay. Most players and adults believed that Justin was the best ball player in the league. Small of stature and not particularly muscular, Justin had all the baseball skills. What distinguished him most from other Little Leaguers was his fearlessness—he was described as a "kamikaze." He barreled into opposing fielders while running the bases and would dive after ground balls that other players considered certain hits. Unlike many Little League batters, Justin showed no fear that he would be hit by the ball—such fear being the single greatest weakness of most players. Indeed, Justin had lost a front tooth several years before when trying to catch a line drive at which most players would have ducked.

Justin had a reputation as a fighter and would regale his teammates about the fights he had gotten into—and won. In third grade he had been asked to leave his parochial school. Of all the players I met, Justin was the most overtly racist, freely calling black children "niggers." On some dimension he was an extremely disagreeable child. Yet, this picture should be put into paradoxical balance. Justin was truly a team leader and rarely criticized a teammate. He led practices for the coaches, gave instruction to the younger players, and complimented their developing abilities. While Justin often criticized himself (crying after the team *won*, if he had made an error), he would not criticize the team—a noble attribute among preadolescents.

While interpretation is dangerous, some of Justin's behavior can be explained by his broken family. His father, a highly competitive man, was a heavy drinker and a womanizer (according to gossip). Some days both of Justin's parents attended his game, seated on opposite sides of the field, with Mr. Kay having a female companion and liquid refreshment. Perhaps due to his home life, Justin developed a very close relationship with Peter Chadbourne and Peter's family. Justin and Peter spent considerable time together away from the Little League diamond.

Harry Stanton. Harry was Justin's best friend but was much quieter—even somewhat moody. Like Justin, Harry was a fine baseball player and probably the best pitcher in the Hopewell Little League, although he lacked Justin's intensity. He was a partner with Justin in his elementary school fights, although he did not engage much in racist rhetoric. A tough kid who could hold his own in a fight (or start one), Harry did not have the same "need" for aggression that his friend had.

Whitney Evans. Both Justin and Harry were twelve years old; Whitney, their classmate, was only eleven. Although Whitney was a fine baseball player, few regarded him as being good as his friends. Whit was a good pitcher and an excellent catcher but somewhat slow of foot and, as an eleven-year-old, not a powerful hitter. He was a close friend of Harry and Justin, and the three boys often spent their leisure time together. Whitney was the most gregarious of the three, ready with a quick grin. He, like his friends, was always ready for adventure, whether streaking or fighting.

The team. These three boys—Justin, Harry, and Whitney—constituted the heart and soul of Sharpstone Auto. When I asked Sharpstone players at the end of the season to name their three best friends on the team, Justin received eleven of the possible twelve peer nominations, and Harry and Whitney each received nine. These close friends represent an elite clique that was widely accepted (see fig. 6–1). Players were asked who on the team they considered to be leaders. Of the twelve players who responded, *all* named both Justin and Harry as team leaders (three also named eleven-year-old Whitney). Players were also asked whom on the team they considered to be *bossy*. Only one player named Harry as bossy; no one

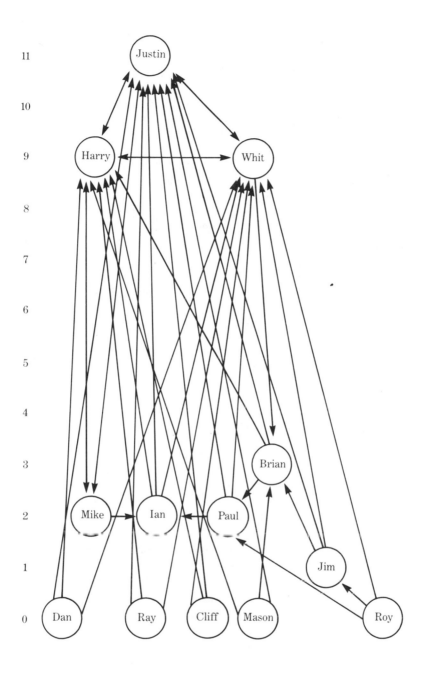

Fig. 6.1 Sharpstone Friendship Choices (End of Season)

mentioned either Justin or Whitney. The team social structure is un-ambiguous and accepted.[5]

Transatlantic Industries

The previous year Transatlantic Industries had won the league championship by defeating Sharpstone in a hotly contested championship game. Like Sharpstone, TI had a distinguished history. The year I observed Sharpstone, its two best players from the previous year had returned, which led Sharpstone to feel confident. In contrast, the two best players on TI had graduated from Little League baseball, and most observers felt that TI would have difficulty winning the championship again. Nonetheless, TI players were confident in their abilities; although not all were certain they would come in first, they were not defeatist, and they optimistically looked forward to success.

As on most Little League teams, the coach of Transatlantic Industries was a player's father. Fred Turner had coached Little League for many years and was regarded as one of the better coaches. Although Fred did not have the baseball or teaching skills of the Sharpstone coaches, he held numerous practices, was concerned with and interested in his players, and instructed them in baseball fundamentals. He was friendly, yet disciplined his players if they strayed from his way of doing things. Whether because of his coaching style or because of the personalities of his players, Fred had few disciplinary problems—with the occasional exception of his son, Frank.

Unlike Sharpstone, Transatlantic Industries did not have any true preadolescent leaders. While there was consensus on who were the leaders of Sharpstone, such consensus did not exist on TI, where five players were named as team leaders by at least four players. No player was named as a leader by more than seven players, suggesting a team without a clearly defined status hierarchy but with many secondary leaders. Two players, Frank Turner and Tom McDarrel, played important roles on TI but were not "true leaders."

Frank Turner. Being the coach's son is difficult in the best of circumstances, but it is even more difficult for the boy who does not excel at baseball. Frank, an eleven-year-old, batted first and started most games for TI at second base. Only two other players—both twelve-year-olds—had more at-bats than Frank. Despite the confidence of his father, Frank batted only .200 (eight for forty). The coach's preferential treatment of his son was recognized by sneering teammates and opponents. While Fred Turner had more confidence in his son's ability than was objectively warranted, Frank was a good eleven-year-old player and was one of the nine best players on TI. While none of his teammates named Frank as one of the "really good" players on TI, four named him as one of their three best friends on the team. He was named as a team leader by no one and as bossy by three boys. He was a boy who was moderately well liked but not well respected.

Perhaps because of the support of his father, Frank felt himself to be a better player than was justified by his performance on the field. He named himself as one of the best players on the team at the end of the season. Frank's high personal expectations influenced his behavior in that he easily became frustrated and verbally aggressive. For example, he told his teammates, "If I whiff with the bases loaded, I'll do something dangerous." Frank frequently threw down his bat, batting helmet, or glove when something went wrong and on several occasions was warned about his "temperment" by his father.[6] Although Frank was not a major behavioral problem, he was more aggressive than the other members of his team and more aggressive than his father wished him to be.

Tom McDarrel. Tom, a quiet, mature, responsible twelve-year-old, was one of TI's best players—his batting average was .458, second highest on the team. At the end of the season he was named as a best friend on the team by five fellow players, as bossy by six, as a leader by seven, and as one of the best players on the team by five boys. Although Tom was not the consensual team leader that Justin and Harry were on Sharpstone, he was respected by his teammates. Tom had a close, almost fraternal, rapport with the coach. From the beginning of the season Fred treated Tom as the team leader, and they discussed strategy. Unlike many of his peers, Tom was not drunk with optimism but was a concerned realist, and Fred continually attempted to convince him that optimism was justified:

> At a practice early in the season, Tom comments privately to Fred that the team needs more strong hitters if they are going to win the championship. Later in practice, after one of Tom's teammates, Darrin Alsop, hits two home runs, Fred turns to Tom and says, teasingly: "Whadda you mean, no hitters?" When Fred repeats this, Tom responds in a friendly tone: "All right, all right, you emphasized it enough" (field notes, Hopewell).

Perhaps part of the team's slight coolness to Tom was the perception that he was a child attempting to be a "responsible adult." Tom was

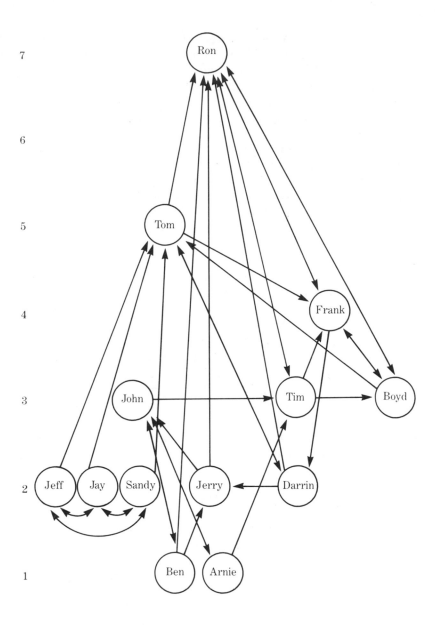

Fig. 6.2 Transatlantic Industries Friendship Choices (End of Season).
Note: Jerry and Arnie name only two best friends on the team.

liked, but there were sparks of resentment when he attempted to impose an adult moral order:

> In one game Fred emphasizes that the team should "talk it up," shouting support to their teammates. When Tom reminds his teammates, "OK, let's hear some chatter," an eleven-year-old teammate mutters, "*I* don't want to hear no chatter" (field notes, Hopewell).

Although Tom received the second-highest number of friendship nominations from the team (five) at the end of the season, he received only one from a fellow twelve-year-old. He was the leader in the eyes of the coach and the younger players but not among his peers.

The team. Unlike Sharpstone, TI did not have an elite clique (see fig. 6–2). The boy who had the most friendship nominations (seven), Ron Winchell, was fourth highest in leadership citations (five) and had the fifth-best batting average on the team. The best batter, Darrin Alsop, received only two friendship choices and four leadership citations. TI was a decentralized team characterized by fewer close ties than Sharpstone had.[7] The team did not have the esprit of many Little League teams, nor was it racked by dissension. In contrast to Sharpstone, no players epitomized the team. In part, as a result of this loose structure, TI never developed a rich idioculture to the extent that Sharpstone did.

Team Cultures

Those who examine cultures comparatively argue that the structure and environment of the social unit influences (or causes) the culture produced. Although this is easier to demonstrate when the populations of groups are markedly different or the environments are notably dissimilar, this assumption also applies to small groups from the same population, operating within a similar environment. Every group contains within it a different mix of individuals that affects which traditions are known and usable; each group has different needs (functional culture); each group has a different status hierarchy (appropriate culture); and each group has experienced a unique set of triggering events. In this analysis, I focus on three elements that distinguish these preadolescent teams and their culture: (1) the effects of the professionalism of the Sharpstone coaches, (2) the effects of the presence of a high-status clique on Sharpstone, and

(3) the fact that players on TI did not live in the area of the Little League field.

Professionalism

The first difference a casual observer would notice between the two teams was their orientation to baseball. While TI had many good baseball players who knew the fundamentals of the game, they were not sophisticated in their performances. Sharpstone players, in contrast, were taught the nuances of the game by their coaches. No team bunted or stole bases nearly as often as Sharpstone. Players recognized this difference:

> I asked Ron Winchell on TI what he thinks distinguishes TI from other teams. He responds that it is their style of play. He says that Sharpstone likes to bunt, while TI hits away (field notes, Hopewell).

Although TI had relatively little idioculture grounded in baseball skills, members were concerned with fielding and the number of home runs hit. Fred Turner's baseball obsession was fielding. He believed that if you could get fielding right, batting would "fall into place." His plan at the beginning of the season was to devote two of the three practices each week to fielding ("with a little batting to break the monotony"). Although he devoted less time to fielding than he promised, TI was a good fielding team. Both Tom McDarrel and Darrin Alsop were powerful long-ball hitters, and they competed to see who would hit the most home runs. Stealing bases and bunting were rarely mentioned.

Attitudes were very different on Sharpstone. Partially because of the baseball interests (the known culture) of the coaches and players (especially Justin, Harry, and Whit), Sharpstone was filled with baseball culture. The team developed a unique series of baseball rituals. It was the only team that regularly had pregame calisthenics. While this practice was originally organized by the coaches, it was later run by the team leaders in the *absence* of the coaches:

> Tom McDarrel of TI watches Sharpstone doing calisthenics and asks, "What are they doing?" Jeff James, a younger teammate responds, "Warming up." Tom jokes, "It looks like they're having an orgy" (field notes, Hopewell).

In addition, Sharpstone players regularly ran "laps" around the field before practice. Several other "professional" rituals developed, unrelated to warming up. Sharpstone players huddled immediately prior to a game, putting their hands together in the center of the circle; then, with a grand shout brought their hands over their heads, to the amusement of their opponents. Although this ritual was instituted by the coaches and derives from other sports rituals, it characterized the team. By themselves the players developed a secondary ritual also derived from professional sports teams. Before the first inning when Sharpstone was in the field, the pitcher, catcher, and infielders would meet on the mound. It was not clear if the coaches approved the ritual, since at one point Peter Chadbourne told them, "Break up that tea party." Further, Sharpstone players believed that the home dugout (the dugout on the first-base side of the field) was their lucky dugout and would always try to sit there. The team became upset and angry on the two occasions when the legitimate home team insisted on its rights to the home team dugout:

> Although they are the "away" team, Sharpstone takes the home team dugout today as usual. Some of their opponents on the Carlson Roller Rink team want the home team dugout, but the Sharpstone players do not leave. When Carlson's coach arrives, he insists that his team take the home dugout, in part because of a taunt by Justin. Peter Chadbourne tries to convince the Carlson coach that Sharpstone is the home team, but to no avail. Finally Sharpstone moves grudgingly to the bench on the opposite side of the field. Ray Coleman, the nine-year-old infielder, calls the away dugout "the stupid dugout," and Cliff Alsop, another nine year old, complains: "This dugout stinks." Ian Cartwright, a twelve year old, adds, "This bench rots. It's bad luck." When Whitney arrives late, the first question he asks of his teammates is why they are using the away dugout (field notes, Hopewell).

Athletic superstitions ("baseball magic"—Gmelch 1971) were important to these boys to reduce the uncertainty of playing but were less so for other teams for whom baseball was not so central.

This professionalism can be seen in other areas, including appearance. By the late 1970s, few adults cared much about children's appearance; yet, Peter and Dave insisted that their players get haircuts and followed through on their belief that players should have short hair throughout the season—at one point threatening not to start a boy unless he got a haircut. Appearance on Sharpstone reflected the "selves" these boys were supposed to develop.

The coaches also purchased for each of the players two red,

white, and blue wristbands. These were distributed the day before the season began and were supposed to differentiate Sharpstone from other teams through "the Sharpstone look" that was to create a sense of comradeship and professionalism. However, Sharpstone lost the first game of the season to TI by a lopsided score (12–3), and the players decided the wristbands brought bad luck. For the remainder of the season, no one ever wore a wristband, indicating the seriousness with which these boys took baseball superstitions.

This "professionalism" was also evident in their athletic slang. Both Sharpstone coaches conversed in "sportspeak." Athletic lingo was widely used, originally by the coaches but subsequently by the team because of the respect of the players for their coaches. The coaches called players "turkeys," a term picked up by the team. When the team quietly sat on the bench, Peter would say "Morgue City out here," or if he wanted the team to come to life, he would say, "Hey, now, it's got to be Melon City out there" (field notes, Hopewell). To get the attention of the fielder (and to have the infielders play "in") he would yell, "Tough on D [defense] now." Such phrases were repeated by the players, although they were not as fluent in sportspeak as their coaches. Many teams used some sports language, but on no other team was this as pronounced as on Sharpstone.

What differentiated the teams even more than the absence of athletic ritual and talk on Transatlantic Industries and its presence on Sharpstone was a constellation of attitudes present on Sharpstone but not noticeable on TI. These attitudes centered around competition. Sharpstone players were taught (and accepted) that they should be tough, hard-nosed competitors. While players on most teams have rough competitive urges, coaches do not support them. Such support was forthcoming on Sharpstone. For example, before an important game Dave Hundley exhorted the team to "Play Sharpstone's brand of ball. Play hard" (field notes, Hopewell). These preadolescents were taught to slide into a base with their legs high in order to break up a double play. Sharpstone had a reputation for this behavior among umpires and other coaches:

> Before the first game of the season, Fred Turner tells Peter Chadbourne that they should not allow players to "plow into" opposing infielders. At first Peter was doubtful about this (in part because of Turner's motivation) but finally agreed. Turner told me that Sharpstone had been guilty of this throughout the previous season (field notes, Hopewell).

This hard-nosed baseball play was known and usable on Sharp-stone. Further, the players believed that because of their style of play the umpires were against them. Although no team likes the umpires, Sharpstone players and coaches went further than believing the umpires were merely incompetent—they believed the umpires conspired against them:

> During the first game between Sharpstone and Furniture Mart, the umpire calls the game on account of fog, with Sharp-stone far ahead, meaning that the game will be started over. Sharpstone players and coaches are furious, particularly since the game on the other field is continuing. Peter tells me the umpires are out "to get" Sharpstone because they win so often. He recalls that last year the team had to play in the pouring rain and lost. Players share Peter's attitude that umpires cheat Sharpstone (field notes, Hopewell).

Sharpstone's preadolescent professionalism was also seen in the influence of the coaches on the playing of the game. Unlike most teams, Sharpstone had an intricate set of signals: if the coach placed his hand on his belt, they were to steal; if the coach placed his hand on his cap, they bunted. Although other teams had signals, most coaches rapidly discovered that the signals didn't work, since the boys forgot what they were and neglected to look for them. Sharp-stone players used these signals successfully throughout the season. Peter and Dave also instructed their players on when they should "take" pitches (i.e., deliberately not swing) to rattle the pitchers (contrary to many coaches, they believed "a walk is as good as a hit"). They also had the catcher talk to the opposing batter to disturb his concentration. More than any other team, Sharpstone was directed by the coaches, much as high school, college, and professional ballplayers are. This style of play was recognized by opponents, such as the TI player who commented scornfully to a Sharp-stone player: "Your coach is so organized. He tells you when to steal." Although other players rejected parts of this ideology of professionalism, Sharpstone players were proud of their orientation. They claimed that, not only did they want to win, but, as one said, they wanted to learn how to play the game as "it should be played." Although their competitive spirit was fierce, they wanted to do more than win; they wanted to win with style.

TI's culture was close to that of most teams in the league in regard to professionalism. Players wished to win, but they were not taught how to win as "professionals." They simply played their hardest, and because they were talented boys, they won. In fact, they beat Sharpstone the two times the teams played during the season. However, Transatlantic Industries developed little in the way of baseball-related idioculture. Players were supposed to call for fly balls hit in their vicinity, a point emphasized by their coach, but otherwise they *simply* played baseball. The players and coaches did not share the known culture necessary for developing a professional sports idioculture.

Elite Cliques and Idioculture

As noted above, Sharpstone and Transatlantic Industries differed in that Sharpstone had a clearly defined and recognized elite clique, whereas the social structure of TI was more diffuse. This difference had implications for cultural production and acceptance. The presence of social leaders reflected a preadolescent authority structure that could accept or reject cultural traditions (the appropriate culture). Because of the position of team leaders on Sharpstone, it had a much larger and robust idioculture, which was shaped by the interests and personalities of the leaders. I will focus on three themes of the Sharpstone culture, largely absent among Transatlantic Industries players: aggression, sexual interest, and racism. Although the coaches had some influence on the development of these themes, they derived primarily from the preadolescents themselves.

Aggression. Each team had one player who was aggressive: Justin Kay on Sharpstone and Frank Turner on Transatlantic Industries. Both threw bats, gloves, and helmets; both moped when depressed. However, the two boys differed in the amount of support they received from teammates and coaches for their aggression. Frank received no support from his teammates, who felt that he was being immature. His father was embarrassed and criticized him for his outbursts. Frank's aggression did not spread to other team members.

Justin's position was more complex. At times he was praised and rewarded for his aggression. Justin was eager to "run over" opposing infielders on the base paths or to barrel into the opposing catcher. When his behavior helped the team, he was praised by his coaches for his hustle, or mildly told not to "overhustle." On one occasion Justin saw that he would have to "take out" the catcher and started to smile broadly rounding third base. Throughout the season, Sharpstone was criticized for playing "hardball," which other adults felt could lead to injuries. The coaches publicly agreed that "hardball" should be avoided, but they claimed there was little they could do about it, citing Justin's personality. To the team, they said and did little to prevent this behavior; although Justin was the "worst offender," other players also adopted this style of play. The only discouragements were mild reprimands—for example, after Justin "ran over" the opposing second baseman, Dave said, "I don't want to see anybody hurt" but never explicitly ordered him to stop. After all, such "kamikaze" baserunning is integral to professional baseball.

This aggression reached its peak in the second game against TI, when Justin again "ran over" the second baseman—this time needlessly in terms of the play. As a result, the Sharpstone batter was called out for interference, and the coaches removed Justin from the game (a game TI won by a single run) to teach him "a lesson." This eliminated such flagrant aggression for the remaining two weeks of the season, but Sharpstone continued playing rough baseball. In the practice following that game, Peter Chadbourne told the team: "I'm going to show you the *proper way* to take someone out at second base," demonstrating more subtle moves, less dangerous but with the same effect. Peter told the team: "If you go into second standing up, a good shortstop is going to put the ball right between your eyes. I can see you guys being aggressive, but I don't want you to end up in the hospital"[8] (field notes, Hopewell). Although the coaches were instrumental in providing an atmosphere in which this style of play was acceptable, it was Justin and also Harry and Whitney who, as role models, made aggressive play characteristic of the team.

Along with its aggressive play, Sharpstone was also known for its inability to accept frustration or failure. Justin again was particularly guilty. After an umpire had made a series of frustrating calls, someone on the Sharpstone bench threw a rock at him. When the umpire tried to discover who had thrown the rock, the Sharpstone players claimed ignorance. Later two Sharpstone players told me gleefully that Justin was the culprit. The following game Justin announced he had thrown the rock—proud of his deed. He showed me the size of the rock, and although he likely exaggerated to indicate his "bravery," it was about the size of a golf ball. The key point is not that one unusual player threw the rock (for such would not characterize the team) but that his teammates admired him for his daring, and the event became a team memorate.

One of the most memorable games of the season was fought between Sharpstone and Carlson—two excellent teams. Sharpstone finally won on a run scored by Justin in the bottom of the final inning. After the game, Justin sat in the dugout bawling, despite the fact he had scored both Sharpstone runs and made numerous excellent plays. Earlier in the game he had made an error at shortstop and couldn't forgive himself. His coaches watched him, amazed that he could be miserable after Sharpstone's best game of the season.

Most players (including Frank Turner) who indulged in such behavior would have been scorned by teammates as "weird," "a baby," or "a faggot." Yet Justin was not scorned. He was regarded as the toughest boy on the team, the most ready to fight, the best ball player, had close friends on the team who supported him, and was treated by the coaches as a leader. This position was acknowledged by his opponents, who respected and feared him. As one TI player noted, "I wouldn't bug him; he'd beat me up" (field notes, Hopewell).

Throughout the season Justin was not criticized for actions that would reap scorn for other boys. Justin's behavior was partially mirrored in the behavior of his close friends, Harry and Whitney:

Harry is picked off first base, and is furious. As he walks back to the Sharpstone bench he kicks a beer can lying on the field and slams it into the fence (field notes, Hopewell).

Whitney is called out on strikes in the bottom of the sixth inning on a pitch that he felt was outside (and thus a ball). This strikeout loses the game for Sharpstone. He starts crying, throws down his bat and helmet, and walks away in anger (field notes, Hopewell).

The behavior of the team leaders is not condemned by the coaches, and their behavior spreads to their teammates:

Cliff Alsop, nine years old, after striking out, starts crying and throwing dirt (field notes, Hopewell).

Dan Quimble, eleven years old, becomes increasingly angry with each pitch; he stands at the plate muttering angrily. When he strikes out, he returns to the dugout in tears (field notes, Hopewell).

Although Sharpstone players did not respond with tears and anger every time something disappointing happened, the majority (at least ten of the thirteen players) at some point of the season behaved in this way. This pattern was supported by the appropriate culture of the team, the fact that it was usable (not sanctioned by the coaches), and functional in that it externalized blame from the team that expected to win to their opponents or to forces out of their control. One insightful preadolescent opponent suggested that they became so angry because they *expected* to win, and when they lost, the impact was greater on them than on others, who expected less.

This explanation is predicated on the role of Sharpstone's elite clique and the anger associated with an elite clique, which I also found on other teams.[9] It is plausible that the structure of the team influences its emotional reactions. The existence of an elite clique of good ball players leads to the expectation of victory. Close, mutual friends who lead a team convince themselves they will be successful. When these views are ratified by other players on the team (and they are an "elite" because they receive friendship choices from others), the expectation for personal and collective success becomes proportionally stronger. As a result, the thwarting of these expectations is significantly more frustrating than when there is less expectation of victory.

A second feature that might explain the relationship between anger and the presence of an elite clique is that such a structure makes clear the locus for blame. Although players on Sharpstone did not publicly criticize Justin, Harry, and Whitney, it was clear to these three (and to their teammates) that when Sharpstone lost it was their fault. Their angry reactions externalize the blame for defeat onto the shoulders of others—the umpires, their opponents, or the world in general. When specific attacks are not possible, the anger is directed outward in a diffuse fashion—in the form of tears and curses, which indicate to preadolescent onlookers that the player does not think this athletic failing is typical of him and that he is angered by its unjustness. On the surface, crying and cursing seem to be very self-involving activities, but they are more properly seen as a technique among preadolescents to achieve role distance (Goffman 1961). When boys cry, they are not really crying at their own actions but at something the world has done to them. Crying comments about these external forces and distances oneself from the implication that one caused it. Tears are particularly likely when an individual or group is routinely seen as responsible for negative outcomes, as is true of teams with an elite clique. On a team with a more diffuse social structure, such as TI, individuals are not held so responsible; no one person or group is *expected* to cause the team to win, and crying and anger are uncommon.

Girls and Gays

As I've emphasized, in our sexualized society, during preadolescence boys attempt to deal with their male sex role. Part of this task is to recognize that they are, or soon will be, sexual beings (see chapter 5). The formulation of this interest takes different forms among different groups. The teams described in this chapter differed dramatically in how they viewed women and homosexuals. TI's culture was largely devoid of discussion of girlfriends or homosexuality (even playful talk), while such subjects comprised major foci of discussion for Sharpstone.

There were several structural reasons why talk about sexuality was known, usable, functional, and appropriate on Sharpstone but not on Transatlantic Industries. The actions of the coaches, the interests of players prior to the baseball season, and the existence of the elite clique on Sharpstone all helped these topics become a central part of Sharpstone's idioculture.

Coaches. Peter and Dave had no parental responsibilities, allowing for a different type of relationship to develop with their charges. Although the coaches maintained their authority when discussing baseball, they had an equal-status relationship with their players on other matters. They relished hearing about their players' "romantic" and quasi-sexual exploits, reinforcing this talk. For example, when Justin and Harry purchased rings for their girlfriends, the coaches wanted to learn all about their relationships; they referred to these girlfriends in a way often reserved for banter among adult males. Although the remarks were not leering, they were "knowing":

> At an early Sharpstone practice three young girls sit in the grandstand, cheering Whitney, Harry, and Justin. One girl yells something to Whitney, and Peter teases them, saying: "C'mon girls, no love life until after practice" (field notes, Hopewell).

When Whitney and Justin told Dave they had gone streaking the previous night, Dave was immensely amused, asking them what they did and what the reaction was.

More significant than this questioning for developing a male sex-role culture on Sharpstone were comments that these role models regularly made during the practice. These included teasing comments about sexuality, or criticizing players for being "girls." For example:

> Peter seriously tells the team before a game: "Hey, you're not girls out here, you're baseball players. Play like men" (field notes, Hopewell).

Although girls were not condemned they were differentiated from boys on the dimension of masculinity. The same applied to "homosexuals" and "effeminates":

> Justin and Harry stand on the field talking to each other, not paying attention to the practice. Peter calls to them: "You know what two guys who stay together are" (field notes, Hopewell).

> Peter feels that Harry is pitching too hard and tells him, "Harry, just throw a little bit like a fag" (i.e., throw lightly with a limp wrist) (field notes, Hopewell).

These comments were not said hostilely and were accepted by the players. Indeed, players were flattered by being talked to in such a "mature" fashion by their coaches. Similar comments characterized the team; players called each other girls and fags and were interested in each others' sexual exploits. Players even joked about sexual matters with their coaches, as when Peter got married and spent a week on his honeymoon, or:

> After a fast line drive hit by Justin passed Dave who was pitching, Justin teases, "Watch out for your balls," and later, "I almost hit your nuts" (field notes, Hopewell).

Such talk would have been unusable on other teams, and these sexual metaphors were never heard on Transatlantic Industries, where a conservative, middle-aged father was the coach.

Players. It is hard to distinguish the effects of the personalities of these boys from their position as an elite clique. As might be expected, Justin, Harry, and Whitney were most actively involved with girls, but several other boys, possibly because of peer pressure, admitted to having girlfriends or publically claimed they would get them soon—in contrast with other teams (including TI) where this topic was discretely ignored.

Justin, Harry, and Whitney were more open about their relationships with girls than are most preadolescents. During the season their girlfriends attended practices and games, and occasionally a boy-girl couple attended a game in which Sharpstone was not involved. A code of appropriate conduct organized these encounters. A boy never talked to his girlfriend at practice, not even to acknowledge her presence; a girl did not talk to her boyfriend, although she cheered when he made a good play. Girls never attended practice alone but always in pairs or threesomes. At games a boy and girl might stand together and talk quietly, but they did not touch each other. These relationships stood in sharp contrast to another set of boy-girl social contacts, which involved teasing, yelling, and chasing. The former were "romantic" boy-girl friendships, treated with dignity and some embarrassment; the latter were also boy-girl friendships but not romantic. The former sort of relationships and their relative openness differentiated Sharpstone from other teams, although the Sharpstone players were more involved in both types of relationships than were members of other teams.

Boy-girl relationships are delicate: so delicate that Justin, Harry, and Whitney formed an informal "gang" in school, "The Hell's Angels," to provide mutual support in dealing with the opposite sex (e.g., giving notes, transmitting messages, and beating up on other boys who "mistreated *their* girls"), and generally to provide a social setting in which these boys could develop their romantic interests without being taunted or shamed. Talk of these boys' sexual exploits did reach the team and entered its joking culture. For example, Harry's teammates learned that he had given an expensive ring owned by his mother to one of his girlfriends, and they teased him about it. When an unfamiliar black dog began barking at practice, Whitney's teammates named the dog Laurel (for Whitney's girlfriend) and Justin made this meaning explicit by saying, "That was Whit's girlfriend barking," meaning that he was going out with a "real dog." Or:

> During a break in practice, Dave notices that Harry is not present and asks, "Where's Stanton? In the dugout sulking?" Whitney giggles, "He's taking care of personal business." At this point Ray Coleman, a nine-year-old player, rushes to the dugout laughing gleefully. Dave remarks, "He must have seen him [Harry] kissing his girlfriend." Harry comes up chasing him, and Ray yells when Harry has almost caught him, "I didn't tell them nothing." Harry stops chasing him, and seems a little embarrassed (field notes, Hopewell).

More than on any other team, boy-girl relationships were important. While this emphasis originated in the attitudes of the team leaders, the interest spread to other team members, who discussed their own girlfriends as well as the activities of the team leaders. Sharpstone was not the only team with players who dated, but it was the only team on which these relationships played such a central and salient role in the team's sense of self. The sexual and romantic activities of the players were part of the team culture—reflected both in talk about sexual activity and in insults of others for being "girls" or "effeminate." This cultural content resulted from the structure of the team—the coaches' interest in such matters was not disguised, and the elite clique defined these activities as a sign of manhood. TI lacked a coach who desired to be a "friend," boys who were known for their sexual maturity, and an elite clique that set a "moral" tone for the team. Although I spent approximately the same amount of time with TI as I did with Sharpstone, I *never* heard the players discuss girlfriends, and I never learned if any of these boys had girlfriends.

Racism

The third topic on which Sharpstone and TI differed was their interest in race. Both teams were lily-white; TI players *never* mentioned race, while race was a frequent and usable topic on Sharpstone. Justin in particular hated some of his black peers, although he had sufficient tact to maintain good relations with several black adults. The Hopewell Little League had four black players, and special animus was reserved for two of them: Roger and Bill Mott, who played for the Carlson team. The Mott brothers were excellent ball players, and Bill's batting average of .606 was the third highest in the league—higher than Justin's .500 average. Throughout the season, Justin was unsparing of Bill and others:

> I was talking with some Sharpstone players about the best home run hitters in the league, and I mentioned that Billy Mott of Carlson was pretty good. Justin replied with disgust, "That dumb nigger." He immediately described how "two niggers tried to jump me" (field notes, Hopewell).

> One of the grounds keeper's helpers is a swarthy adolescent. Justin told Harry and Whitney that the boy is a Puerto Rican and therefore, is "half nigger and half white." Justin calls him a "punk," and Justin and Whitney both call him "half and half." The boy, who is within earshot, is becoming angry; Justin, Harry, and Whitney run away laughing (field notes, Hopewell).

These racial attitudes were shared and were publicly expressed by other members of the team (although I did not hear *every* Sharpstone player use racist language):

> Mike Marchio says that he calls the "colored people" in his neighborhood "jungle bunnies." Later Ray Coleman says that "all the people who live around me are niggers" (field notes, Hopewell).

The reactions of the coaches also allowed this talk to be usable; the coaches, while embarrassed, defined this racism as a *strategic* problem—a problem of impression management rather than of moral decay:

> Bill Mott, pitching for Carlson, hits a Sharpstone batter. Justin calls to him, "Come on, you nigger." Peter tells Justin, "Don't be stupid." Justin responds, "That's what he is." Dave warns Justin, "You'll get thrown out of the game." Justin concludes, "I don't care if he calls me whitey." This ends the discussion (field notes, Hopewell).

The coaches believed that boys should not use these words because other adults would sanction them or they might be attacked. When nine-year-old Ray Coleman called his neighbors "niggers," Dave told him, "That's not nice" and changed the subject. The reactions of the adults, while not encouraging the talk, did not make it unusable; no moral appeal came from these adults.

Although such language was presumably known to all players, only on Sharpstone was it usable. It is dangerous to suggest the reasons for these attitudes, but it may be relevant that two years previously, in Justin's first year, Sharpstone had a black coach and black players; this coach, who reportedly disciplined his players harshly, may have provoked resentment. This, however, is only speculation, particularly because Justin did not complain about this coach, nor did he give any indication that he considered the Motts like him. The rivalry between Justin and Bill Mott was a prime factor in the racial talk. Justin and Bill were regarded as two of the best players in the league; a boy of Justin's intense competitiveness and aggressiveness must have found this hard to accept. Justin's position on the team and the lack of intense objections from the coaches spread this racial talk to the other members of the team, who otherwise might have remained silent.

Geographical Dispersion

The Rhode Island township of Hopewell includes several towns covering approximately sixty-four square miles. Included are the towns of Hopewell, Whisper (a de facto part of Hopewell, although technically another political unit), Jamesville, and North Jamesville. The Little League field is located in Hopewell itself and can be reached by bicycle from Hopewell and Whisper, but it is too far from Jamesville and North Jamesville for a bicycle ride.

The two teams differ in where their players live. Eleven of thirteen Sharpstone players live in Hopewell or Whisper (the two from Jamesville and North Jamesville are ten years old). However, six of the thirteen players on TI (including three of the twelve-year-olds) are from Jamesville and North Jamesville. Where players live affects the teams and their cultures. Sharpstone had a much more robust and fully developed culture than Transatlantic Industries, with more frequently repeated (salient) cultural traditions. Sharpstone players arrived at games and practices early, becoming well acquainted. They were more likely to see each other around town, and many attended games in which their team was not playing. These factors contributed to the intensity of their friendships and bolstered their culture. This contrasts with TI players, who depended on their parents for transportation.

Parents of players on Sharpstone were more likely to attend games than the parents of players on TI. The average Sharpstone parent attended 11.3 games, while the average TI parent attended only 9.2.[10] There are several reasons for this. First, it requires more time and gasoline for the parents of boys who live in Jamesville and North Jamesville to attend games (TI parents had a car pool so that only one or two mothers each day would drive the boys to the game). Second, the parents from Jamesville were not as well integrated into the parental "network" as were parents from Hopewell. To the extent that one reason for attending Little League games is social contact with other adults, parents from Jamesville had less reason to be present.

Significantly, one of the few distinctive aspects of Transatlantic Industries' idioculture dealt with the lack of parental attendance at their games, which they felt reflected poorly on the team:

With one parent in the TI grandstand, Frank Turner comments sarcastically to his teammates: "How do you like our fan?" Several other TI players continue the discussion (field notes, Hopewell).

Frank Turner says to his teammates, "Look at all the fans we got," referring to the small number of TI parents in the grandstand and in their cars. He tells me that Sharpstone always has a lot of parents who come to their games, and that when a Sharpstone player gets a long hit or a home run, their parents honk car horns; whereas when a TI player gets a hit, there is silence (field notes, Hopewell).

Although it was generally players from Hopewell and Whisper who made these comments, they were not directed at the boys from Jamesville but at all parents (and thus functional in differentiating this team from their parents). Such talk seems on the surface to indicate an antiparental attitude on TI led by Frank, but the team culture wasn't sufficiently developed so that this became evident.

Culture and Its Implications for Structure

Sharpstone and Transatlantic Industries were two teams with distinct idiocultures, Sharpstone's far more developed than TI's. Sharpstone, with a clearly stratified and consensually accepted team structure, developed cultural traditions around several major themes: baseball professionalism, aggressive play, sexual maturity, and racial antagonism—which reflected themes that were known, usable, functional, and appropriate. The recognition of these themes by players directed their behavior, provided a common identity, and gave Sharpstone a distinctive style of play and talk.

Transatlantic Industries, without these clear themes, was not seen by its players as being so distinct from other teams in the league. The cultural elements developed by Transatlantic Industries lacked a thematic uniformity and few were repeated with any regularity. Thus, the fact that I have not presented many idiocultural elements from TI does not indicate that the team had *no* idioculture, but rather that the idioculture was diffuse, like the social structure of the team, and not salient.

Although both teams were successful during the season, their success differed, in part as a function of their culture. TI was comprised of a number of boys who could play baseball very well—good pitchers and long-ball hitters. Each player performed well. Sharpstone, because of its internal team loyalty and outward aggressiveness, seemed much more of a *team*. Its emotional togetherness and baseball teamwork were partially attributable to the structure of the team, partially to its idioculture, and partially to the interaction of structure and culture.

Even though the two teams were similar in their environments and even in their outcomes (baseball success), events within each group and in its culture were not necessarily similar. Sharpstone and TI were particularly distinctive in their appropriate culture and in their usable culture, and, as a consequence, their specific traditions and behavior differed. The contrasting idioculture of similar teams was a result, not only of differing sets of random behaviors (triggering events), but of the constraints and options open to a team. Boys can and do shape the general preadolescent culture to distinctively different ends. This suggests that the content of group interaction is not random detritus but worthy of sociological analysis in its own right for the study of group dynamics.

7

Preadolescent Subculture

Having examined the processes by which preadolescent culture (and, by implication, all culture) is created and transmitted in groups in which participants know each other, I now focus on cultural transmission in larger social units. Here I treat American preadolescent males as a community, recognizing that any one preadolescent boy knows relatively few others, despite being embedded in a social network. I ask how preadolescent culture can be relatively similar across communities. Unlike chapter 5, in which I discussed the general form of "developmental imperatives," this section describes the more specific interactional linkages that permit the wide dissemination of cultural material. It is self-evident that contemporary Western societies are not culturally homogeneous. Nations are split by divisions such as ethnicity, religion, class, occupation, and age. Social-structural divisions correspond to divisions in the knowledge of societal members. The cultural massification in America has not yet wiped out the vitality of specialized cultures. These societal segments have been termed subsocieties, and the knowledge they share is their subculture (Fine and Kleinman 1979).

In conceptualizing subculture, writers have frequently treated it as if it were a closed and formal structure, a social system devoid of interaction (e.g., Miller 1958; Cohen 1955). In contrast, I emphasize the role of face-to-face interaction in the creation and use of culture (Spector 1973). However, this approach, with its concern with interaction, leaves open the question of how culture becomes spread throughout a subsociety in which members do not interact with each other. How do many items of culture remain relatively invariant and become widely known? In order to claim that a preadolescent (male) subculture exists, I must show, first, that there are shared cultural traditions—traditions that seem not to be widely known by other segments of society—and, second, that these cultural elements have spread throughout the preadolescent population in America.

162

Cultural traditions are created through individual or collective manipulation of symbols. From the point of creation, the cultural form is communicated to others and diffused outward from the original interaction partners (Jacobs 1893). The transmission of culture within a large group results from interaction, although in some cases this diffusion may be limited unless the information reaches wider audiences via the mass media. After diffusion through the media (e.g., children's cartoons, G or PG rated films, hobby magazines, radio shows), additional diffusion may occur through interpersonal channels or repeated media communication (Katz and Lazarsfeld 1955). Particularly when dealing with preadolescent culture, one must not equate the extent of information spread with the method of transmission. Much that the mass media attempts to communicate is never transmitted by its audiences. Further, many cultural items that are never transmitted by the media are known throughout a cultural system. A considerable amount of information is "common knowledge" among young people—dirty jokes, sexual folklore, aggressive humor, drug lore, pranks and teases— that could not be transmitted by the adult-controlled media, which are highly protective of children's supposed innocence and delicate sensibilities.

Iona and Peter Opie have marveled at the speed at which some childlore can spread between far distant communities; they suggest, "It seems that the schoolchild underground . . . employs transworld couriers" (Opie and Opie 1959; 7). This rapid transmission can be observed by examining the spread of topical parody songs. One scurrilous parody dealing with the abdication of King Edward VIII was spread in London, Chichester, Liverpool, Oldham, and Swansea in Great Britain within three weeks. The Opies claim that these versions were not communicated through conventional media sources. Youth cultures (of various ages) are excellent examples of subcultures that provide a set of communication channels external to the mass media. They are specialized information conduits defining the boundaries of a particular culture. Most adults remain blissfully unaware of what is communicated. Subcultural traditions that derive from group cultures support Mannheim's (1952; 307) explanation of the formation of youth cultures as originating in concrete groups ("generational units") of young people who create new perspectives and develop distinctive cultural patterns that may be diffused subsequently to others.

The subculture construct serves as a gloss for communication within interlocking groups, and for the knowledge and behaviors shared by these groups. The extent of the subculture consists in the boundaries of knowledge within the group's pattern of relationships. As Shibutani (1955, 566) notes, "culture areas are coterminous with communication channels."

With this theoretical underpinning, I ask whether preadolescents form a subculture in contemporary American society and, if so, what are the communication links that allow information to be diffused. In this discussion I examine preadolescent language (or "slanguage") as an indicator of the presence of subculture. The development of a special language for groups operating within the framework of a larger society is a common phenomenon and, if a subculture exists, we should find words used by preadolescents that are not widely spread among other groups but are known in several preadolescent communities.

Common Content

Folklorists long ago discarded the idea that similar cultural forms develop in isolation—an approach known as polygenesis (Brunvand 1978; Dorson 1972). In other words, the presence of a cultural tradition in several groups simultaneously indicates contact among them. The existence of common lore and language suggests that children form their own societies which differ in content from those of their elders. In the works of Douglas Newton, "The world-wide fraternity of children is the greatest of savage tribes, and the only one which shows no sign of dying out" (Opie and Opie 1959, 2). Childlore is remarkable for its temporal continuity and its geographical spread. This culture, much of which has been forgotten by adults, is part of what Mary and Herbert Knapp (1976) term "the secret education of children." Stone and Church (1968, 370) suggest the extent of this children's culture in America: "Among his friends, the middle-years child lives in a special culture with its own traditional games, rhymes, riddles, tricks, superstitions, factual and mythical lore, and skills, transmitted virtually intact from one childhood generation to the next, sometimes over a period of centuries with no help from adults and often in spite of them."

To indicate that a preadolescent subculture exists in America, I shall show that words and phrases are known by preadolescents in several communities and that these terms are not known, or at least are not widely used, by adults. Obviously this analysis is speculative, because my sampling base is not sufficiently large to determine the extent of word usage. For example, some terms might well be known throughout the South, Southwest, or West and be totally missed by this research, which examines only five communities in New England and Minnesota. Since the purpose of the research was not a systematic study of children's informal vocabulary or slang, even in the communities studied, much slang went unreported; I underrepresent the common knowledge that actually exists. The words collected were in the vocabulary of at least one speaker in the community; the extent of knowledge obviously varies according to sociometric position, attitudes, age, interests, and abilities. Even within a very limited geographic area, cultural knowledge is not known to the entire preadolescent population. For this chapter, I assume that any word collected in a community was spoken in that community.

Information can be shared by individuals on two analytically distinct dimensions I term *horizontal* and *vertical*—metaphors borrowed from the study of social structure. The horizontal dimension corresponds to the geographical region in which a term is known. Thus, a slang item may be widely known or may be known only by two neighbors. Most important studies of the diffusion of adult words (e.g., Allen 1973) focus on geographical diffusion. Vertical diffusion represents the extent to which words (knowledge) have permeated segments of society, defined structurally rather than geographically. Some vocabulary is known only to a particular group or class within society, while other items are known more widely. Although class distinctions are frequently schematized in terms of their vertical organization, with higher classes being layered on less prestigious ones, the analysis of this vertical dimension uses altitude metaphorically. This vertical dimension includes, not only class distinctions, but groupings by occupation, race, religion, and age. In terms of age, most individuals find themselves living in intimate proximity with those of other ages—but not sharing all they know.

These two dimensions are analytically separate and empirically distinct. I treat these dimensions, for heuristic purposes, as crosscutting each other and divided in two (see fig. 7.1). Thus, culture elements can be placed into one of four quadrants. Common speech is characterized by both high horizontal spread and high vertical spread. Slang words in general circulation, including the once infamous but always widely traveled "four-letter" words, are also in this quadrant. Localisms (see Kurath 1970) are characterized by wide vertical diffusion but narrow horizontal diffusion. Words with narrow horizontal spread and narrow vertical spread are a particu-

Horizontal Diffusion

Wide   Narrow

Common Speech "Four-letter words"	*Regional/Local Speech* Ish Soda Pop
Preadolescent Speech Duh Doofy Buck Wuss	*Local Preadolescent/* *Idiosyncratic Speech* Schmedley Angy

Fig. 7.1   Horizontal and Vertical Dimensions of Folk Speech

lar class of localisms—indicating the existence of an idioculture among the speakers. Family words (Read 1962), rituals (Bossard and Boll 1950), or folklore (Cutting-Baker, Gross, Kotkin, and Zeitlin 1976) are examples of this phenomenon. The fourth type is my particular concern in this chapter: words or phrases that spread widely among a particular subsegment but that are not known to others in the society who do not share identification with these individuals and who are not part of their communications network (i.e., wide horizontal spread and narrow vertical spread). If a preadolescent subculture exists in America, a portion of preadolescent talk should be in this fourth category. The boundaries of preadolescent talk are not exact, as former preadolescents will recall these terms and may use them in suitable situations, and not all preadolescents are equally conversant with the shared knowledge of their peers. However, the existence of a subcuture presupposes shared knowledge within a group and relative ignorance among those outside the bond of brotherhood. It is important to recall that a division exists in preadolescent life between male preadolescents and female preadolescents, with significant gaps between the groups on many issues. One might suggest that they have two separate subcultures.

Traditional Speech

All competent members of a society acquire a set of words and phrases that allows them to communicate with others. Through shared symbols people are able to construct collective meanings— meanings that may go well beyond the denotive implications of the vocalizations themselves (see Garfinkel 1967; 24–31). By the time a boy has reached preadolescence he has mastered a remarkable number of social meanings and the words that elaborate, describe, and index these meanings. By preadolescence a child is a facile interactant with adults and peers on most social topics. In conjunction with the formal vocabulary that adults strive to teach children in the school and in the home, or indirectly through the mass media, the child gains a working knowledge of much general slang—terms that are part of "colloquial speech."[2]

Preadolescents are well aware of sexual and aggressive slang used by male adults and in informal, private conversations refer to balls, boobs, chicks, dicks, fags, faggots, fairies, jerks, and niggers. These terms are part of the general American slang vocabulary (cited in Wentworth and Flexner 1975), although they are likely to be used more frequently by some groups than others (those male, young, and secular). As researchers (Poston 1964; Kratz 1964; Olesen and Whittaker 1968) have pointed out, the fact that a group (in that case, college students) uses slang words does not necessarily make them part of the slang *of that group*.

Regional Vocabularies

Words characterized by narrow horizontal diffusion but extensive vertical diffusion are regionalisms. Possibly because of the homogenizing impact of the mass media, I found few regionalisms. *Ish* was used in all three Minnesota leagues but not in New England. *Ish* is the Minnesota equivalent of *ick* or *yeech* in other parts of the country—mild disgust. Although I cannot establish *Ish*'s geographical spread, it is known to Minnesota residents of all ages. *Oofda* in Minnesota as a synonym for *my gosh!*, and *pop* in the Midwest as opposed to *soda* in the East to refer to a sweet carbonated drink are examples of regionalisms spread among large segments of society.

Group Slang

Words that have narrow horizontal and vertical spread reflect a group culture. Family words are of this type, as are words or secret languages confined to friends (Oring 1984). Much preadolescent slang is localized and group based. Words are created in an idioculture; many die stillborn, others gain a continuing group existence, and a very few others gain national or regional currency. Boys in Sanford Heights claim to have created the word *angy* to mean "thank you"; in Maple Bluff, *schmedley* was the cue for two boys to go outside and share a cigarette together; the onomatapoetical *blutchuck* in Bolton Park referred to vomit; in Beanville, a *glom* was an awkward kid, a creep. *Prang, gremtight, humaned, leon, raga, ruminent remain,* and *royal patoon* are some of the localisms these preadolescents created that do not appear to have spread outside their own community and are not known to adults. The creation of some local phrases requires a considerable imagination, such as a Beanville word for flatus: *Rip Roaring Flying Mountain Lion Ahem* or the Sanford Heights obscene curse: *Royal Bohemian Superior Butt-Fucker, It's on Fire.* These preadolescents delighted in their mastery of these off-color tongue twisters. Most of these words are significant primarily because of their novelty and because their meanings are hidden from adults and other non–group members—but generally they have little staying power. Words are constantly being created, used, and discarded without any record of their existence.

Subcultural Slang

Subcultural slang originates in an interacting group, but it is not limited to that group. It is characterized by relatively small vertical spread coupled with a substantial horizontal spread. Of the 387 words collected from preadolescents (see Fine 1979–81), 98 words (25 percent) were collected in more than one location.[4] As I noted, this figure understates the actual amount of shared vocabulary in that such data collection was not a central focus of this research endeavor but a side involvement, and so many words were uncollected. Yet, while the count is reduced because of the lack of intensive collection, it is also true that many of these common words are not limited to preadolescents. Some of the words collected are part of the general slang culture in America: balls, fairy, or fart. Others of these slang words may be known by adults, although rarely used by them—being recognizable or *known* but not usable. Both preadolescents and adults have this subset of words in their own culture, but for adults these words are not usable (perhaps because of their childish, immature implications); for preadolescents they are.

In order to estimate how many of the words I collected are part of preadolescent vocabularies in more than one location and not part of adult vocabularies (with their preadolescent meaning), I compared the list with the Wentworth and Flexner's *Dictionary of American Slang* (2d ed.), the authoritative American slang dictionary. Of the 97 words, 58 (60 percent) are also listed in the *DAS*, which does not specifically include children's slang. This, then, leaves 39 words "preadolescent slang." I cannot conclude that these words are not also found in adolescence. Indeed, I suspect many are, since "pre-

Table 7.1   Preadolescent Slang

1. **Adoi,** *adj.* Stupid; e.g., "they have such adoi players" (BP, SH)
2. **Bite,** *v.i.* Insult with homosexual implications, as in "you bite" (BV, BP, SH)
3. **Booger,** *n.* Mucus (MB, HW, BP, SH)
4. **Buck,** *n.* Ride on a bicycle as the second rider (MB, SH, BP)
5. **Bumpers,** *n.* Old sneakers (not stylish or manufactured by a "name" company) (BP, SH)
6. **Buzz,** *n.* Short haircut; crewcut (BP, SH)
7. **Ding Dong Ditch,** *n.* Prank involving ringing a doorbell and running from the house (also Ding Dong Door Ditch, Ring and Run, Nigger Knocking) (BP, SH)
8. **Dink,** *n.* Penis (often diminutive); disliked boy (BV, SH, MB)
9. **Doi,** *int.* That's stupid, duh (BP, SH)
10. **Doof,** *n.* Foolish, awkward boy (BP, SH)
11. **Doofy,** *adj.* Foolish, awkward (HW, BP, SH)
12. **Dork, Dorko,** *n.* Disliked boy (BP, SH)
13. **Duh,** *int.* That's stupid (BV, BP, SH)
14. **Egg,** *v.t.* Throw eggs at an object as a prank (usually a house or car) (HW, BP, SH)
15. **First base,** *n.* (1) Kissing (as in "getting to first base"); (2) Lips (HW, BP, SH)
16. **Gaywad,** *n.* Disliked boy; homosexual imagery (BP, SH)
17. **Get on your horse,** *v.i.* Run fast (BP, SH)
18. **Goober,** *v.i.* Drool (BP, SH)
19. **Heinie,** *n.* Buttocks (BP, SH)
20. **Ish,** *int.* Exclamation of disgust (see "ick") (MP, BP, SH)
21. **Mo,** *n.* Homosexual (BP, SH)
22. **Motormouth,** *n.* Boy who talks constantly (BP, SH)
23. **Mutt,** *n.* Disliked or ugly girl (BP, SH)
24. **Nail,** *v.t.* Hit (as in "nailing" a car by throwing an egg at it) (HW, SH)
25. **Pusslick,** *n.* Disliked boy (possible effeminate implication; derivation from slang for cunnilingus) (BP, SH)
26. **Sad,** *adj.* Unsatisfactory, bad, poor (BV, BP, MB, SH)
27. **Scabby,** *adj.* Unsatisfactory, bad, poor (BP, SH)
28. **Sleezy,** *adj.* Lucky, often with the implication that the luck was undeserved (as in "sleezy catch"). Sometimes "sleeze" will be used as a noun to describe a boy who is undeservedly lucky (BP, SH)
29. **Slug bug,** *n.* Game in which the boy who first calls out that he sees a Volkswagen Beetle can hit the other game player. This game is usually played while driving in a car, until parents stop it. Variations of the game include "Orange Slug Bug" (BP, SH)
30. **Snuggy,** *n.* Prank which involves sneaking behind a boy and yanking or tugging at his underwear (see also "wedgie") (BP, SH)
31. **Swirly,** *n.* Prank in which boys stick another boy's head or feet in a toilet bowl and flush the toilet (from the "swirl" of the water being flushed) (BP, SH)
32. **Tinsel teeth,** *n.* Boy who wears metal braces on his front teeth (HW, BP)
33. **Ultra,** *adj.* Very sophisticated or "cool" (BP, SH)
34. **Wanky,** *adj.* Crazy, foolish, silly (BP, SH)
35. **Way to be,** *int.* Supportive comment, meaning "Keep it up" (MB, BP, SH)
36. **Wedgie,** *n.* Prank which involves sneaking behind a boy and yanking or tugging at his underwear (see also "snuggy") (BV, HW)

Table 7.1 (continued)

---

37. **Whore,** *n.* Disliked or ugly girl (also "prostie," "slut") (MB, SH)
38. **Woman,** *n.* Disliked or effeminate boy (MB, SH, BP)
39. **Wuss,** *n.* Effeminate boy (BP, SH)

Notes: Slang expressions collected in more than one location and not cited in Wentworth and Flexner (1975). BP = Bolton Park; BV = Beanville; HW = Hopewell; MB = Maple Bluff; SH = Sanford Heights.

---

adolescent culture" is a gloss for a system of knowledge that does not have clear age boundaries.

In order to examine the knowledge of adults about children's words and activities, the fourteen parents interviewed in Sanford Heights were asked if they were aware of their son doing a series of activities. Of our parental sample, 43 percent believed their preadolescent boys did not use nasty or rude words, 50 percent believed that their sons did not tell dirty jokes, and 57 percent believed that their sons did not play pranks. While it would be wrong to assume that *all* boys engage in these actions, it does suggest at least that some parents either were not aware of their son's behavior patterns or were politely refraining from mentioning these behaviors to an outsider. While the latter explanation cannot totally be discounted, I did not sense that parents were dissimulating; as best as could be judged, parents were being sincere—particularly since it was clear I knew what these boys actually did with their friends. Some parents were unaware of their sons' activities.

One of the clearest instances of parental ignorance was in the case of "funny phone calls."[5] Only two of fourteen parents (14 percent) believed that their children had performed this prank, whereas *half* of their offspring admitted to this activity. Parents also reveal considerable ignorance of preadolescent speech (see table 7.2), and even in those cases in which they claim to have heard their child use a particular word they are unaware of its situated meaning.

Other genres of culture such as games, jokes, legends, and folk beliefs differentiate children from adults and indicate that preadolescent culture is not simply an argot but an "organized world" (Speier 1973, 142; see Schwartz and Merten 1967). One example of this age-specific culture is the simple trick of tugging on someone's underwear, called a *snuggy* in Minnesota and a *wedgie* in New England. This trick involves sneaking up behind one's victim (an age mate or a younger boy) and tugging on his underwear as hard as one

Table 7.2   Knowledge of Preadolescent Culture by Parents and Sons

	Parents[a] Who Knew Item's Correct Meaning[b] (N = 14)		Boys Who Knew Item's Correct Meaning (N = 14)	
	N	%	N	%
Buck	4	29	8	57
Ding Dong Ditch	1	7	9	64
Doofy	1	7	5	36
Dork	9	64	10	71
Hot Box	6	43	13	93
Mutt	2	14	11	79
Polish Home Run	1	7	9	64
Polish Rope Trick	0	0	1	7
Prange	0	0	5	36
Royal Bohemian	1	7	4	29
Snuggy	5	36	12	86
Swirly	1	7	4	29

[a]Sample includes seven mothers and seven fathers.
[b]Meanings of these terms can be found later in this chapter.

can—a prank that recognizes the emerging sexuality of these young boys, and that is structurally similar to bra snapping (Knapp and Knapp 1976, 84). In Bolton Park I was told that a boy had been hung by his underwear for two hours until someone rescued him; in Beanville the perpetrator would tug so hard on the victim's underwear that it would rip, and then the perpetrator would rub the cloth in his victim's face. Giving a boy a snuggy/wedgie is part of the preadolescent male subculture.

Another major element of preadolescent male slang (discussed in chapter 5) is talk of homosexuality (and oral sex). Boys call each other a *faggot* or *fag, fairy* or *feather, gay* or *gay wad. Cocksucker* is an ultimate put-down because it makes explicit what is hidden in the other terms, and it is dangerous in that the emotions the child is repressing (either because of psychodynamics or for reasons of impression management) are revealed. One is struck by the emphasis in the informal talk of preadolescent males on "sucking" (found in all five leagues), "biting" (e.g., *bite me*—found in Beanville, Bolton Park, and Sanford Heights), and "eating" (Bolton Park and Sanford Heights). Even when the reference is to a female "victim," the metaphor is frequently oral—as in the case of *snatchbite, twatlick,* or *pusslick.* Boys may say to their friends, rivals, and enemies (with different tones, of course): "bite my ass," "bitehead," "bite my bag," "eat my goober," "eat me out," "french my hole," "go suck a cow," "go suck an egg," "head me," "lick my ass," "suckhead," "suck me royal," "suck my willie," "suck my twang," or "suck my summer sausage." Homosexuality is an important theme for some members of this age group; sexual lore generates prestige in the interpersonal marketplace of communication.

Diffusion

Recognizing that preadolescents share a culture that differentiates them from other groups (although the boundaries of the subsociety are not always clear), how are these cultural elements diffused among preadolescents? The existence of a cultural element in several groups suggests communication. While the preadolescent community in a local area can be treated as a closed system, the members of this community interact not only with each other; even at this age, these communities are connected with others through a set of *interlocks* or social linkages. These connections take a variety of forms and can be analyzed in terms of either individuals or groups. Individuals, for example, may share membership in several groups simultaneously or sequentially. Groups connect with other groups through mechanisms such as intergroup communication (i.e., communication from one group to another), multigroup communication (communication from one group or a single individual to a number of groups—as in the mass media), or communication between groups by nonmembers who have a role status that requires or encourages such communication. Through these interlocks, cultural information and behavioral options are diffused, resulting in the creation of a shared universe of discourse. I conceive of this social network, rather than the demographic age boundaries of preadolescence, as the referent of the term *subculture*. Not all preadolescents are knowledgeable about "preadolescent culture," while some early adolescents and social scientists are.

Multiple Group Membership

A direct mechanism for the interchange of culture within a population results from the fact that people may belong to several groups simultaneously. Cultural elements that are found in one group can easily be introduced into other groups through overlapping memberships. This is evident in the modern preadolescent's busy schedule—boys may belong to several youth groups in areas outside of their local neighborhood. For example, one boy in Bolton Park attended a gun-safety school which met in another suburb. A boy in Sanford Heights missed a week of the season because of an outing of boys in school patrols. Sports, contests, or summer camps allow the preadolescent to meet peers from all over the region—or the nation (e.g., the Boy Scout Jamboree or the National Spelling Bee). A cultural item can be transmitted readily if it meets the idiocultural criteria necessary for introduction to the group to which the boy belongs. When the group joined is short-lived (camps, jamborees, etc.), the boy may decide to communicate dramatic and salient information to gain the attention and esteem of his new acquaintances (Sherif et al. 1961; 76, 79).

When boys return from their adventures, local friends are eager to learn what happened; these personal narratives are a source for the introduction of culture, particularly preadolescent "deviance" such as sexual talk and aggressive pranks. The idea of a *swirly*— sticking a boy's head in a toilet (either clean or unflushed) and flushing—was learned by some Sanford Heights youngsters attending a summer hockey camp in northern Minnesota; one of them almost had that prank pulled on him.

Interchanges among groups in which individuals participate simultaneously are less dramatic, but the new cultural item may be mentioned when relevant. Preadolescents who belong to several groups characterized by few joint members provide a crucial linkage for the spread and alteration of cultural traditions. Memorable cultural products, such as song parodies, spread quickly. These are among the first things individuals perform when they enter another group. Diffusion is motivated by the perceived value of the information.

The extreme case of joint membership is the migrating preadolescent.[6] Obviously mobility varies as a result of socioeconomic, environmental, and historical factors of communities and families, and rates of mobility in and out of the five areas studied were low. For example, of the forty-eight twelve-year-old Sanford Heights Little Leaguers, two had moved into the community within a year of the beginning of Little League season (one from a St. Paul suburb and one from a small town in the south-central part of the state). In the few months after the season, two others left the area—one to a small exurban town north of Sanford Heights and the other to Wisconsin. Occasionally boys move considerable distances—one boy in Bolton Park moved to Florida, a teammate had just moved from Chicago. This migration allows for cultural traditions to be spread even when media channels do not exist. Transient communities (such as those near army bases or universities) may experience a higher rate of cultural change than more stable communities.

When a preadolescent migrates, his entire store of knowledge moves with him and is transferable to his new peer group; this produces homogenization of traditional material. The boy from the suburb was quiet and had low status in his new environment, but Hardy Wieder, from southern Minnesota, soon became a leader of his preadolescent peer group, particularly knowledgable in the sexual ways of the world; his sharing of preadolescent traditions broadened the knowledge of his friends.

Weak Ties

No matter how dense or tightly knit their social networks, boys are likely to have acquaintances outside the groups in which they are most active. Interacting networks are never totally bounded or finite (Barnes 1969). Granovetter (1973, 1974) argues that contacts outside of one's close circle of friends are of crucial importance for disseminating information throughout a social system. A series of "small-world" studies conducted with adults (e.g., Milgram 1967; Travers and Milgram 1969) has demonstrated the extent of these network strands, which often stretch across the nation. Because of the social and geographical mobility characteristic of modern society, Americans may have social ties with others at great physical distances and beyond social and demographic lines. These ties provide opportunities for cultural diffusion if there is suitable motivation. Studies of the spread of rumor, hysterical contagion, and news demonstrate that information and behavior can spread rapidly under favorable conditions—that is, when the information is regarded as worth communicating and the structural characteristics of the situation are conducive to dissemination.

My data do not allow me to assess the precise extent to which these weak ties are found among children. Because preadolescents do not have easy access to transportation and because their telephone calls are dialed at the discretion of parents, their acquaintances outside their community are limited compared to those of adults, but they do exist.

The geographically mobile child may maintain friendships over many miles, and it is not uncommon for a boy's former friends to be invited to visit. The childhood pastime of corresponding with pen pals is another example of this same phenomenon. Likewise, the distant (spatially and genetically) cousins who populate American extended families give children others with whom to compare their life situations and cultures. Family reunions provide the opportunity for members of a clan to become acquainted with each other and to share local and family traditions (Ayoub 1966). Family visits are common, particularly with preadolescent children, who are old enough not to create too much trouble but young enough to be willing to be shown off and to have no choice but to accompany their parents. At these visits children may meet kin their own age; if these kinfolk live elsewhere, the child may be exposed to novel preadolescent culture. Since children's culture has regional and local variation, kinship ties provide a mechanism by which cultural traditions jump geographical chasms. For example, Barry Rymer, a twelve-year-old Sanford Heights Little Leaguer, was visited by his ten-year-old cousin from a farm near Mason City, Iowa. Although he was teased about being a farmer with "dirty fingernails," he and Barry's friends traded cultural information. For example, instead of calling girls "mutts," the Iowan male subculture calls these creatures "hogs" and uses "moron" rather than calling someone "sick" (field notes, Sanford Heights). Information was traded that may have provided cultural options for Sanford Heights preadolescent boys and for those in Mason City.

Conversations with infrequently met acquaintances facilitate rapid dissemination of large amounts of new information in a relatively short time—a process Yerkovich (1976) terms "updating." Through extended questioning, participants can cover significant topics in greater detail.

Closer to home, a preadolescent boy may know several adolescents or young adults who are willing to tell him about sensitive topics—sex, pranks, insults, etc. A major font of this information is older brothers (though for some topics, older sisters can perform this function). Some older brothers felt a responsibility to their siblings to teach them those cultural traditions helpful for achieving status among the younger boys' peers. Although siblings may not be "close friends" (particularly since they run in different social worlds), these elder siblings are sources for the continuation of cultural tradition. Children without elder siblings learn from those preadolescents who have them. Likewise, a seventh-grade boy may become attached to an older schoolmate who will take him under his wing, and the younger boy will then inform his peers.

Consider the spread of the slang expression *zoid*. *Zoid* was defined by its originator as referring to a boy who is a "loser" or who has a poor reputation and is not a member of any group (as in the sarcastic put-down: "You're a zoid; ya know it?"). The word was created by a twelfth-grade boy in Sanford Heights[7] and spread to his regular baseball friends. The word subsequently was learned and accepted by the originator's ninth-grade brother, and the brother used *zoid* with his friends. One of this ninth-grader's friends had a sixth-grade brother playing Little League baseball. This boy added *zoid* to his vocabulary. When the forty-eight twelve year olds were interviewed after the season, eleven other boys said they had heard the term. He had named ten of these boys (91 percent) as his friends (53 percent of the boys that he named as friends). The structure of cross-age kinship ties supplements the diffusion that occurs among close age-graded friends.

Specialized diffusion. The mere existence of a communication linkage does not mean that all types of information will be transmitted: such connections may spread specialized information. Information flows within a network according to interest (Dégh and Vázsonyi 1975; Fine 1980b). As a result, within a community several communication channels may operate simultaneously—for example, one for dirty jokes, a second for school happenings, and a third for discussions of sports. People may specialize in the information they transmit, and some relationships may be specialized in what the participants feel it is appropriate to discuss. Thus, sensitive cultural information (e.g., sexual knowledge) may reach only those who are likely to be receptive. My data in support of this assumption of specialized channels are not definitive, but they do suggest the existence of such a process.

In order to examine the specificity of network relations I use data from the sample of forty-eight twelve-year-old boys who played Little League in Sanford Heights. The density of this communications network became evident when each boy characterized each of the other boys in the sample as a close friend, a friend, or a speaking acquaintance. Of the 2,256 dyads in the sample, 18.2 percent involved close friends, 31.2 percent were friends, and 23.6 percent were speaking acquaintances,[8] for a total of 73 percent of the relationships.

Boys were asked whether they were aware of thirty-five traditional cultural items, which I knew from observation were known by at least some Sanford Heights preadolescents. Boys who said they had heard the item were asked to name all those from whom they had heard it. In this analysis transmission links within the sample were coded with a *1;* if there was no transmission, the item for that dyad was coded *0*. The thirty-five items were reduced to twenty-four for the analysis, using the criterion that for each item at least one transmission chain must exist for at least one-quarter of the sample. Thus, there were twenty-four variables for each dyad.

I divided these twenty-four terms into five cultural categories: (1) heterosexual activities, (2) insults, (3) pranks, (4) baseball terms, and (5) a residual category of nonsexual and nonaggressive activities. Heterosexual activities consisted of four terms: *spin the bottle* (Sutton-Smith 1959); *Getting to second base with a girl* (i.e., fondling her breasts); *truth or dare* (a children's game in which the child of the opposite sex either must answer a question truthfully: "Do you like Patti?" or take a dare), and *kiss or kill* (get kissed or be "killed"). The insult category consisted of seven terms: *gaywad, bite me, doofy, dork, mutt, prange* (a general insult, local to Sanford Heights), and *Your royal Bohemian butt-fucker, it's on fire* (a local insult in Sanford Heights). The eight pranks were: *funny phone calls, egging a house, ding dong ditch* (ringing a doorbell and running away), *mooning, giving a snuggy* (yanking someone's underpants from behind), *giving a swirly* (sticking someone's head in a toilet bowl and flushing), *shooting a polish cannon* (a homemade explosive device which shoots tennis balls), and the *Polish rope trick* (two boys stand on opposite sides of a street at dusk, pretending to hold two ends of a rope—hoping to stop cars). The fourth category consisted of two baseball terms: *being in the hole* (being up after the on-deck batter), and a *Polish home run* (a ball hit over the backstop). The final category consisted of three terms that are neither hostile nor sexual: *giving a buck* (a ride on the back of one's bicycle), *hotbox* (a game which simulates a baseball rundown), and *smear the queer* (a wrestling-tag game in which players attempt to tackle the boy who holds a designated object).

If diffusion follows lines of interest, transmission patterns should be similar for items within the categories but distinct between categories. In other words, I hypothesize that the sexual material should be transmitted through different conduits than the pranks or the insults.

I found qualified support for this hypothesis based on a factor analysis of transmission links (a Verimax Rotated Factor Analysis, using ten iterations to convergence) and also a Guttman-Lingoes Smallest Space Analysis. Since the results from both techniques are similar, I shall report only the factor analysis. Both techniques determine which variables are the most similar—or go together best. In this analysis comparing reported instances of diffusion, I examine which communication paths are the most similar. Using the standard Eigenvalue criterion of 1.0, five factors together explained 51 percent of the variance in the transmission patterns of these twenty-four cultural items. For purposes of this analysis I shall use .40 as the criterion level as to whether an item is significant on any given factor. Since the factors are by definition independent, they represent different patterns of transmission. Were all cultural elements transmitted through the same channels—that is, conduits that spread all material—we would expect a single factor. Likewise, if certain cultural items were transmitted together, but this transmission was not based on content or interest, the factors should be inexplicable.

The clearest evidence for the existence of specialized conduits within a communcation network is the second factor (see table 7–3). The highest loadings on this factor are for the four heterosexual terms: *truth or dare, kiss or kill, getting to second base with a girl,* and *spin the bottle.* The transmission pattern for learning about these heterosexual items is different from that of the other items. The fourth factor is also clear, reflecting aggressive insults. The highest loadings are for *bite me, gaywad,* and *prange.* Calling a girl a *mutt* and saying *your royal Bohemian butt fucker, it's on fire* also have moderate loadings on this factor. *Doofy* and *dork,* two relatively innocuous insults, do not have high factor loadings. This apparently is a channel for aggressive insults; no noninsults load on this factor.

The fifth factor includes the nonaggressive nonsexual activities. All three items in this possible "residual" category load on this factor, indicating that perhaps this is a peer activity conduit (*buck,* however, doesn't reach our criterion level). *Egging a house* also loads on this factor; while *egging* is a physical activity like the other three items, it is also a prank. The other pranks do not have high factor loadings.

The other two factors are less clear. The first factor, the strongest factor, reflects the diffusion of *some* pranks. Of the eight pranks in the sample, four load highly on this factor: *giving a snuggie, funny phone calls, the Polish rope trick,* and *mooning.* The other pranks are not part of this conduit. Complicating the interpretation, calling someone a *dork* and *giving a buck* also load on this "prank" factor.

Factor three is difficult to categorize. Although both baseball terms load highly on it (a *Polish home run* and *being in the hole*), *doofy, mutt,* and *giving a swirly* also have high loadings. Rather

Table 7.3 Conduit Factor Analysis
(Varimax Rotated Factor Analysis)

	Factor 1	Factor 2	Factor 3	Factor 4	Factor 5
Spin the Bottle	.36	.47[a]	.04	.05	.16
Second Base	.03	.55[a]	.25	.14	−.02
Truth or Dare	.37	.70[a]	.02	.06	.17
Kiss or Kill	.15	.54[a]	.08	.07	.10
Gaywad	−.02	.01	.04	.49[a]	.05
Bite Me	.05	.21	.37	.46[a]	−.10
Doofy	.04	.01	.44[a]	.08	.06
Dork	.57[a]	.10	.30	.09	.08
Mutt	.07	.25	.49[a]	.25	.23
Prange	.24	.14	−.03	.53[a]	.05
Royal Bohemian	.13	.06	.03	.28	.13
Funny Phone Calls	.56[a]	.17	.11	.31	.18
Egging	.15	.37	.16	.10	.44[a]
Ding Dong Ditch	.11	.38	.10	.29	.18
Mooning	.57[a]	.27	.19	.33	.13
Snuggy	.52[a]	.12	.23	.10	.12
Swirly	.06	.20	.50[a]	.01	−.13
Polish Cannon	.11	.32	.18	.10	.27
Polish Rope Trick	.72[a]	.22	−.11	.01	−.04
In the Hole	.08	.00	.41[a]	−.02	.03
Polish Home Run	.09	.10	.44[a]	.01	.20
Buck	.61[a]	.11	.11	.01	.31
Hotbox	.43[a]	.11	.07	.17	.48[a]
Smear the Queer	.30	.28	.07	.16	.47[a]

[a]Above .40

than attempting to force some label onto this collection of cultural items, I admit my puzzlement.

Of the five factors, three are relatively clear and support the existence of specialized conduits in cultural transmission. A fourth factor may serve the same function, although this interpretation is tentative. Of course, stronger (or weaker) evidence might be found from a different set of variables or alternate categories. These categories, derived from my theoretical expectations, and not from a post hoc examination of the data, do suggest that some cultural traditions are disseminated along lines of interest. There appear to be differences in transmission patterns among preadolescent boys between sexual and aggressive material. This suggests a more complicated sense of preadolescent propriety than might otherwise be thought and a more complex and highly differentiated social network.

Structural Roles

A third way in which cultural information spreads within a social system is through individuals who perform particular structural roles in intergroup relations. These are individuals who are not part of these groups but have contacts with them. In terms of preadolescent lore, relatively many individuals have the potential to serve in this capacity. Preadolescents are processed by numerous adult and adolescent guardians; these guardians, such as teachers, may have access to the preadolescent for a period of time and subsequently take charge of a new set of preadolescents. Because of the nature of adult-child relations (see Fine and Glassner 1979), not all types of preadolescent lore can be transmitted in such situations, but some can be.

Camp counselors, for example, tell ghost stories and mildly off-color anecdotes for the amusement of their campers. In turn, preadolescents may teach this guardian some of their culture. If the camp counselor is with these campers for two weeks and then a new set of campers replaces them, the counselor may become a key linkage in the diffusion of preadolescent lore. Although he is not a full member of the group, his role allows for diffusion of lore. Unfortunately, little research has been systematically conducted on the role of the camp counselor (or similar role inhabitants) as the transmitter of cultural material. Sheldon Posen (1974; see Mechling 1984) has begun to study this phenomenon through an interesting analysis on the role of the prank and practical joke in summer camp, noting that the continuity of campers and counselors from one summer to the next allows for the continuation of camp traditions and the dissemination of these traditions within the camp. Posen claims that both campers and the staff are responsible for these traditions, and notes that, particularly in cases in which the prank was costly, extravagant, or gross, its memory is kept alive through oral recall. While the primary role obligation of counselors is not the diffusion of preadolescent cultural traditions, this is an indirect result of their multigroup contacts. These adolescents link groups that lack direct ties. Little League coaches, who work with the same boys over several seasons with 50 percent turnover each year and may coach other sports, also may spread preadolescent lore.

Media Diffusion

The fourth pattern is transmission through the mass media. Television, radio, and films each play a large role in children's lives, and the fact that the media are either national (as in the case of network television and films) or responding to national influences (as in the case of Top 40 Radio or local television programming) implies that the culture displayed by these outlets is relatively uniform. Many groups of preadolescents are simultaneously affected by a single communicator (or communicating group). The effects of a popular television program on children's culture should not be underestimated—as underlined by numerous references to the Fonz or Kojak during this research. One pair of friends named themselves Starsky and Hutch after the television characters. While I was conducting research, the film *The Bad News Bears* was distributed nationally. Boys frequently referred to the film to describe their experiences and so, a Hopewell boy challenged another boy invoking the film's memorable line: "Stick it where the sun doesn't shine." Another boy referred to one of Hopewell's teams as the Bad News Bears because of their lack of athletic skill. In the film the Bears improved to the point that they nearly won the league championship, but the *meaning* of the Bad News Bears in children's interaction is of a team filled with incompetents who curse and belch.

Jingles from television commercials and popular songs enter the culture of childhood through their frequent repetition on radio and television and provide children with a shared store of knowledge and common sources from which to create and transmit parodies (Opie and Opie 1959, 6–7, 91–92; Knapp and Knapp 1976, 162–66). Each local group takes the raw materials provided through the media and fashions them through interaction to fit the needs of members in their peer activities.

Audiences for media productions are not limited by age alone. These raw cultural elements will generally be viewed by other groups; however, the way in which this culture is used is a function of age and social status. In the case of *The Bad News Bears*, the insults in the film fit the preadolescent culture of aggressive insults, many of which have anal overtones. One might expect that the elements this age group selected from the film are strikingly different from those of their adult guardians. The film ostensibly is about the dangers of overcompetition and adult involvement in youth sports. Although accessible to all, media productions are not consumed by a random sample of the population but are selected on the basis of prior interests—interests that reveal the boundaries of the subculture.

These four types of cultural linkages or interlocks illustrate possible transmission mechanisms and together explain how a culture of childhood in American society is possible, even when geographical mobility is restricted and in the absence of child-sponsored media.

Identification

Those who study subcultures often ignore the emotional components of social life. From that perspective one might argue the analysis of the culture of childhood should be limited to "substantive" features—such as values, norms, behaviors, and artifacts. However, a discussion of these items alone misses a critical aspect of a subculture—that is, the ability of a person to see himself or herself as a member of a group or, in Mead's (1934) terms, as an "object of appropriation." The acquisition of a self-identity includes the development of self-indication (Blumer 1969), whereby the individual can view himself or herself as a member of a group, marginal, or an outsider.

Even within an age category, individuals have alternative views of the type of self they present and the cultural system with which they identify. Although I have presented the culture of childhood as uniform and homogeneous, there are considerable differences among groups of children as to what they know and what they believe is appropriate behavior—one feature that leads to childhood cliques. Even at preadolescence a boy finds himself with several cultural models available. These models are known by the preadolescents and discussed openly. For example, at one school in Bolton Park, kids are classified as to whether they are daredevils (kids who get into trouble), jocks, or burnies (burn-outs—preadolescents who smoke, drink, and use drugs). Most Little Leaguers consider themselves jocks and, like some older athletes, scorn the burnies (field notes, Bolton Park). Three boys who attended the local Bolton Park parochial school told me that in their school there are three groups of kids: rowdies, in-betweens, and goody-goodies (or Holy Joes)—not surprisingly all considered themselves to be in-betweens. Similar groupings were found in other schools. These distinctions caution against assuming the existence of a homogeneous children's culture and emphasize the importance of understanding the child's identification with his own group. Being part of any subcultural system requires motivation and identification with those who are members. Values, norms, behaviors, and artifacts constitute a subculture only if individuals see themselves as part of a community whose members give meaning to these "objects." Being classified in a particular age category is not by itself sufficient to predict cultural orientation.

Individuals, even during preadolescence, may identify with specific groups of which they are members or with the large social categories to which they belong (the subsociety). In terms of preadolescent identification the orientation tends to be directed toward the interacting group or institution (the team or group of friends and even, in some cases, the community). "Class" consciousness has not fully developed by this age, although it does as the child becomes an adolescent and begins to see himself explicitly as a member of that socially defined subgroup. During preadolescence children realize they are members of a subgroup, but identification is not explicit in that the rhetoric for talking about their age group as a specific group has not developed. Yet, the importance of belonging to an age cohort is implicit in the criticism that boys may receive for hanging around with others a few years older or younger. I noted that one sixth grader in Sanford Heights was roundly criticized by his peers for having a girlfriend in ninth grade. Even single-year age cohorts may be identified with because of school grade (and this identification is perhaps stronger than identification with the period of preadolescence as a whole, as when fifth and sixth graders are rivals).

Identification for preadolescents, as for adults, is situational; the child's orientation changes as a result of his social context. This may be related to the development of parent-peer cross-pressures that begin to develop at this period (Kohen-Raz 1971, 103), and become quite intense during adolescence (Brittain 1963). The child operates under two distinct normative orders, which become salient because (1) both have sanctioning power—the ability to give rewards and punishments, and (2) the child wishes to belong to both groups when situationally appropriate, and thus identifies with both peers and parents. The child can manage the dual identification with peers and parents without much difficulty except when both are present simultaneously and identification with each presupposes a different course of action. That preadolescents increasingly spend time with their peers has implications for the development of identification of oneself as a peer rather than as a family member. The role of peers is indicated by the time-budget study I conducted in Sanford Heights among twelve year olds shortly after the season. When I asked about the previous Saturday (after the season ended), the sample claimed to have spent an average of 4.4 hours with friends but only 3.8 hours with parents. While this is not a significant difference, it does suggest that these boys have moved from their parents' orbit. The changing activity patterns of children permit the development of a preadolescent subculture—a subculture that involves identification as well as shared content. The age segregation found in American society (Conger 1972) is part of this process in that, not only do children spend less time with their parents, but historically they have come to spend less time with all adults who might provide nonpeer identification.

The media and adults typically define preadolescence as a social category about which generalizations can be made; members of that age category come to think of themselves in relation to stereotypes offered by older members of the community. This identification with peers, sponsored in part by adults, leads preadolescents to adopt behavior patterns and artifacts defined as particular to their age group.

On the basis of shared cultural content among American preadolescents, the evidence of the existence of communication channels between different communities, the presence of identification with one's own age group, and the stereotypes by outsiders, one can speak of a preadolescent subculture. Although this subculture may not apply with equal force to all preadolescent boys, and may not involve a completely homogeneous core of knowledge for all who participate in it, some cultural elements seem to characterize preadolescents. The subculture does not refer to the age group itself but to the core of common knowledge—knowledge shared by participants in a childhood communications network, who recognize in themselves a community of interest.

8

Sport, Culture, and Preadolescence

As I write this conclusion, it is the beginning of baseball season in Minnesota. Preadolescents are emerging from their snowy cocoons to appear throughout our parks and fields with their bats, balls, and gloves. Something feels very right about seeing boys engage in this most American of pastimes. Hopefully, too, the setting of this analysis of preadolescent culture will seem apt. By emphasizing sport, I hope to have uncovered something of all culture; by describing preadolescent boys, I hope to have revealed something of all of us. The issues behind involvement in baseball and peer groups are not limited to preadolescents—or to males, or to Americans—although the forms that behaviors take are molded by circumstance. I have used the lens of interactionism to explore how people create meaning, behavior, and structure in those settings in which they find and place themselves. Although I focus on topics that might seem, on quick glance, "quirky" or "trivial," they reveal in their very smallness the play of emotions and concerns that reside in larger realms.

In this conclusion I shall briefly examine the several major themes of the book, restating my concerns and attempting to make explicit their generalizability. Specifically I describe (1) the development of the male sex role within and outside the world of baseball, (2) the process of socialization within Little League, (3) the status of preadolescent baseball as work and play, and (4) the creation and organization of cultures—both idiocultures and subcultures.

All this is part of the desire by preadolescent boys to be "men" in the "moral" sense of the term. I do not mean by this that preadolescents will behave as men do, but only that they select from among the repertoire of behaviors that they perceive that men (particularly media men and other role models) display. They select those behaviors that are congruent with their own needs for independence and separation from the world of girls and younger children. They must show themselves not to be a part of these protected classes. For this, the stereotyped role of the male (some of which is reflected in their coaches' demands) serves admirably. It is one of the most

185

distinctive features of male development at all ages that boys constantly feel the need to differentiate themselves from those who are female, weaker, and younger. This research represents a case study of this process in one age period and in a small number of settings.

Often students of sex roles have focused their attention on females. Those who have written about males typically have not conducted observational field research. This, of course, is ironic in that most social science research is conducted among males. Yet, such subjects are typically treated not as males, but as people. In contrast, much research on female groups explicitly recognizes that these subjects are people *and* women. As one concerned about the relationship between the sexes, I see this research imbalance as unfortunate. Obviously some of the material in chapter 5 (and elsewhere) will be deeply troubling to students of a fair and just social order. I hope that, as the bearer of "bad news," I might escape some of the traditional consequences of that role. At the very least my discussion should sensitize readers to the fact that there is a male sex role that is capable of being empirically observed and described. Only by being with the boys can we understand what it means for them to be mature. Our sons seem much more like Clint Eastwood than Alan Alda; more like Johnny Carson than Phil Donahue. Most males—of all ages—do.

Socialization

Almost everyone agrees that Little League baseball players are socialized; the question is, What do they learn—and how? I argue that the moral socialization that occurs in Little League baseball—and implicitly all moral socialization—is inherently problematic (see Stevenson 1975). Much situated moral teaching is rhetorical. I don't mean this socialization is "false," dishonest, or hypocritical. Rather, it is designed to persuade those to whom it is directed of its moral appropriateness, but it has only an uncertain relationship to the world that actors experience and the behavioral reality that an outside observer might see. For example, by talking about "hustle," coaches make claims about being able to depict the inner workings of the players' minds, and being able to judge what is limited by ability and what is limited by motivation. Likewise, sportmanship is grounded in moral expectations about presentation of self—expectations rarely stated explicitly. Even in similar techniques of socialization by the players themselves, boys rely upon implicit attributions of what others must be thinking. Moral socialization is always difficult in that it is designed to change not only hands and feet but hearts and minds.

The dynamics of moral socialization are generally similar from location to location, and there are few social settings in which some moral socialization does not occur—although the extent and content of this moral teaching varies. In all these cases persons must read into others what they think these others are feeling, and they will decide how they should be feeling. To do this, people need to take the role of the other: in this case not to know how they themselves should behave but to tell the other how to behave. Fortunately, people are rather good at figuring out what is going on in the minds of others (or at least so that others agree to their readings); so, more often than not, these challenges to moral propriety are not resisted. In Wittgenstein's terms, we express our prior knowledge of the conventional behaviors being used. We know the outward criteria for inner process (Wittgenstein 1968, para. 380).

This connection between inner and outer life allows for a wealth of moral comments in social interaction. Because of their impressionable subject pool and because of the didactic intentions of their parent organization, Little League baseball programs stress the moral nature of their teachings more than most, but all group activity reveals character through behavior. All interactants see themselves as potential moral barometers and enforce their own standards on others (even if, in some circumstances, these are standards of pluralism and nonintervention). Perhaps because the technical side of sport is typically seen as secondary, the moral component is given considerable weight—particularly outside the professional arena. Most people accept that sport should be teaching values, whereas few make this claim explicitly for mathematics.

Working, Playing

The relationship between work and play poses one of the most significant dilemmas in understanding sport. After all, sport is not the same as play. One thing that distinguishes sport and play, both classified as leisure activity, is that sport requires an outcome, and this outcome is based upon the competency of performance. How well one performs makes a crucial difference in sport, whereas in play such qualitative judgments are decidedly secondary. Goffman (1961) notes that fun is the only legitimate reason for playing games; yet, such an explanation is not wholly adequate for addressing the reasons why individuals engage in sports, especially team sports.

Agreeing to participate in sports involves making a commitment to the group and to the activity; that agreement is seen as providing a "contract" that should not be broken because of lack of "fun." Later, when these contracts become more formalized in adulthood, such is explicitly recognized (and little differentiates sport from work), but even in preadolescence participants believe that once one has committed oneself to play Little League baseball one should not quit, one should attend games and practices, and one should try as hard as possible during the game. Ideally one should constantly pay attention and be serious. While this is not always enforced (and thus some features of play are accorded to preadolescent sport), these values are widely held and point up the contrast between Little League and the voluntaristic characteristics of play.

Significantly, boys are frequently exhorted to "hustle" but rarely are they encouraged to "enjoy." Surely one reason for this is that boys "naturally" enjoy baseball, but also baseball is seen as something to be worked at for its long-term payoffs. "Good" and "bad" play are readily defined in terms of success or failure, wins and losses. The danger, some critics feel, is that the idea of "fun" shrinks to unimportance in contrast to the technical demands of the games. Likewise, competition may be transformed from a self-generated contest that is common in preadolescent informal activity to a task in which the end (victory) overwhelms the means of achieving that end. This process reflects the inherent ambiguity and ambivalence in our understanding of sport and suggests that the seemingly opposite categories of work and play will never be truly separate.

Throughout much human activity there is a strain between treating the activity as a moral requirement and as a purely voluntary activity that, when it isn't engrossing, can be put aside. Consider most occupations. Obviously in discussing occupations we consider activities that on prima facie grounds should be treated as work. Indeed, much occupational activity is work—it is serious, rationalized, and motivated by economic incentives. Yet, occupational roles are not without some aspects of play. First, work is never so structured that there isn't some leeway for "time-outs," for some occasions in which play is able to sneak into the corners of work. These are the informal moments (Fine 1986; Bradney 1957; Roy 1959–60; Swanson 1978; Nusbaum 1978). Workers always find time to "break away" from the formal requirements of their roles to engage in activities that give them pleasure. They oscillate between the demands of work and the pleasures of play. This same process characterizes Little League baseball. Attention is not devoted solely to the game itself but shifts according to the options at the moment. These shifts are not due entirely to the fact that we are dealing with pre-adolescents (although this surely does influence the attention span) but also to the human tendency to change one's focus and gain some autonomy over the conditions of one's activity. This change in focus seems essential to many types of human activity, both in public, so-cial settings, and also in private ones, where daydreaming can take the place of playful interaction.

A second way that play and work are integrated depends on breaking down the distinction between work and play. Work, for its part, need not be "painful." Some workers at some times—like the Little League players described here—do enjoy what they do. Fur-ther, they adopt a "playful" attitude toward it. That is, they infuse some measure of joy into their work, they transcend the formal rules of their activity, even when not breaking them. Work is in this sense "performance" (e.g., Abrahams 1978; Jones 1980), and perfor-mances occur in several ways. Performances need not be by rote but can be playful, spontaneous, joyous enactments within whatever rules are accepted. To attempt to constrain role performances by a set of rules is likely to be a misguided attempt at order and an in-effective one as well (Hilbert 1981). The ways in which one performs what one should perform are variable over time and among partici-pants, and in this way Little League baseball and other activities may be seen as containing elements of playlike and worklike orienta-tions to the displayed behaviors. In this way, too, there are analo-gies between the struggle of work and play found within Little League baseball and that which constrains people throughout the display of all roles.

The Threads of Culture

One of the threads running throughout this analysis, becoming explicit in chapters 6 and 7, is the process by which preadolescent culture—and by implication, all cultures—is created and becomes connected to a group. I have not attempted to do justice to every theory of culture that has been put forward. This is not a theoreti-cal treatise on culture but an empirical one; moreover, my analysis is grounded in the interactionist perspective, which paints culture in social-behavioral hues. Psychoanalysis, structuralism, Marxian thought, to name but three of the views I haven't dealt with, are brilliant syntheses but do not address what are, for me, the critical questions: How is culture *used* in groups, and how is it transmitted within a community?

Idioculture

How does culture (idioculture) enter small-group activity? I suggested five elements were necessary for a cultural element to enter the life of a group: that its components be *known*, that it be *usable*, *functional*, *appropriate* in terms of the status hierarchy in the group, and *triggered* by some experience. Groups that interact intensively over a long period of time and whose members have a sense of commitment toward each other are relatively likely to be able to create a strong and vibrant idioculture. Little League baseball teams often exemplify this sort of group, although, as I pointed out, some teams approximate this ideal more than others. Sports teams, with their emphasis on the socioemotional side of shared activity and with their clear and explicit task goals, seem particularly likely candidates to develop collective traditions and shared meanings.

However, if the existence of idiocultural traditions were only to be found on Little League baseball teams, the concept would have relatively little utility and robustness. I argue that this construct is applicable to all small groups of whatever type. Necessary for the creation of a common culture is a sense of shared direction, the coming together of lines of action. This means that those attributes of members and those events that happen to them collectively or individually become potentially relevant and meaningful for interactants. Perhaps more evident than the importance of idioculture for a sports team is its role in a family (Bossard and Boll 1950). All families establish traditions that serve to characterize them and to distinguish them from other families, and that direct their behavior in unique ways. Rather than just throwing up one's hands and proclaiming that differences between families are not susceptible to social-scientific analysis, we should attempt to gain a more effective handle on the establishment, change, and usage of culture within a family. This is the task I have set myself in studying Little League baseball teams. I put forth no lawful "generalizations"—only process and filtering mechanisms.

The concept of an idioculture or group culture serves as a *mediator* between (1) those external factors influencing a group and internal demographic/personality factors that constrain the behaviors of individuals, and (2) the outcomes of group interaction. I explore the role of shared meaning in group dynamics—suggesting the process by which structure is transformed into behavior. Too often groups have been portrayed as aggregations of persons who deal with each other in purely structural ways. The *content* of group interaction has often been ignored in the discussion of social dynamics. It is this crucial mediating role of content and meaning that I wish to reclaim for social psychology. I hope to do more than merely transform nomothetic analysis into idiographic description. The cultural traditions of a Little League baseball team are more than random items that just happen to be particular to the group: they are valuable social-scientific clues in their own right.

Subculture

There is a world beyond the small group. Culture spreads outside of its community of origin, lodging itself in numerous communities and spreading within them. I argue that a subsociety is comprised of numerous interlocking groups in which members identify themselves collectively as a meaningful social segment; a subculture is composed of those cultural traditions that flow through these social networks and that are perceived by members of the subsociety and by outsiders as being particularly characteristic of this social segment.

Admitting that these boundaries are somewhat vague, I argue that there does exist a preadolescent subculture, and that patterns of diffusion within it can profitably be seen in terms of social interlocks—linkages that connect portions of this subsociety. These interlocks—overlapping group memberships, acquaintanceship ties, structural roles, and mass-media diffusion—are characteristic of other social worlds, not just age-based subcultures. Housewives, for example, may have (or once have had) a subsociety based in similar dynamics. These women share various voluntary activities—bridge clubs, garden clubs, Junior League, PTA, etc.—in which they meet other like-minded women who live outside their immediate neighborhood. Since some of the groups are national, there is an opportunity for meeting others at great distances. Second, many of these women have acquaintances in other communities. Perhaps they have moved their domicile because of their husband's career, or they may know others through their kinship network or by remaining in touch with college friends. Others may be in structural roles for communicating information within this subsociety: beauty salon operators or Avon representatives may spread culture. Finally, housewives have access to a medium almost entirely their own (daytime television), which they—like preadolescents—don't control. Advertisers and network programmers recognize this and cater directly to this audience. Whether this particular subsociety of housewives still exists is an empirical question, but the type of analysis I have proposed is certainly applicable beyond preadolescents. We are each part of various socially and personally defined societies with their own traditions and values. Although a subculture will be more diffuse than an idioculture of a group that is characterized by face-to-face interaction, it is more definable than a national culture. If we understand culture as disseminated through social relationships, we can then examine these meaningful connections in order to understand the patterns and variations of tradition.

Coda

All research projects represent a beginning rather than an end. Every good study, however complete, is a "pilot" study in that it provides direction for additional research. The analytical lens I used for preadolescent sport and culture can be focused on all ages—and should be. A more explicit longitudinal project might allow for inferences about how the naivete of early childhood is transformed to the knowing sophistication of preadolescence or how the naivete of preadolescence is transformed into the knowing sophistication of adolescence, or how all this is transformed into adult male concerns, demonstrating the manifold ways in which the child is father to the man.

The theoretical concerns of this monograph focus on the sociology of culture in all kinds of groups. Culture content is never divorced from social-psychological and structural dynamics, although tracing the connections can be perplexing and incomplete. This realization has perhaps been heeded in the study of the world of fine art more than it has been in examining the cultural grounds of routine activity. Other cultural units need to be scrutinized with thoroughness and an emphasis on the social construction of meaning. Again, a more longitudinal study might capture some of the processes of change that I have only been able to hint at in this observational research. A focus on *sets* of groups that share members might also prove profitable (e.g., the personal connections among baseball teams, gangs, church groups, scout troops, and summer camps); so, too, would the study of groups that "barely" interact over distances (e.g., examining the group structure of Boy Scout jamborees). Obviously this research has not exhausted the topic, only the observer.

Ultimately my study is one of a particular social world. Little League, perhaps more than most settings, is a stage. Players and coaches perform, and through these performances they enact a wide range of emotions. These games are a nexus for much that is important in the life of a preadolescent boy. If we wish to understand these creatures of the dusk, we could do far worse than by examining this game that asks a boy to be both an adult and a child, controlled and uncontrollable.

Appendix 1:

The Effects of Little League Baseball

Perhaps in some future century an anthropologist will use Little League baseball as an example of the exotic child-rearing practices that American adults inflicted on their offspring. Such an anthropologist could readily find twentieth century parents and educators to agree. Throughout most of its nearly half-century, Little League baseball has been at the center of a maelstrom of criticism. The fact that the league has grown and prospered during this period indicates that the debate is by no means one-sided.

Critics of Little League baseball have been loud and vociferous, and they have had an impact on adults involved with the game, who occasionally seem defensive, and on those who vow never to let their children participate in such a quasi-militaristic organization. Despite the criticism of Little League baseball, the organization has not lacked vocal supporters, who have argued that Little League baseball has highly beneficial aspects. Little League Baseball, Incorporated, has recruited well-known public figures, including Walt Disney, Walter O'Malley, and J. Edgar Hoover, to sit on the executive committee. Just as Hall of Fame pitcher Robin Roberts has spoken out against Little League, other professional baseball figures such as Hall of Famer Bob Feller praise it extravagantly.

Roberts claims:

> There is a lot of pressure on these young people to do something that is unnatural for their age—so there will always be hollering and tremendous disappointment for most of the players. For acting their age, they are made to feel incompetent. This is the basic fault of Little League. . . . What would seem like a basic training ground for baseball often turns out to be a program of negative thoughts that only retards a young player (1975, 11)

Feller disagrees:

> Little Leagues not only foster friendships, develop coordination and good health habits in the boys, but they break down social barriers to make a more closely knit community. . . . No

one pays any attention to how much money the boy's father has, or his social standing. . . . Where else is there a more practical training for democracy? (Feller with Lebovitz, 1956, 80–81)

Claims for Little League Baseball

Five major benefits of Little League baseball are proposed by supporters: (1) Little League reduces delinquency; (2) Little League promotes tolerance; (3) Little League teaches baseball skills and provides a regular program of exercise; (4) Little League has psychological benefits for children, particularly in the area of self-esteem; and (5) Little League has social benefits for children, particularly in promoting leadership. I shall examine the evidence for each of these assertions before turning to the criticisms of Little League.

Little League Reduces Delinquency

J. Edgar Hoover once claimed that Little League baseball would be the greatest deterrent to crime in American history (Ralbovsky 1973, pt. 3, 1). While others are not as expansive as the late G-man, Hoover was not alone in his belief. The Williamsport, Pennsylvania, police found that the expansion of Little League in their community occurred simultaneously with a drop in the juvenile crime rate (see also DeSantis 1953, 189–90). Although crime data have not been systematically analyzed, coaches concur in this assessment and point to the fact that Little League provides boys with a constructive activity to fill their free time:

> The boys that participate in sports usually are not the boys that are having a lot of other problems. Now they may not be very good, but they're active. They're tired at night; they use their energies competitively in that they learn good sportsmanship; it's gotta help their character. . . . The more time we can get these boys and girls involved into sports is that much time they're not thinking of doing something else. You gotta keep their little minds busy (coach interview, Bolton Park).

The belief that youth sports keep children out of trouble by keeping them off the street (Watson 1973, 102) was once widely accepted by professional criminologists and social workers (Thrasher 1927; see Berryman 1975). Evidence to support or refute the causal assertion is difficult to find, although in particular instances a care-

fully thought-out sports program can have a positive effect (Yablonsky 1962). Data do suggest that athletes are less likely to be
delinquent than nonathletes (Schafer 1969; Landers and Landers
1978), but whether this is due to selection or the moral elevation of
sport is not clear. While the rate of delinquency may be lower for
athletes, Little League baseball is clearly no panacea. The existence
of such a belief does suggest American values about athletics. Edwards (1973) and Ogilvie and Tutko (1971) suggest that rather than
athletics building character, the causal relationship may be reversed. They suggest that sports do not build character, but that
the selection process of sport may exclude children who manifest
undesirable moral characteristics.

Little League Increases Tolerance

Former representative William Cahill (R-N.J.) once told the House
of Representatives that Little League baseball could reduce prejudice: "What better medium for improving race relations in the
United States and developing better international relationships
through the world, than this great sport of baseball played as it is
under the ideal conditions prescribed by Little League baseball"
(Ralbovsky 1974, 54–55).

Despite a lack of ethnic contact elsewhere, Winoque Indian boys
and white boys on the Maine–New Brunswick border played Little
League harmoniously. Even in the South, Little League could overcome some racial boundaries—as in Harlingen, Texas. Harlingen,
like all Texas during the 1950s, was segregated along racial lines. At
one Little League practice in 1953, a black youngster appeared,
wishing to play on the First Methodist Church team. The church,
not willing to make this moral decision on its own, took the problem
to the league, which decreed that the black youngster (and a few
other blacks) could practice with the league. Despite threats from
irate whites, one black youngster was chosen for a team and played
without incident (Redmond 1954).

Little League, Incorporated, is on record as supporting equal access to teams for all males (and now females as well) regardless of
background. As early as the 1950s, the Little League charter stated
that the league is "for the promotion of sportsmanship and the development of character among boys of the community without regard to race, creed or color" (Redmond 1954, 175). With an emphasis on team cooperation, shared goals of team members, status
based largely on ability, and institutional support from the league
organization, Little League baseball meets the conditions postu-

lated by Allport (1954) for successful racial contact, at least in theory. The practical difficulty is that, because of residential segregation, relatively little economic and racial diversity exists in most suburban communities. Of the forty-two Little League baseball teams studied, only four had any black players. While no racial epithets were overheard on these four teams, players on rival teams revealed considerable racial prejudice (see chapter 6). An increase in tolerance, while a potential benefit of Little League, probably is negligible in most leagues, whereas team competition may exacerbate prejudice in some cases.

Little League Teaches Athletic Skills and Provides Exercise

It is hard to argue that Little League—teaching the mechanics of baseball—does not provide youngsters with regular exercise. The main criticism comes from those such as Robin Roberts who argue that preadolescence is too young to learn specific baseball skills, but even he accepts the legitimacy of *some* athletic training at this age. Even a casual observer can recognize that Little Leaguers are better ball players by the end of the season than they had been when the season began, and this improvement is not only a result of physical maturation. Some coaches impart fairly sophisticated skills, such as hook slides, suicide bunts, taking pitches, and the finer nuances of baserunning. Many former Little Leaguers claim that the experience was valuable for teaching them the basic skills of the game, although Little League is also the beginning of a severe selection process that eliminates boys less able athletically from formal sports participation. Despite the fact that participants in Little League do not represent a random sample of preadolescent males, and thus Little Leaguers are better players than those not involved, observation convinces me that Little League is successful in teaching basic athletic skills. This is the clearest benefit of Little League baseball, in my opinion. However, both proponents and critics see Little League as far more than a baseball program, and in terms of the moral and psychological effects of Little League the debate rages.

Little League Has Psychological Benefits for Players

There is more evidence for the proposition that Little League baseball has positive psychological effects than for the counterassertion that Little League injures children psychologically, and so I include this topic as a proposed benefit of Little League. The major studies on this issue are inconclusive about long-term effects of Little League baseball on preadolescents. This is perhaps not surprising, because, despite the intensity of the debate, Little League participation covers no more than ten hours a week for only three months. Only a remarkable program could have dramatic permanent effects in that time.

Individual parents do conclude that the league has had considerable effects on their offspring. For example, one Hopewell parent commented, "My son reaped huge benefits from participation. I noticed benefits in buildup of self-concept and attitudes of caring and cooperation with teammates" (mother of eleven-year-old). Unfortunately research findings do not match the certainty of this parental assessment.

Seymour (1956) compared matched groups of boys aged ten to twelve who either had been involved in Little League baseball or had not been involved. He found little difference in the number of problems expressed by the two samples. There was also little difference between the samples on personality measures, with the exception that Little League participants scored higher on leadership and on a sociometric measure. However, these differences were found *prior* to the season as well as in the postseason measures. Although there were indications that participants entered the program more successful on some measures of personality, these differences did not increase during the season, nor did other differences appear.

Dickie (1966) compared a group of Little League players with a sample of nonparticipants using the California Test of Personality and found no significant differences between players and nonparticipants on a total adjustment score either before or after the season. He did note a slight tendency for Little Leaguers to show more improvement on this test during the course of the season. However, problems of sampling and a substantial attrition rate make the results highly speculative. Research by Brugel (1972) indicates that Little League baseball does not affect the self-concept of eight- and nine-year-old Little League participants as compared to nonparticipants, although eight-year-old participants did significantly improve their self-concept scores over the season.

Most studies that find a difference between participants and nonparticipants do not use a pretest/posttest design, and as a result it is impossible to tell whether differences are due to characteristics of the sample, the effects of the program, or some other factor. Skubic (1956) found that players do better in school, possess greater motor skills, and are better adjusted socially and emotionally than nonparticipants. Salz (1957) examined three groups of preadolescent males: the winners of the Little League World Series the previous year,

players on a team that did not win a championship, and nonparticipants. He found that the Little League champions were somewhat
superior to the other Little League players on a number of measures and that both groups of players scored distinctly higher than
nonparticipants on many of the measures, including schoolwork, responsibility, sociometric measures, and friendliness. The boys on
the championship team also scored higher than the nonparticipants
on measures of cooperation, integrity, community relations, family
relations, and total social adjustment. While Salz could not claim
that Little League caused these effects, he felt confident in claiming
that Little League was not detrimental to development.

In 1962–63, the Little League organization itself conducted a
study involving 1,300 physicians who were parents of Little Leaguers. One question asked how Little League baseball affected
their son's emotional adjustment. Sixty-four percent claimed Little
League had a favorable effect; 33 percent claimed the league had no
significant effect; and only 3 percent noticed a negative effect on
emotional adjustment. Only 4 percent of the doctors reported that
their sons developed extreme aggressiveness because of Little
League; another 6 percent claimed that aggressiveness was "sometimes" a problem. Fully 94 percent of the doctor-fathers felt that
Little League was beneficial to their children. These findings are
consistent with studies of sports participation in schools (Powers
1955; Biddulph 1954), although cause and effect are unclear.

Most claims that Little League baseball produces undesirable
side effects are based on individual instances. Some children do find
Little League traumatic. For example, one boy in Hopewell could
not tolerate the pressures of competition, and when these pressures
were compounded by a minor head injury, he decided to quit baseball. However, I know of no systematic research study that has
shown any harmful psychological side effects of Little League. On
the basis of my observations, I suspect that there are two types
of players for whom Little League may have particularly strong
effects—*either* positive or negative: the boy who has difficulty controlling aggression and the shy child. The specific effects of Little
League appear to result from several factors: the success of the
team, the attitude of the coach, and the composition of the team. In
those instances in which the league exacerbated aggression, the
situation often involved (1) a boy not fully accepted by his peers (or
at least not a leader among them), (2) on a team that was not playing
as well as it was expected to, and (3) with a coach who was unable to
find an appropriate outlet for the player's aggression and unwilling

to take effective disciplinary action to prevent future outbreaks. In four of the five clear instances of this problem, the player was one of the better players on the team but not the best, and as a result resented the team leader. In several other instances, players with similar problems were helped. In three of the clearest instances of positive effects, the coach explicitly or implicitly made the boy team leader, and so the boy was able to redirect his aggression. This tactic is doomed to failure if the boy is not a superior ball player, as others will not accept his authority. The chemistry of a Little League baseball team is complicated and difficult to specify; however, a sensitive coach, knowing his players, may use them as resources in developing the character of his players.

The Little League experience may also be particularly significant for shy, withdrawn boys. Generally these boys are not among the better players, and some quit before the season's end or only show up sporadically. Coaches may forget the boy who causes no trouble while all around are riotous. Often this boy is suffering from nothing more serious than a problem in his athletic self-confidence, and this can usually be resolved by placing the player in the starting lineup occasionally and giving him encouragement. Cheering from teammates can be helpful, although insults can be devastating and can lead to feelings of failure. Finally, if the boy does have some talent, and if sparks of his talent occur at critical times, successful social integration is possible. While Brugel (1972) is probably correct that Little League baseball has no general effects on self-image, in particular cases it may have dramatic consequences.

Although Little League cannot hope to produce dramatic changes in most participants, a sensitively run sport program can provide a congenial environment in which such changes are fostered. On the basis of my research and that of others, it is not possible to say that Little League has a substantial positive effect on players; however, there are positive outcomes for some players. Further, there is no systematic evidence that Little League has harmful effects on personality.

Little League Has Social Benefits

Proponents of Little League baseball argue that the program improves the leadership abilities of children, makes them more popular, and strengthens the relationship between fathers and sons. Little League is described as a method of inculcating "constructive living" (McConnell 1960). However, once again little evidence exists that these desirable outcomes are produced by Little League, although there is some evidence that participants have more leadership ability and are better liked than nonparticipants.

Leadership Seymour (1956) indicates that teachers rate Little Leaguers as displaying more leadership than nonparticipants— both prior to and after the league season. In addition, the *increase* in participants' scores was significantly greater than the change in the scores of nonparticipants. However, traits that often are associated with leadership, such as cooperation, social consciousness, and responsibility, did not show similar effects. Salz (1957) discovered that Little League champions scored significantly higher than did nonplayers on a measure of leadership, but there was no difference between nonchampionship players and nonplayers. This study did not measure leadership before the season, and since boys on the championship team may have been chosen precisely because they had displayed leadership, causal inferences are not warranted. It is no doubt true that organized sports do sharpen the leadership skills of certain individuals, particularly those with athletic skills (see Tryon 1939; also Reany 1914; Cowell and Ismail 1962; Kleiber 1978); however, organized sports may also teach some children how to be followers and passive. Perhaps Little League trains boys to adapt to several positions within an organizational hierarchy—both of leadership and of being dominated.

Popularity Supporters of Little League claim that players are better able to make friends than nonparticipants. Athletes, at least in childhood, do receive higher sociometric ratings than nonathletes, although again the direction of cause and effect is uncertain. Seymour (1956) found that Little League participants received higher social acceptance scores from both boys and girls than did nonparticipants. However, this difference occurred both before and after the season, and changes in social acceptance during the season were not significantly different for the two groups. Salz (1957) discovered that Little League champions received higher sociometric ratings than regular players, who in turn received higher ratings than nonparticipants. Several other researchers, although not studying Little League specifically, have compiled evidence that athletic children are better liked than nonathletes (Hardy 1937; Cowell and Ismail 1962; Flowtow 1946; Buchanan, Blankenbaker and Cotton 1976).

One explanation for this phenomenon is that boys playing team sports have a greater opportunity to meet peers. Although this social-contact hypothesis probably explains some of the difference, it does not explain the entire effect, particularly the higher ratings given to male athletes by girls (in Seymour's study). Several additional factors may be operating. First, as noted above, there is some evidence that athletes are more physically, emotionally, and socially mature than nonplayers. Second, athletes may be known to others to a greater extent than nonplayers, through reputation if not by direct contact. Third, athletes because of their personal attributes may be in a better position to provide rewards to others, a feature of children's interaction that leads to attraction (Hartup, Charlesworth, and Glaser, 1967). Fourth, being an athlete in American society is a valued status, and nonatheletes may wish to associate themselves with these "culture heroes."

Father-son contact Little systematic reserach supports the belief that Little League brings fathers and sons together. Mostly one finds personal accounts (e.g., Voigt 1974a). Bob Feller comments: "Little League is fostering the healthiest kind of father-son relationship. In baseball, a father and son can meet on a common ground from which blooms companionship, respect and real love" (Feller with Lebovitz 1956, 81). Dickie (1966, 44) demonstrated that a player's total adjustment score on the California Test of Personality was positively correlated with parental attendance at Little League games, although here again the direction of causality is uncertain.

Parents in two Illinois leagues (one middle class and one working class) were asked what they felt they gained from attending their son's games: 34.5 percent named the pleasure in observing their sons play baseball (Watson 1974). Of the parental sample, 31.3 percent claimed to have attended every game, 42.7 percent attended most games, and only 5.3 percent did not attend at all. In Hopewell I asked parents after the season to estimate how many of the fourteen games they had attended. Fathers on average attended 9.4 games, and mothers attended 10.3 games. Much as Watson found, 31.8 percent attended all games and 3.5 percent did not attend any games. However, these figures do not indicate how children react to the presence of their parents. In the in-depth interviews in Sanford Heights and Bolton Park, I asked fifty-one players three questions related to the role of parents in Little League:

1. Do you think that parents sometimes take Little League baseball too seriously and force their kids to play?
2. Was this true of your parents?
3. Do you like having your parents come to watch you play?

Since the results from the two leagues did not differ significantly, only combined figures will be given. As is often the case, players felt that pushy, competitive parents belonged to other children. Seventy-four percent believed at least some parents take Little League too seriously and force their children to play, but only 8 percent felt this applied to their own parents. Eight-eight percent claimed they liked having their parents watch them play. Only four children (8 percent) preferred not to have their parents present.[1] While these data do not directly address the question of whether Little League promotes parent-child interaction, they do suggest that parents and children relate on a friendly basis.

There is no evidence that Little League baseball widens the gap between parents and children, although such may happen if an incompetent father coaches his son, or if the son is surly and hostile. Little League seems conducive to positive interaction in that it provides for a shared "universe of discourse" for the family. Watson (1973, 261–63) argues that Little League effectively socializes the parents to the child's world, a world to which they might not ordinarily be exposed. While it is unfortunate that one needs to resort to organizational structures to build bridges among family members, such is the pattern of age segregation in American society.

Criticisms of Little League Baseball

Having described some of the proposed benefits of Little League, I now examine six complaints of those who doubt the effectiveness of the organization and the validity of its mission: (1) Little League causes physical injuries; (2) Little League is too competitive; (3) coaches are unqualified; (4) parents as spectators destroy the game; (5) Little League exploits players; and (6) games organized by adults do not permit children to structure their own leisure.

Little League is Physically Dangerous

One of the most fearful arguments for league officials is that the games are dangerous. If true, this claim would negate a fundamental goal of Little League: physical fitness. My discussion is divided into two parts: short-term, "surface" injuries and long-term, "hidden" injuries.

Not even the harshest critics of Little League advocate that children not play baseball, despite the risk of injury. If Little League did not exist, children would play baseball outside the supervision of adults and would probably suffer more injuries than now. The national headquarters staff has made a concerted effort to make the game as safe as possible, claiming a better safety record than any other youth athletic program in the world, and justifiably points with pride to the Little League tradition of physiological research and equipment innovation. Injuries are rather rare and typically not serious (see Hale 1967, cited in Yablosky and Brower 1979, 159).

The chronic effects of Little League are more difficult to assess; some critics have argued that organized athletics for preadolescents are damaging because bones, cartilage, joints, ribs, and muscles are not sufficiently developed (Bucher 1954; Michener 1976; Zinser 1979). Particular attention has been given to a condition known as "Little League elbow" (DeHaven 1976, 65), or epiphyseal injury, a stress on the still-growing bone ends around a pitcher's elbow. For nonphysiologists this debate is quite complex; estimates of the frequency of this condition range from 90 percent to 5 percent (e.g., Larson, Singer, and Bergstrom 1976; Cahill, Tullos, and Fain 1974; Adams, 1965). Most recent medical findings suggest that the danger is not as great as once thought (Caldwell 1977), and many orthopedic surgeons believe that the Little League pitching regulations are appropriate (a maximum of six innings each week with three days' rest if the boy had pitched more than three innings in a game).

The real problem with "Little League elbow" is not medical but sociological. While the Little League rules are adequate in themselves, there is nothing to prevent a child from playing on other teams, practicing with his father, and pitching in informal games with friends. As a result, stresses on the preadolescent's arm are magnified. Further, boys typically regard the curve ball as the most prestigious pitch, not knowing or caring about the special stresses it places on their arms. Coaches have difficulty convincing players not to throw curve balls. Because the deliberate curve is difficult to spot at this age, boys sometimes deny throwing it, while continuing to— winning games and gaining peer status. Even when players heed the warnings of coaches in the Little League game, they may attempt to perfect the curve with friends. Not until the "social meaning" of the curve ball is altered will the problem of "Little League elbow" be solved.

Little League Is Too Competitive

If one had to describe the central core of criticism of Little League, one would immediately focus on competition. Whether competition for preadolescents is healthy is the central question of this debate (see Scott 1953; Anderson 1953). However, the effects of competition result from how it is defined by participants.

Critics cite horror stories of the effects of excessive competition. Children do—at times—cry when they have not lived up to their own expectations and those of peers or parents. On other occasions children take out their aggressions on adults—the umpire or coach. One tournament game between the Riverdale Tigers and the Bolton Park Astros was in the top of the sixth inning with Bolton Park behind 1–0 when one of these incidents occurred. After getting the first Bolton Park batter out, the Tiger pitcher walked the next batter on what he apparently considered a strike. At this point the pitcher became angry at the umpire and gave him "the finger." While the Astro players remained quiet, their adult coaches yelled that the umpire should throw the boy out of the game for unsportsmanlike conduct. After a few moments the umpire did remove the boy from the game. At this the pitcher, who was calming down after his moment of defiance, became furious and through his tears cried, "Every one of them fucking umps is against me. . . . I'm too good for them." Despite an attempt by his coach to quiet him, he ran from the field. This situation is atypical, a function of the pressures of tournament play on this preadolescent.[2] However, those who criticize Little League claim that this incident differed only in degree from many others. Chicago pediatrician John L. Reicher summarized the critics' views on Little League competition:

> Strong emotional reactions are too often engendered by high-pressure competitive games. Hero worship of the star, the sense of failure in the boy who does not make the team or who fails to make the crucial play, the obvious disappointment of the parent when the boy fails, or the excessive pride and praise when he wins, the apparent difference in social acceptance between the winners and the losers—all these can have a profound effect on a child's emotional development and social adjustment (McNeil 1961, 80; see also American Academy of Pediatrics 1956).

Critics cite the overstatements of Vince Lombardi ("Winning is not everything. It is the only thing") and George Allen ("Every time you win, you're reborn; when you lose, you die a little.") Despite these fears, there seem to be no differences in social adjustment between boys on winning and losing teams (Dickie 1966, 43).

Other adults support competition for children, noting that when they become adults they will have to compete and it is valuable for them to start early. By the age of six, children have learned to compete (Sherif 1976). In the Little League survey of doctor-parents, only 10 percent felt that children played under excessive emotional pressure; 22 percent felt that this occurred occasionally, and 68 percent felt their children were not under excessive emotional pressure. Several studies suggest that whatever the effects of the pressure, they are only transitory (Hanson 1967; Skubic 1955). I asked players and parents in Sanford Heights and Bolton Park about their attitudes toward competition and winning. Players were asked, "Do you think Little League in general is too competitive?" Parents were asked:

1. In general, would you say that coaches overemphasize winning, underemphasize winning, or are just about right?
2. On the team your son played on this year, would you say that the coaches overemphasized winning, underemphasized winning, or were just about right?

Four randomly selected twelve year olds from each team were interviewed;[3] one mother and one father (of different children) were randomly selected as the parental sample from each team.

Although the opinions of participants are not the only measure by which to judge competition, they indicate its perceived extent. As can be seen in table A.1.1, over three quarters of the sample believed that Little League is not too competitive. Sanford Heights, the lower-middle-class league, is seen as somewhat more competitive than Bolton Park, the upper-middle-class league ($X^2 = 4.76$, $df = 1$, $p<.05$, combining "yes" and "somewhat" versus "no"). This statistic does not address whether the difference is due to the circumstance that the upper-middle-class league is less competitive, or that the lower-middle-class boys are more sensitive to the negative effects of competition. My sense is that the former explanation is probably more accurate. Coaches in Sanford Heights emphasized competition as a virtue more than coaches in Bolton Park (see also Watson 1977).

Parents also are generally satisfied with the emphasis placed on winning (see table A.1.2). Most parents in both leagues felt that Little League in general and their son's coach in particular did not overemphasize winning. Respondents are likely to be more satisfied with their son's team than with Little League in general. As above, the lower-middle-class league is described as more oriented towards winning than the upper-middle-class league, although the difference is not statistically significant.

My orientation to competition follows that of Sherif (1976, 18): "The participants [in the debate over competition] almost always start with preconceived judgments about the effects of competition that no amount of talk can alter. To some, competition is regarded as

Table A.1.1 Is Little League Too Competitive?

	Yes		No		Sometime	
Bolton Park						
Players on successful teams	0	0	11	92	1	8
Players on unsuccessful teams	0	0	11	92	1	8
Total	0	0	22	92	2	8
Sanford Heights						
Players on successful teams	1	7	11	73	3	20
Players on unsuccessful teams	4	33	7	58	1	8
Total	5	19	18	66	4	15
Total		10		78		12

Notes: Question asked: Do you think Little League in general is too competitive?
Successful teams are those with season winning percentage over .500; unsuccessful teams are those with winning percentages below .500.

Table A.1.2 Parental Views on Coaches' Emphasis on Winning

	Bolton Park		Sanford Heights		Total
	N	%	N	%	%
In General					
Overemphasize winning	1	8	5	36	23
Emphasize winning just right	9	75	8	57	65
Underemphasize winning	1	8	0	0	4
Don't know	1	8	1	7	8
On Son's Team					
Overemphasize winning	0	0	3	21	12
Emphasize winning just right	10	83	9	64	73
Underemphasize winning	2	17	0	0	8
Don't know	0	0	2	14	8

natural, healthy, and essential for building character. To others competition is regarded as harmful, psychologically injurious, and detrimental to cooperative activity, which is endowed with all manner of beneficial effects and seen as the highest state of human relations." This suggests the debate over competition is essentially ideological, not empirical, and that "competition" must be examined in context. In addition to the psychological significance of competition, its interactional significance must also be considered. In other words, it is not the game per se that affects children, but the way the child's athletic significant others (the coaches, parents, and fellow players) define the game.[4] According to the questionnaire results and from my observations, competition is not a major problem.

Coaches Are Unqualified to Teach Youngsters

Several Little League critics have charged that most coaches are unfit for their responsibilities. This charge is particularly worrisome in that in most leagues coaches are unpaid and unscreened volunteers. Enough "horror stories" about coaches can be cited to prevent our dismissing this charge, and these examples led one writer to claim that newspapers have ignored the "child abuse" in Little League (Ralbovsky 1974, 79). Coaches have been accused of fighting with each other (Ma, It's Only a Game, 1961), attempting to "buy" star players (Baby Bonus Babies, 1958), playing illegal players (*Sports Illustrated* 1969), attacking parents and umpires with baseball bats (Ralbovsky 1974, 67, 72), and "throwing" baseball games (Cohane 1961).

One successful businessman presented an ingenious, although incorrect, explanation for the failure of Little League coaches: "The people who run Little League and PONY League and all the rest of them are usually on the lowest part of the sociological curve, guys who can't quite make it in their business, married, or social life. So they take it out on the kids of everybody else" (quoted in Brosnan 1963, 120). Walter Matthau brilliantly depicted this stereotype in his portrayal of coach Morris Buttermaker in *Bad News Bears* (Woodley 1976). This view reflects the class bias in the debate over Little League—with highly educated, socially liberal critics attacking athletically inclined traditionalists. While Little League coaches may have slightly lower SEI statuses than the parents of the boys that they coach, this does not suggest that they are deficient in their public or private lives.

The average head coach (in Bolton Park and Sanford Heights) is forty-one years old, with four children and three years of schooling beyond high school, typically in a trade school or technical institute. In the upper-middle-class league in Bolton Park the head coaches were an insurance broker, a truck driver, an internal-audit manager, a transportation consultant, a manufacturer's representative, and a dentist. In lower-middle-class Sanford Heights, the coaches were an engineer, an oil salesman, a real estate agent, a mover, a mechanical estimator, a mail carrier, and a welding instructor. In Hopewell the sample of ten father/coaches had an average Duncan SEI rating of 53.5, compared to a rating of 60.2 for noninvolved fathers, a nonsignificant difference. In the more homogeneous Bolton Park community there was no difference between coaches and parents.[5] Comparing the fourteen father/coaches with the fifty-six noninvolved fathers revealed virtually identical SEI scores (69.5 versus 68.7).[6]

Some critics note that most coaches lack formal training, and in none of the leagues studied was there any systematic attempt to train coaches to deal with the problems of children. Most coaches are parents who have no formal instruction in child development, and this may be seen as a significant problem: "The talent required in managing a team of boys of varying ability, with all the physiologic and psychologic problems that this entails, is beyond that of many parents, even with the best of intentions" (Beleaguered Little Leaguers 1964, 1015).

Although there is little training by local leagues, many coaches do work in other youth programs. An early study claimed that 65 percent had some training in youth work (Solomon 1953, 172). Twelve of the thirteen managers in Sanford Heights and Bolton Park had had experience with other youth groups—Cub Scouts and other sports teams. Thus, the father-coaches are not totally inexperienced, although most are not professionally trained.[7] Studies indicate that a properly organized preseason training program for coaches seems valuable in providing an opportunity to discuss appropriate methods for implementing Little League guidelines and relating to children. Children who played for coaches with such training showed increased self-esteem compared to a group who played under coaches with no such training (Smith, Smoll and Curtis 1979; Smoll and Smith 1981).

Despite the coaches' lack of formal training, most players and parents are satisfied with the adult leadership. In the Bolton Park parental sample (twelve parents), 82 percent of the noncoaching parents approved of their son's coach. In Sanford Heights, 92 percent of the fourteen parents approved. Among players there was also considerable support for the coaches. In Bolton Park 88 percent of the twenty-four players were satisfied with their coach, another 4 percent had mixed views, and 8 percent were dissatisfied (this latter 12 percent all had the same coach). In Sanford Heights players expressed greater dissatisfaction; still, 56 percent of the twenty-seven players interviewed were satisfied, 19 percent had mixed views, and another 27 percent were not satisfied—all four respondents from one of the seven teams criticized their adult leadership.[8] In my own judgment only 2 of the nearly 100 coaches I observed could seriously be faulted as unqualified to work with children (in my opinion), although many could have improved their coaching skills.

Case one: The screamer. Felix Dimaggio, a reasonable man off the diamond, as an assistant coach could not control his anger and regularly berated his players for minor errors. He seemed at times to represent the worst stereotype of the Little League coach. His insults seemed untinged by fondness: "If you miss many balls, I'm gonna put my foot on your body," or "You're playing like a puppy dog. Play baseball!" Once after a one-run defeat he told his team scornfully, "You can't go any lower." The comments in and of themselves are not unusual in terms of volume or even content; what was disturbing was that the criticism was continuous and the tone hostile. While this may not have represented his beliefs, he *appeared* to dislike the children he was coaching. His behavior became so disruptive that in the middle of the season, league officials asked him not to coach.

Case Two: The hypocrite. Al Wingate publicly claimed to have little interest in winning, telling me on one occasion that "after all, it's only a game; it's more important that the kids get a good workout." However, these statements contrast with a man intensely devoted to winning at any cost. His public smile might deceive those who did not hear him sarcastically tell a twelve-year-old opponent: "Where did you come from, under a rock?!" On another occasion he threatened a twelve-year-old opponent, who reported the following story:

> Last year me and some other kids, we weren't playing that night, but his team was. We were fooling around, and he goes "Come on, get out of there." So we were playing there, right? And he goes to me, "Come here. . . . If you want to still be playing Little League, you will get out of here, 'cause I can get your uniform and make you not play again" (transcribed interview).

Particularly serious was the double-bind or incongruity between his verbal content and paralinguistic cues. He stood behind his team's bench talking with his assistant coach, berating a boy for a lack of ability; yet when the boy came within hearing range Al would heartily congratulate him on his effort. This might not have been bad, except that the original comment had been made within earshot of other players, who learned they could not trust his praise.

Preadolescents, who face a variety of teachers and other caretakers, are remarkably resilient. On the basis of available evidence, there does not seem to be a greater number of unqualified Little League coaches than one might find in any random sample of child caretakers. However, local leagues should place greater emphasis on the recruitment of coaches by examining temperament, if not formal training. Although most coaches are good role models, this does not excuse a lack of diligence in recruitment and training.

Parents Are a Harmful Influence on Little League

Parents have been accused of ruining preadolescent sports. One enthusiastic journalist, letting his typewriter get the best of him, claimed, "the Little League parent . . . of whatever sex, is the most obnoxious phenomenon of our time" (Sumner, 1978, 10). In fact, some parents do become overly involved in the game:

> [A former Little Leaguer] recalls: "One April day, my mother handed me a paper bag, containing two bologna sandwiches, an orange, and some cookies, and said, 'If you don't get into Little League, you better not come home for supper'" (Robbins 1969; 10).

In a game between the league-leading Phils and the challenging Cards, a father of one of the Phils gets excited at the umpire's call. The coach of the Phils had (unintentionally) called time out while the ball was still in play, to which the coach of the Cards objected. The umpire ruled in favor of the Phils in that the time out was accepted. This father, who appeared to be drunk, did not realize that the decision was in favor of his son's team and began to scream at the base umpire: "What's the matter with that stupid ass out there! I'm not dumb. I know what's going on!" He threatens to "get" the base umpire. At this point the home-plate umpire threatens to eject him from the park area if he doesn't control himself, and the incident ends (field notes, Sanford Heights).

The empirical question, never to be answered to everyone's satisfaction, is the extent of parental discipline problems. One indicator is the frequency with which coaches report problems with parents. All thirteen coaches in Bolton Park and Sanford Heights were asked, "Have you ever had problems with parents while you have been managing?"

Coaches who answered affirmatively were then asked to enumerate and describe these problems. Six of the thirteen coaches answered affirmatively, mentioning ten parental problems. Most of these involved parents who overvalued their son's abilities. As might be expected, coaches were always vindicated in their own eyes, and these stories were told as moral exemplars of proper parent-coach relations. These thirteen coaches had spent a total of sixty-three years in Little League, and if the figure of ten incidents is accurate, there was an average of one parental incident every 6.3 coaching years. Obviously this figure is low: coaches wish to make it appear that they get along with parents; what constitutes a "problem" varies from coach to coach; and those coaches with the most parental problems are unlikely to continue. All that we can deduce from these responses is that coaches do not claim that their relations with parents are a major problem.

In the parental interview, I asked about attitudes toward other parents. As I noted in chapter 1, results from both Sanford Heights and Bolton Park revealed that most parents felt other parents *in general* placed a proper emphasis on winning: 81 percent felt that winning was properly emphasized, 12 percent felt winning was underemphasized, and only one parent (4 percent) thought winning was overemphasized. No parent spontaneously suggested that the league could be improved by altering parental behavior or banning parents from games. Neither players nor coaches mentioned parental problems when asked for specific difficulties or improvements.

Observation supports these responses. Rarely are parents a major irritant. In each league there were "incidents," but these were infrequent and isolated. Parents do yell during Little League contests, and some are quite loud, but excesses can be dealt with by league officials by reminding parents of appropriate role distance (i.e., "It's only a game"). Parents, like their children, are aware of the need to present themselves in a favorable light.

Little Leaguers Are Exploited by Adults

Modern sport is a commercial enterprise, and some critics have noticed the potential for adults deliberately or inadvertently to exploit children who participate in Little League (Rarick 1978; Moore 1966; Guegner 1955; Anderson 1953). Although it is generally conceded that the star players receive the benefits of Little League, these stars also are those most exploited by greedy adults.

An extreme example of this exploitation was an offer by a Pennsylvania Little League coach to two boys in a neighboring league that if they played for his team, he would give them a trip to New York City. James Michener suggests that such offers may be increasing: "Cases are surfacing in which overzealous coaches have roamed far afield to recruit talented youngsters to play for them. There have even been cases in which coaches have persuaded parents actually to move into their districts, so that a nine-year-old star can bolster the home team" (Michener 1976; 144–45). The professionalization of

Little League through player contracts, franchises, farm teams, all-star teams, and the world series (Schwertley 1970; see also Vaz 1982) has caused concern for some adults. The *Christian Century* suggests: "If [parents do not prevent the professionalization of] Little Leaguers, we shall have to conclude that the blight of professionalism, which threatens all American sports, is so deeply rooted in some defect in the character of our people and our culture that the only amateur left will be the husbandly frier of steak at an outdoor grill" (Little League baseball produces rhubarb, 1959, 870).

Exploitation may also be reflected in the involvement of business in Little League, which some contend makes preadolescents serve as junior "sandwich boards" for their "sponsors," advertising fast food, gas stations, government agencies, funeral parlors, or, in the case of the fictional Bad News Bears, Chico's Bail Bonds.

Joey Jay, the first Little League baseball player to reach the professional major leagues, noted: "I've known a lot of kids who were treated like little heroes. Afterward, they expected everything to be handed them on a silver platter, and it wasn't. They couldn't adjust" (Wake Up, Wake Up 1960, 69).

However, there is no systematic evidence on this point. In the leagues I examined, I doubt the presence of any significant exploitation. Sponsorship may be a painless way of keeping the registration cost of Little League low. A league that charges $250 a year for sponsorship (a reasonable figure) can gross $2,000 from an eight-team league and can eliminate raffles or decrease registration fees. Sponsors seem content in giving money and then leaving the team alone, satisfied with the tax deduction, advertising, and community spirit that the contribution brings.

In the five leagues examined, players were not publicly honored for having won the championship, and whatever fame they acquired was modest and fleeting. Some criticism of Little League is based on semantics rather than substance. The fact that one speaks of drafts and contracts does not imply that these carry meanings similar to those on the professional level. Whatever "exploitation" occurs seems modest compared to the way in which American media and industry might exploit children if they chose.

Little League Destroys Childhood Spontaneity

This final criticism reflects Americans' images of preadolescence. How should preadolescents spend their leisure time? What are preadolescents like in a "state of nature"? The answers to these questions are based on an image of the "child role," grounded in the way in which adults selectively recall their own childhood.

Probably the prevailing ideology of child educators is that children should be left alone to enjoy their leisure (e.g., Knapp and Knapp 1976; Yablonsky and Brower 1979; Mitchell 1954; Denzin 1977) and to develop their own social system, moral order, and culture. According to critics, adult organization destroys the vitality of preadolescent activity: "Little Leaguism" is threatening to wipe out the spontaneous culture of free play and games among American children, and . . . it is therefore robbing our children not just of their childish fun but also of some of their most valuable learning experiences . . . it nearly monopolizes the field and drives almost to bankruptcy the natural and spontaneous culture of play and games among American children" (Devereaux 1976; 37, 53).

While Devereaux's position is common (Opie and Opie 1959; Beleaguered Little Leaguers 1964; Kleiber 1978, 1981), there is no empirical justification for the belief that children's culture is being destroyed. Indeed, Sutton-Smith and Rosenberg (1961) found that over a fifty-year period children's preferences for informal group activities were *increasing*, although they did note a constriction in the number of boys' games. Clearly there is a finite number of hours in a child's day, and filling several of them leaves less time for other activities; however, even with Little League there is still much free time. Kleiber (1978), comparing preadolescents playing organized sports with those who did not, found, to his surprise, that there were no differences in the amount of child-directed games played.

Two other arguments can be raised against those who suggest that children should be free of adult influence: (1) the need for organization in American society, and (2) the aggressive nature of children's informal interaction. Reminiscences by adults of their preadolescent baseball experiences often focus on games in a vacant lot. However, less open space now exists, and as a consequence, there is a need for regulation fields and formal organization ("The Case for Little League" 1976; 13). Although baseball would exist without Little League, it would be on a smaller scale. Pickup games with thirty boys are rare; ten players is considered a large crowd. While there are advantages to baseball played by small groups, one loses the interrelationship of positions that constitutes a full game.

The second argument concerns the content of preadolescent interaction. Some adults describe children's play as idyllic, based upon romanticized childhood memories. Actually preadolescents are often cruel to those who are disliked (e.g., Olweus 1978; Fine 1981a). In sports, boys may not allow disliked others to participate in informal games. Status structure in informal games may be more dramatic than in Little League, where most coaches attempt to treat every boy fairly. Some time ago Martin Levin (1969, 4, 6) wrote a witty and wise comparison of the Official Rules of Little League with the "rules" of his informal baseball days:

> A browse through the Little League Baseball Official Rules indicates that times have changed since my sandlot baseball days. I'll tell it like it is now, and then try to tell it like it was then. . .
>
> PROTESTS—Protests shall be considered only when based on the violation or interpretation of a playing rule or the use of an ineligible player. No protest shall be considered on a decision involving an umpire's judgment.
>
> Protests—A protest was considered only when you were awfully sure you would lick the other guy. There was no umpire, unless some kid was on crutches and couldn't play. Nobody paid any attention to his calls, because he was just another kid.
>
> FIELD DECORUM—The actions of players, managers, coaches, umpires, and League officials must be above reproach.
>
> Field decorum—There was no managers, or coaches, or any of those big people. Only players who swore and spat. Anyone caught being above reproach got clobbered.

While this account is humorous, it contains a measure of truth. Preadolescent leisure is structured by the naked show of force, controlled by a sometimes ruthless hierarchy.

As I have emphasized, one's evaluation of Little League is grounded in the perspective of the evaluator. Thus, it is appropriate to ask the players about their attitudes toward organized and informal baseball. During the middle of the season, players in Bolton Park and Sanford Heights were asked, "Which do you prefer, Little League baseball or informal baseball games with your friends in the park or in someone's backyard?" In Bolton Park, 94 percent of the eighty-three players preferred Little League to informal baseball. In Sanford Heights, 73 percent of the ninety players preferred Little League, with 24 percent preferring informal baseball and 2 percent liking both equally.[9] Obviously this sample was self-selected in that these boys had chosen to play Little League and the question was asked during the season, but still the responses must lead one to question the traditional wisdom about the desire for free play. Players claim to prefer Little League because it has fewer arguments and more fairness. By virtue of their authority, adults can end disputes and solve problems that, when preadolescents are together, remain sources of tension (Davies 1982, 30):

"I never play with my friends. You get in too many arguments" (Twelve-year-old, Bolton Park Royals).

"It's [Little League] more organized. You don't get in bad fights with your friends" (twelve-year-old, Bolton Park Orioles).

These children value the organized character of Little League. The long-term effects of Little League are unclear because of the many other variables that affect participants and nonparticipants; however, there is little evidence that Little League destroys children's culture. Even if it could be proven that children's culture is significantly altered by Little League, this would not necessarily be harmful.

Summary

Having examined proposed benefits and drawbacks of Little League, I now address the general satisfaction of parents and players. Parental satisfaction was assessed through a question asked of the parent sample in Bolton Park and Sanford Heights: "Overall, in terms of the league your son participates in, are you: 5. Extremely Satisfied. 4. Very Satisfied. 3. Satisfied. 2. Somewhat Satisfied. 1. Not at All Satisfied."

The results indicate that parents in these two communities were supportive of their leagues. Mean parental satisfaction ratings were 3.3 in Sanford Heights and 3.8 in Bolton Park. Only two (of twenty-six) parents were "Somewhat Satisfied," and none was "Not at All Satisfied." If these results do not indicate that the leagues are problem-free, neither do they suggest that the basic structure of the leagues is harmful.

Players are even more satisfied. One direct behavioral measure is the number of preadolescents who voluntarily quit the league during the season. Since Little League is voluntary, a boy can discontinue his participation. Obviously strong social forces, such as peer and parental pressure, tend to prevent this, but quitting does occur (e.g., Broadus and Broadus 1972, 26–27), and it reflects extreme dissatisfaction. In the four leagues from which complete data are available (all except Beanville), only nine (2 percent) of the 391 play-

Table A.1.3   Satisfaction with League and Team

	League Satisfaction		Team Satisfaction	
	$\bar{x}$	N	$\bar{x}$	N
Beanville, first year	—no data—		4.3	32
Beanville, second year	4.6	30	4.1	30
Hopewell	4.5	99	4.1	99
Sanford Heights	4.2	90	3.8	90
Bolton Park	4.5	83	4.3	82
Maple Bluff	4.0	107	3.8	107

ers quit during the season for reasons other than vacations and family relocations. Four boys quit in Maple Grove and in Sanford Heights, one boy quit in Hopewell, and none left a team in Bolton Park. Of these nine boys, only two quit bitterly over their lack of playing time.

At the end of each season players were asked about their satisfaction with the Little League program and about the team they played for. Specifically they were asked:

1. How much do you like Little League baseball: 5. Extremely much. 4. Very much. 3. Much. 2. A little. 1. Not at all.
2. How happy are you to be playing for the team you are on: 5. Extremely happy. 4. Very happy. 3. Happy. 2. Somewhat happy. 1. Not happy.

Generally players were very satisfied with the performance of the league and their team, even if they played for unsuccessful teams. The mean satisfaction score for all leagues is 4.3 (409 cases) and the equivalent mean for team satisfaction is 4.0 (428 cases). The correlation between satisfaction with one's team and the league is +.56 ($n = 408$, $p = .001$). All five leagues reveal the same pattern of results (see table A.1.3).

While certain leagues seem slightly more successful than others,[10] the consistency of the results is striking. Although the Little League program does not meet the needs of every boy, it appears to serve the majority of children well.

To examine the extent to which league satisfaction and team satisfaction result from competitive success, teams were grouped on the basis of whether their winning percentage was .500 or better, or below .500 (See table A.1.4). It is not surprising that boys on winning teams were happier than those on losing teams and that this difference also affected satisfaction with the league as a whole.

Table A.1.4 Mean Levels of Little League Satisfaction

League Satisfaction[a]

	Successful Teams[c]		Unsuccessful Teams			
	Satisfaction	(N)	Satisfaction	(N)	t	p
Total Sample	4.39	(237)	4.20	(172)	-2.26	.024
Beanville, 1975	.... no data collected					
Beanville, 1976	.... both teams successful					
Hopewell, 1976	4.60	(52)	4.30	(47)	-1.98	.051
Sanford Heights, 1977	4.21	(53)	4.27	(37)	.32	.750
Bolton Park, 1977	4.57	(42)	4.49	(41)	-.58	.561
Maple Bluff, 1977	4.13	(60)	3.79	(47)	-1.76	.081

Team Satisfaction[b]

	Successful Teams		Unsuccessful Teams			
	Satisfaction	(N)	Satisfaction	(N)	t	p
Total Sample	4.31	(247)	3.62	(193)	-7.05	.001
Beanville, 1975	4.80	(10)	4.05	(22)	-2.19	.037
Beanville, 1976	.... both teams successful					
Hopewell, 1976	4.46	(52)	3.64	(47)	-4.76	.001
Sanford Heights, 1977	4.23	(53)	3.27	(37)	-3.95	.001
Bolton Park, 1977	4.62	(42)	3.90	(40)	-3.84	.001
Maple Bluff, 1977	4.05	(60)	3.43	(47)	-2.77	.007

League Satisfaction (by age)

	12-Year-Olds		9-, 10-, 11-Year Olds			
	Satisfaction	(N)	Satisfaction	(N)	t	p
Total Sample	4.23	(218)	4.42	(179)	2.25	.025
Beanville, 1975	.... no data collected					
Beanville, 1976	4.83	(12)	4.50	(18)	-1.66	.109
Hopewell, 1976	4.41	(49)	4.50	(50)	.60	.550
Sanford Heights, 1977	4.20	(50)	4.28	(40)	.39	.701
Bolton Park, 1977	4.38	(39)	4.66	(44)	1.95	.054
Maple Bluff, 1977	3.93	(68)	4.07	(27)	.62	.534

Team Satisfaction (by age)

	12-Year-Olds		9, 10, 11-Year-Olds			
	Satisfaction	(N)	Satisfaction	(N)	t	p
Total Sample	3.99	(229)	4.18	(199)	2.85	.005
Beanville, 1975	4.50	(12)	4.15	(20)	-1.00	.325
Beanville, 1976	3.83	(12)	4.28	(18)	1.37	.182
Hopewell, 1976	4.06	(49)	4.08	(50)	.10	.922
Sanford Heights, 1977	3.58	(50)	4.15	(40)	2.25	.025
Bolton Park, 1977	4.08	(38)	4.43	(44)	1.76	.089
Maple Bluff, 1977	3.76	(68)	3.93	(27)	.59	.559

[a]Based on the question: How much do you like Little League baseball:
5. Extremely much. 4. Very much. 3. Much. 2. A little. 1. Not at all.
[b]Based on the question: How happy are you to be playing for the team you are on:
5. Extremely happy. 4. Very happy. 3. Happy. 2. Somewhat happy. 1. Not happy.
[c]Successful teams are those with a .500 winning percentage or better; unsuccessful teams are below .500.

However, the small differences between the attitudes of boys on the stronger and weaker teams suggest that players are able to separate their frustrations with defeat from their evaluations.

Having determined that team success affects satisfaction, is satisfaction influenced by personal success? During the final week of the season, all players were asked to estimate their current batting average. Using a reported batting average of .350 as a cutoff, the sample was divided into two groups on the basis of their reported batting average. There was no difference in satisfaction between these two groups, either for the total sample or for any of the leagues. Players seem to separate their personal success from their evaluation of the season and the league.

Perhaps players' reported batting average might not be as effective a measure of personal success as an "objective" measure. To examine the relationship between satisfaction and skill, two additional measures were gathered in Sanford Heights and Bolton Park. On the basis of the scorebooks collected from coaches, I computed the "actual" batting average of each player. These "objective" measures are not completely "objective" but are also social and political, as certain players may be given "special" treatment—most notably coaches' sons. However, such records probably have a greater likelihood of being reliable than players' reports. A second "objective" measure is based on a set of questions asked of all coaches in Bolton Park and Sanford Heights at the end of the season; coaches were asked to rate each of their players on a five-point scale in terms of their overall ability: 5. Better than almost anyone in the league. 4. Better than most others in the league. 3. Better than the average player in the league. 2. About average. 1. Not as good as most players in the league.

Neither measure correlates significantly with team satisfaction ($r = .07$, $n = 172$, $p = .18$ for batting average, $r = .04$, $n = 147$, $p = .31$ for coach's rating) or league satisfaction ($r = .01$, $n = 173$, $p = .47$ for batting average; $r = .12$, $n = 147$, $p = .07$ for coach's rating). Skill and satisfaction are not related.[11]

Age does affect player satisfaction: younger players (those under twelve years of age) were significantly happier playing Little League than those older, although the magnitude of the differences was not large (see table A1–3). This age difference was not consistent across leagues. The differences seem to be greater in those leagues in which there is a sharp status difference between major and minor leagues—Sanford Heights and Bolton Park—although by this criterion differences were expected in Hopewell. Beanville did not run a minor league program, and Maple Bluff permitted all eleven- and twelve-year-olds to participate in the major league. It is reasonable to assume that, in leagues with sharp status differences, participating in the elite league would be inherently satisfying for the younger players, whereas older players might have taken this position for granted.

On the basis of the data presented in this chapter, I must hand down a Scottish verdict on criticism of Little League: not proven. The arguments of the critics of the program, although valid in individual cases, appear invalid generally. Similarly we must view with caution claims made by the proponents of the program that Little League has major benefits. While the conclusion may not be glamorous, Little League does not seem to have the dramatic effects that its proponents hope or its critics fear. Basically Little League is fun for those preadolescents who participate, and while we should never stop trying to curtail its flaws, we should be satisfied that it brings a little joy to the lives of our children.

Appendix 2:
Participant Observation with Children

Every research setting has its own peculiarities—special problems that must be dealt with in the course of data collection. The purpose of the methodological appendix in qualitative research studies is to describe these problems and to comment on how they were dealt with. Further, the methodological appendix should discuss how the exigencies of the field situation affected the data. I shall focus on that part of the research that involved participant observation (the main methodological focus of the research), without describing the problems involved in collecting interview or questionnaire data from children.

The key feature that confronts the adult participant observer conducting research with children is that no matter what one's intentions, one cannot pass unnoticed in the society of children. Because of the structure of age roles in American society (Lofland 1970; Conger 1972), it is not possible to enact the complete participant role (Gold 1958), sometimes described as the ideal of ethnographic involvement. Contemporary American society insists on age segregation between adults and children and, as a result, it is unexpected for an adult to "hang out" with children's groups.

The difficulty in breaching expectations is reflected in the small number of research studies involving participant observation with children. While several researchers have established long-term relationships with individual children (Coles 1967; Cottle 1973), there has been little group research with preadolescents. The closest to such research were the summer camp studies conducted by Muzafer Sherif and his colleagues (Sherif and Sherif 1953; Sherif et al. 1961), but these were artificial groups, and no attempt was made to establish equal status relationships, as the adults were counselors as well as observers. Other researchers have studied children in natural settings through formal observational techniques (Polansky et al. 1949; Barker and Wright 1951; Goldstein 1970; Lever 1976; Whiting and Whiting 1975).

Relation of Researcher to Ethnographic Subjects

Research with children is distinctive in that the usual ethnographic relationship between researcher and subject is altered. In the traditional ethnographic model one assumes that one's subjects are equal in status to oneself or, at least, should be treated as such. This status is part of the respect the researcher grants to subjects. In participating with children, this assumption is not tenable, at least in its most obvious sense, because the roles of the participants are structured by attitudes toward age, cognitive development, and physical maturity.

As a result of these unavoidable differences, issues and problems arise that must be confronted by any researcher participating with children. The issues on which I focus consist of the role chosen to deal with children and the implications of that role, the ethical responsibilities of the adult researcher in dealing with children and ways in which these responsibilities can be met, problems involved in achieving rapport and access with children, and how the adult role complicates the understanding of children's social meanings. Although the problems encountered are not entirely separate from those in research with adults, the forms these issues take are distinctive.

The Research Role

I have argued elsewhere (Fine and Glassner 1979; Fine 1980a) that participant observation roles with children can be distinguished on two dimensions: (1) the extent of positive contact between adult and child, and (2) the extent to which the adult has direct authority over the child. After postulating these dimensions (treated as dichotomous), I proposed four roles the adult researcher may adopt: leader, supervisor, observer, and friend.

Leader. The leader has authority over the children and also attempts to maintain friendly relations with them; popular teachers are leaders.

Supervisor. The supervisor role involves authority over children, but without an attempt to establish friendly relations (e.g., authoritarian teachers).

Observer. The observer in the ideal form of this role has neither positive contact with the subjects nor authority but simply records events without becoming personally involved.

Friend. The friend role is an attempt to couple a positive relationship with a minimal amount of authority. To the extent this can be managed, this is identical to the traditional participant observational role used to deal with adults.

For this research I decided the optimal role was that of the friend. While I recognized that I would always be a special type of friend, the less authority I had the better, particularly because I hoped to discover those aspects of children's behavior that are otherwise inaccessible to adults.

Because friendship is not a typical relationship between adults and children (although there often are friendly authority relations), time is necessary to develop it. I vividly recall that in my first weeks in Beanville I was surprised at how "nice" the boys seemed and how few obscenities they used. Only after several weeks had I become sufficiently accepted for the children to drop their reserve.

With minor exceptions, a similar process occurred in each league. At first the children would ignore me, not quite knowing what I wanted. In Beanville, the first league I studied, and the league in which I made the most mistakes, I did not announce to the players until several weeks into the season what my purpose was and so in the early days I was accorded the (non)status of a nonperson. In other leagues, learning from my discomfort, I introduced myself early (with the approval of the coaches). I explained I wanted to learn what "kids like you" think and do, and said I would be "hanging around." This explanation did not answer all the unspoken questions in the children's minds, and it took time to convince the players that I was not an authority and would not report them for their attacks on the adult social order. Eventually I gained rapport with the preadolescents, both during the games and during their private leisure activities. This acceptance was dramatically evident at the end-of-the-season party for the Bolton Park Orioles, one of the teams I had studied in depth. Toward the end of the party, players snuck up behind me and tossed me in the swimming pool, fully clothed. The Sanford Heights Dodgers, on a more decorous note, presented me with a baseball autographed by all team members. Other preadolescents gave me nicknames, notably "Electric Hair" by one team because of my sometimes unkempt, frizzled hair.

Yet, despite the attempt to establish a relatively equal status relationship with the players, my adult role never totally disappeared. In some cases I had to intervene; in other cases the players would assert my authority and then personally support it. For example:

I am distributing the final questionnaire of the year to the Royals, and Hank Gumbel says that he doesn't want to fill it out.

Before I respond, Bruce Faye, another Royals player, tells him he must and that the entire team will gang up on him if he doesn't. Without further comment Hank completes the questionnaire (field notes, Bolton Park).

This situation, while rare, was not unique and, while I made use of the support given by players, I felt uncomfortable, for it seemed to derive from the recognition that as an adult I was to be accorded special privileges. Likewise, there were limits on my involvement with these preadolescents, such as not watching them play aggressive pranks or observing boy-girl parties. A fine line existed between what I was permitted to see, hear, and hear about, and that which was inappropriate. I was a "friend" of a sort, but without all the privileges (and responsibilities) that being a peer entails.

The Personal Equation

The researcher's "personal equation" affects the "friend" role. I shall focus on three components of my personal equation, believing that although they influence all participant observation to some extent, other personal topics may be more relevant for other researchers in different situations. I examine compatibility with research subjects, competence in the skills of one's subjects, and the dangers of overengrossment.

Compatibility. A basic requirement for a participant observer is that he or she can feel comfortable with those being studied (Johnson 1975). Most individuals feel comfortable with some groups and ill at ease with others, and there must be a match between observer and subject. I had worked with children for five years prior to the research in other settings, and believed that I would feel comfortable observing them. Although I experienced those tensions common to the beginnings of participant observation (Bogdan and Taylor 1975), I confidently expected rapport. Some colleagues commented about how difficult getting to know children must be. For them, this research site would have been infeasible. My ease in dealing with middle-class children contributed to the development of relationships.

Competence. Although the participant observer who is open about his or her role is not expected to do everything that other actors do, there are typically some activities, often supportive of the group, in which the researcher must engage. The researcher must decide, considering personal competence and morality, how to respond to these challenges.

During the research I was asked and expected to engage in several baseball-related activities. An honest appraisal of my baseball abilities would reveal that objectively I am not as competent an athlete as were my Little League friends and certainly not as skillful as most of the coaches. Although this did not present major difficulties for the research, it did limit my role. The first season I was asked to help the Beanville Angels:

> An intrasquad game was organized by the coach of the Angels. Since they did not have the necessary number of players, I was asked to play center field. In the field only one ball was hit toward me and fortunately was sufficiently far from where I was standing that I didn't need to be embarrassed about not catching it, and actually made a fairly decent throw to hold the batter to a double. At bat I struck out my first time up, grounded out in my second time up, becoming known as an "easy out." Finally, in my third at bat, I singled (field notes, Beanville).

Particularly in Beanville and Sanford Heights I was teased by players for my lack of playing skills and had to make excuses to coaches:

> *Dick Fowell* (Coach of the Expos): "Do you want to pitch batting practice?"
> *GAF:* "I don't know that my arm is ready for it" (field notes, Sanford Heights).

Although my lack of skills prevented some forms of interaction with the players and didn't permit me to help the adult coaches, it also may have had a beneficial effect in that I was treated as more of an equal and not as a baseball expert; second, by not playing baseball, I had more opportunities to observe and take notes.

A second potential avenue of participation was becoming an umpire for Little League games. Occasionally an umpire would fail to appear for a scheduled game, and the adults present searched for a man capable of filling that position. Since I was officially unaffiliated with either of the teams, I was asked to umpire. I had decided prior to the research that I would never umpire and I stuck to this decision despite some pressure to change my mind, knowing that coaches or parents could always fill in (and indeed no game was cancelled for lack of an umpire). My decision was predicated on three considerations: (1) being an umpire would sharply limit the ability to observe; (2) because I was not fully versed in all the nuances of Little League baseball rules, I felt that I would not be able to give a competent performance; (3) an umpire, particularly one not extensively schooled in his role, often provokes the enmity of one (or both) of the teams. This was particularly sensitive since typically I was studying one of the teams. If I ruled against them, my rapport might have been weakened. For this reason, the psychological pressure to make decisions that would help the research would be enormous, polluting the fairness of the sport. On several occasions I was asked by boys to umpire their informal pickup games and I agreed because the conditions militating against my umpiring formal games did not seem applicable, given the loose nature of these contests.

One's skills influence the role that one can play. On the positive side, I knew how to keep score, and this skill was a considerable advantage for my research in that I was able to remove a burden from the coaches; became the center of attention for the players as they questioned me on the score, batting order, and batting average; and gained an opportunity to take notes without being too obtrusive. An added bonus was that as a result of my keeping score, players' batting averages could be calculated and used for other research purposes.

Overinvolvement. Sports events compel involvement by participants and spectators (Goffman 1961, 1974; Fontana 1978), including the supposedly unbiased participant observer. In a sense it should not matter which team wins or how it wins. In terms of the success of the research, any outcome analyzed dispassionately yields insight into preadolescent sports involvement. Yet, a dispassionate view is difficult to maintain. I found myself rooting (at least silently) for the team I was studying and for the boys I knew as friends. Even when I was studying a team accustomed to failure, and whose continued failure was helpful to the research, it was hard not to become excited at their occasional successes. During some important games, I found myself unable to take extensive notes because the contest had become too engrossing.

The most dramatic example of this phenomenon occurred during the first year of research. Both the coach and the assistant coach of the Beanville Angels were to be absent for a game late in the season, and either I coached or the team would forfeit:

> I found that coaching is hard work—one must constantly make decisions, keep the players in line, and watch out for injuries. I decided to play the game conservatively and didn't allow much stealing. I let one of the better players on the team be my assistant coach, and that helped somewhat, but even so I found it difficult to take notes. I discovered the pressures a coach operates under, and found coaching personally exhilarating, especially since the Angels, who did not have a winning record,

beat the Rangers, who had one of the best records in the League. Some of the Angels suggested I was their good luck charm and others asked me to be their permanent coach (field notes, Beanville).

Personal involvement is, of course, not unique to this research setting (Bogdan and Taylor 1975); however, in social worlds such as sport, in which engrossment is a function of identification with the participants, involvement is to be expected. While such self-involvement is a natural outgrowth of identification, it must be guarded against to ensure it does not interfere with data collection.

In order to create personal role relationships with one's subjects, such as the friend role, one must recognize the significance of such personal factors as compatibility, competence, and overinvolvement. In dealing with children these factors acquire a special significance because traditionally in adult-child interaction these are achieved on the adult's terms.

Adult Role–Related Ethical Issues

Although ethical issues in participant observation have been discussed from many perspectives (e.g., Barnes 1967; Douglas 1976; Roth 1962), typically the discussion has assumed relations among peers—actual or theoretical equals. Yet, one should not pretend that adults and children could comfortably interact in situations in which equality was enforced. While there are research advantages in lessening the power differential, as in the establishment of a nondirective "friend" relation, the elimination of this difference cannot be achieved and does not seem advisable.

Accepting the inevitable difference between adults and children raises several ethical issues that derive from this role relationship. Unlike participant observation with adults, those involved in research with children must consider the subjects' "immaturity" and the fact that they have not reached the age of legal responsibility. A participant observer working with an adult deviant group is interacting with legal peers, and interference with their actions would generally be condemned as irresponsible, particularly from the standpoint of research. However, this is problematic in research with young people, and in some research on gangs the "researchers" have even presided over the liquidation of the gang studied (Greeley and Casey 1963). This problem is reflected in three issues for researchers engaged in participant observation with children: (1) the responsibility of the adult in handling potentially harmful situations; (2) the implications of the adult "policing," or disciplinary, role for the expectations of other adults and the behavior of children; and (3) the problems involved in obtaining "informed consent" and in explaining the research in a comprehensible fashion.

Adult Responsibility

Difficulties may arise when one deals with children in situations in which there is no formal adult authority. Children are mischievous, sometimes aggressive and, on occasion, distressingly cruel; some control may be necessary when other adults are absent. At Little League games I felt little responsibility for controlling behavior; however, when I was with preadolescents in their unorganized leisure time the issue was more problematic. A basic requirement of participant observation research is to ensure that subjects suffer no personal harm (American Sociological Association 1968). Some researchers report that the mere presence of an adult observer may actually increase the amount of aggression displayed by children and adolescents (Glassner 1976; Polsky 1962); this aggression may be designed to test the observer to determine what they can "get away with." In my research I found this testing, although relating more to verbal aggression than physical aggression. The vitriolic component of boys' criticisms of each other seemed to increase as they tested how much I would accept without becoming angry or reporting them.

Developing fixed rules defining when intervention is appropriate is impossible. When I felt these children were close to hurting themselves or others, I intervened:

> A fight nearly started between Wiley and Bud. At the beginning of the game Wiley had walked along the Rangers' bench knocking off caps from the heads of his teammates. Later, when the Rangers were losing, Bud attempted to get even by knocking off Wiley's baseball cap, and Wiley got angry. I was worried about this because Bud, who was known for his violent temper, was holding an aluminum bat. They pushed each other, but didn't come to blows. I suggested that they should keep their attention on the game and the situation ended (field notes, Beanville).

The adult participant observer has a moral obligation to protect children. Other adults, who might intervene if the participant observer were not present, might refrain from acting, feeling that the children are under adult supervision. In the event of physical danger, the adult cannot play an entirely passive role, even though he or she will alter the behavior of the group.

Few situations are dangerous. Boys do fight each other, and when these conflicts seemed "playful," I watched carefully, believing that children's jurisprudence could handle the situation. Children's groups contain members whose skills include the ability to break up fights. This is particularly true of high-status boys, secure in their positions, who can tell others to "knock it off." Yet, if a situation gets out of control, the observer must be held partially responsible—morally and possibly legally. Among the preadolescents I observed, no situation requiring direct involvement (such as separating boys involved in fights) arose when I was the only adult present. However, this issue should be recognized by every researcher who conducts research with socially protected groups. The ideal goal of observational techniques—not to alter natural behavior—is just that—an ideal goal.

Situations that involve direct physical harm to children are rare. Yet other situations, while not physically dangerous, involve behaviors generally condemned by society. In the course of my research, the two major foci of socially unacceptable behavior involved racism and theft.

Racism was present in all five leagues to a distressingly great extent. Once when I was driving some Beanville boys home, we passed some young blacks riding bicycles in that almost entirely white suburb. One boy leaned out the car window and shouted at the "jungle bunnies" to "go back where you came from." In Sanford Heights the preadolescent prank of ringing a doorbell and running away before the door was answered was known as "Nigger Knocking" as well as by its more common name, "Ding Dong Ditch."

The methodological problem is what to do or say in reaction to these behaviors. In most cases I offered no direct criticism, although a few times, when the situation was appropriate, I reminded the boys of the past prejudices against their own ethnic groups—a tactic that seemed particularly effective with Irish-American boys, some of whom had not realized that their own group had been the target of bigots. Despite this gentle chiding, little was done to criticize the children (or, of course, reinforce them) in the belief that a better tactic was to record the event, indicate the scope of the problem, and avoid being seen as moralistic. I suspect that nothing I could have done would have affected their behavior, although during the research I wondered whether my actions were methodologically sound and morally justified.

The other instance of problematic behavior was stealing or "ripping off." On one occasion I accompanied some Beanville players to an ice cream parlor; while I was paying the check I noticed that the players were stealing gum and candy. My first reaction was to stop them and to insist they return what they had stolen. This reaction was attributable to generalized ethical concerns, the desire to teach these preadolescents what was morally right, and the egocentric fear that if patrons or staff had observed these events I might be blamed and humiliated. Simultaneously I recognized that by making a public display I would not alter their actions over the long term but would ensure that I would never be privy to such behavior again, and thus this preadolescent deviance, rarely examined, would be lost. In addition, I had developed attachments to these boys and recognized that public notice might cause them embarrassment or legal trouble. I decided not to do anything, a decision grounded as much in indecision as in specific research objectives. In retrospect, I think the decision was sound since, on the drive home, the boys spontaneously brought up the incident (indicating my acceptance in the group) and, through nonevaluative probing I discovered that considerable stealing (or "ripping off") occurred in school, where lockers were regularly broken into and books, notebooks, and pencils stolen.

In these cases I answered the question of adult responsibility by adopting a "scientific" rationale—that the situation should be disturbed as little as possible. I do not claim that this is correct in an absolute sense; rather, the best rule of thumb is that participant observers must behave so that they can live with themselves (Polsky 1962). Gold (1958) has argued that on occasion it is imperative to subordinate oneself to one's role in the interest of participant observation, but even so, in dealing with children there are times when the adult must enforce moral imperatives.

Adult Policing Role

A second, related ethical concern is the extent to which adult participant observers should allow themselves to be placed in a policing role. This problem is especially salient when one observes in a setting with several power levels and one's research focus is on the low-status individuals. Geer (1970) found that she needed to make explicit to the administration of the college where she was observing that she would not spy for them. Nothing is more damaging for the participant observer than not to be perceived as an "honest broker." Many groups, including preadolescents, are concerned about the use of the information they provide, and the observer must create a role that is not seen as an extension of those of other authorities.

The problem is not only that children are suspicious of participant observers, although at first they are; adult authority figures do attempt to use participant observers for their own ends—sometimes cynically, often out of a desire to help the child. Birksted (1976) discovered, for example, that by observing adolescents he performed a useful service for the school by keeping them busy and out of trouble. Yet, he ran into a conflict because he did not see his role as requiring that he control the students to the same extent that teachers did. I felt similar pressures when I was asked to run practices or watch the boys. Needing rapport with adults, I performed these activities as nondirectively and nondictatorially as I could, but I felt uncomfortable taking on the adult mantle of authority, contrary to the friend role I was attempting to foster. Several times I was asked by parents or coaches for advice about children with minor behavior problems. Although I desired to help, I did not divulge any information I had collected and could only address the parental concerns in the most general terms. Similarly I emphasized to coaches that I would not enforce their rules—my role was not "assistant coach." While this point was made explicitly before the season and was never overtly raised by coaches, I had the impression that enforcement was desired, and on some occasions, when pragmatic needs came before theoretical considerations, I did aid coaches in establishing order; mostly this involved dissuading the players from running about and yelling when order and calm were needed. The problem with my nondisciplinary role was that I sometimes appeared to be the "good guy" while the coach was perceived as the "heavy."

Informed Consent

Virtually every type of legitimate social research requires that the investigator inform subjects of the nature of their participation and about the intentions of the research. This need for informed consent has perhaps not always been sufficiently recognized in participant observation, where secrecy is still frequently practiced and sometimes justified for methodological reasons. Today there is increasing concern for ensuring that one's subjects are informed as to the nature of the project—in some cases to promote research collaboration (Kahn and Mann 1952; Whyte 1955).

I have pointed out elsewhere (Fine 1980a) that we can describe informed consent in terms of the "cover" used by the researcher. Some explanation is necessary to legitimate the researcher's presence. Of course this is true, not only for participant-observation research, but for all long-term relationships. In nonresearch situations one might cite the sponsorship of an acquaintance or the existence of some biographical interest that lends legitimacy to one's presence. These explanations are routinized and conventionalized and are not problematic; in natural interaction the explanation the participant gives will be the one he or she explicitly accepts; it is, in brief, "the real reason" for the person's presence. However, in participant observation these two may not be identical.

Three approaches may be used to explain the participant observer's presence. First, the participant observer may provide the research subjects with a rather complete and detailed explanation of the purposes and hypotheses of the research, fully meeting ethical requirements but possibly inducing respondent bias; this I have termed "explicit cover." On the other hand, researchers may hide their role from subjects—a technique that, if successful, allows for the observation of behavior untainted by respondent bias but possibly is unethical; this I term "deep cover." Finally, a middle ground, that of "shallow cover," can be staked out. By this compromise the researcher explains that research is being conducted but is vague about its goals—not telling subjects the specific hypotheses involved or the topics on which the researcher is taking notes.

For this research project I adopted the third option, which involved the "sin" of omission. While I explicitly mentioned that I was a social psychologist, interested in observing the behavior of preadolescents, finding out what they said and did, I did not expand on this in great detail. To gain access to a league I first approached the president of the Little League I wished to study. I explained that I wished to examine how Little League baseball players played the game and what they did in their leisure. I described the basic plan of the research—I would observe but would not be actively involved in the league structure as an umpire, coach, or grounds keeper. When I gained the league president's approval, I asked to meet the coaches and other adults involved with the league. This was done at league board meetings prior to tryouts (except in Beanville, where the meeting was several days after tryouts). I explained the goals of the research—finding out about preadolescent behavior, telling the coaches they could request that I not study their team—either on specific occasions or for the whole season (this problem only occurred on one team, as will be described below). I emphasized I would not disrupt their control of their teams. While some coaches later admitted scepticism about my project, I encountered no complaints at this time. Once I had the approval of the coaches, I asked for permission to explain to the players the goals of the research. This usually occurred at an early practice (often in conjunction with distributing the first questionnaire). Again, the explanation was general—about my desire to learn what they did and said in Little League and in their other leisure activities. In my informal introduction I emphasized they need not answer any questions I asked nor have anything to do with me. Only one boy explicitly refused to fill out a questionnaire, and no one rejected my presence at the league games. Obviously some of this acceptance was due to the fact that I was usually introduced in a supportive fashion by the adult authority, the coach; in some cases, the coach was too supportive, telling the players that he expected them to answer all my questions. In my presentation I attempted to be informal, asking players to call me by my first name and telling them I would not report them for what they told me privately. At the end of the talk I handed each player a letter to give to his parents; it explained the central focus of the research, invited parents to call me or speak to me with any questions, and informed them that if they had objections to their child's participation in the study I would respect their wishes. Only two parents (neither on teams I studied intensively) registered objections, and their children were not asked to fill out the questionnaires.

The advantage of a vague research bargain is that it permits many informal research bargains to be struck—relations that may be dissimilar. Specifically, these allowed some players to treat me as an intimate, sharing their dirty stories and vile exploits, permitted other boys to use me as a protector against the bullying of their peers, gave isolates someone to listen to their baseball concerns, and provided parents and coaches an opportunity to describe their frustrations in raising children.

The fact that a researcher explains his or her presence does not mean this explanation will be accepted or understood. This is particularly evident when dealing with preadolescents, whose conception of the world may be quite different from that of adults. Subjects attempt to fit the researcher's behavior into their own conceptions of motivation (e.g., Trice 1956; Mungham 1976). I was surprised to learn at the end of the season in Sanford Heights that one local youngster believed I was a drug dealer. The first year I observed the Beanville League, I carefully explained I was a graduate student, a category players had difficulty understanding; when I simplified that to explain I was a student working on a report, understanding and sympathy were immediate. Throughout the season players inquired about the report and knowingly said I was sure to get an A because of all the work I had done observing them. One player told me that my teacher had better give me an A "or else!" Children identify with the concept of doing "homework" (Gordon 1957), and this was a satisfactory explanation for my presence.

I also did not hide the fact that a book might be the eventual outcome of this research. This immediately caught the imagination of the players, and I (like LeMasters 1975) was often told I should include particular details. At times it seemed I was regarded by players as the "official" historian of the league. This interpretation of my goals by players was helpful, as it let me be a central repository for information by those wishing to become immortalized.

Openly taking notes contributed to my central position in the information network, although this was not without disadvantages, as in each league I had to guard my writings against players too eager to know what I thought was important. I soon developed the skill of writing illegibly and without looking at the pad; each skill intrigued the preadolescents.

Perhaps the major theoretical problem that relates to informed consent with children is how to handle confidentiality. Confidentiality is assumed to be necessary in order to hide the identity of specific persons who might be subject to reprisals or embarrassment. The rule is, I believe, fundamentally sound and one to which I adhere in this book. The dilemma was that many players preferred and, in some cases, insisted I use their real names. The possibility of fame outweighed any potential embarrassment. Most players were enthusiastic about being depicted in the book, and some wondered whether they would become famous. Although some players were concerned about the possibility of their parents learning of the things they did, most were unconcerned. Further, several claimed they wouldn't mind if others said negative things about them, feeling they could handle the situation:

> I was talking with Bill Anders and Rod Shockstein about whether to use their real names in the book. Both boys wanted

their names used. Rod added that if anyone says anything bad about him, "I will kill him" (field notes, Sanford Heights).

Despite my sense that Little League players preferred to have their names used, all names in this report are pseudonyms. Although I considered using the real names of those who requested it, I concluded they were not sufficiently aware of the possible ramifications of their decisions. Several youngsters made remarks with aggressively sexual or racial content and, even after several years, they might be blamed for these statements. Further, not keeping players anonymous would have violated my original research bargain with the participants and would have violated the agreements made with university research committees. Yet, I recognize that by disguising identities, I am not permitting these players to get the credit they might otherwise have received for their insight and I am, to some extent, disregarding their wishes.

Dealing with Adults

While the focus of this research project was on preadolescents, I needed to establish positive relationships with adults, both to facilitate support for my presence and to understand the social meanings adults assign to Little League baseball. At the same time I was establishing ties with preadolescents, I established friendly relations with the adults. Several coaches confided to me after the season that they were hesitant about my presence, afraid—in the words of one Bolton Park coach—that I "would blow things out of proportion." During this research, Little League baseball was under considerable criticism over its supposed overcompetitiveness, exclusion of girls, and poor coaching. As a result, some adults wondered, despite my protests, whether I would do a "hatchet job" on them. It was a reasonable concern. During the season they found that my attention was on the players and that I was a sympathetic listener who made supportive comments to them when they were under stress. Soon I became accepted by the adults and was often asked for advice. Coaches came to see me as on their "side." When one coach in Hopewell made remarks to his players that might have seemed moralistic or trite to a more worldly adult (such as him or me), he would wink at me to indicate our shared recognition that this statement did not represent his "true" self.

Toward the end of the third year of research, a local newspaper did a short article on the research that my research assistant and I were then completing. I discussed my findings, which indicated that players were on the whole quite satisfied with the structure of Little League. This article caused much favorable comment from adults in the three leagues under study at the time. While I was dubious about the wisdom of permitting press notice, fortunately the results were more than satisfactory (see Adler 1984).

Because adults and I shared a similar perspective, the idea of university research made sense to them and was seen as a legitimate activity. Most adults were eager to learn the outcome of the research, and some helped distribute questionnaires and ensured they were returned. Even here, some difficulties had to be surmounted. The first year of research, I asked the Beanville coaches to collect questionnaires for me, explaining they were confidential and should be given to me immediately. One coach, although well-meaning, was so curious about his team's reaction that he read the questionnaires before handing them to me and commented to his players about their responses. Fortunately this questionnaire, distributed at the beginning of the season, elicited few negative comments, but the incident required that I change the method of collection to ensure that coaches would not be middlemen. In working with children and adults simultaneously it is necessary to recognize that the two groups have different understandings about the nature of the research and different fears about what it might uncover.

While my relations with most coaches and parents were personally rewarding, I had to deal with one hostile coach. This was during my research in Beanville and may have been a result of my inexperience in explaining my research. I decided to focus on the four teams in the "Central League" (the Rangers, Angels, White Sox, and Astros) and in particular on the Rangers and the Angels. At first all four coaches treated me well, and each seemed eager to help. My early notes have references to how supportive each of the men was. However, several weeks into the season I sensed that Al Wingate, the coach of the White Sox, was no longer enthusiastic. Although he had helped me hand out the first batch of questionnaires, he soon became irritated at my presence. After an occasion on which I tried to collect the questionnaires from his team, he took me aside and informed me that "you can take those questionnaires and shove them up your ass!" In accordance with my agreement with all the coaches at the beginning of the season, I politely informed him that, given his attitude, I would not study his team. Later in the season, when the Astros coach asked me to give him their lineup card, he refused to give me his, saying that he would only give it to "an official member of the Astros organization." Naturally, his attitude was depressing, particularly as it occurred in my first weeks in the field, and I was afraid his view indicated what other coaches felt privately. Fortunately for the research, Wingate was considered a difficult, unpleasant person by the other coaches. In fact, when other coaches learned he had refused to cooperate (I didn't repeat his exact words), I received sympathy, and the incident may have given me credibility. In retrospect, I suspect that part of the problem was due to my not recognizing Wingate's relationship with the other adults in the league. The fact that I chose two teams coached by men who scorned him may have led him to perceive me as a foe. Had I been aware of this I could have spent more time with him, showing that I was sympathetic to his problems. Further, his team started the season very poorly, partly due to the ragged performance of his son. Thus, his expectations for a successful season were dashed early, and perhaps he felt that others gloated. I was an easy target, and, not sensing this, I did nothing to resolve it.

Issues of Rapport and Access to Children

For participant observation to be successful, the researcher must gain access to a variety of social situations—particularly those that are not publicly observable. Such access requires rapport with the participants. While rapport is an issue in all participant observation, the problem takes particular forms in work with children because of the nature of traditional adult-child interaction.

Central to all attempts to gain access is the establishment of a relationship of trust. Participants must believe the observer can be admitted to private conversations and actions without negative consequences. The development of trust goes beyond the explanations given as justification for the observer's presence. Yet, it is difficult to specify how the fragile commodity of trust develops. One boy accorded me the title of "honorary kid" as an indication of my trustworthiness. Similarly:

> Rich Janelli invited me to a cookout that he was having for his friends; when some of them looked dubious, Rich added, "He's a good guy" (field notes, Beanville).

> Rod Shockstein whispered something to Hardy Wieder in my presence. Hardy told him, "You can tell Gary. He's one of the boys" (field notes, Sanford Heights).

Preadolescent culture can be likened to a deviant subculture in that participants attempt to shield certain topics from their adult guardians. This care in their presentation of self is necessary for maintaining a morally proper self and in avoiding punishment.[1] The observer of children, therefore, is in a similar position to the researcher who studies deviant groups. Polsky (1967) argues that the researcher who seeks acceptance by a criminal group must (1) be willing to break some laws (if only as an accessory to crimes and not reporting information to the authorities), (2) make one's contacts believe these intentions, and (3) convince them he will act in accord with these intentions. In regard to preadolescents the issues are structurally similar. Controlling one's desire to intervene at the slightest provocation leads to being allowed to observe on other occasions. Before preadolescents would broach a sensitive subject, they would often attempt to gauge my probable reaction:

> I ask some of the players on the Sanford Heights Dodgers what they joke about. The players giggle, and one player says they are "naughty." I indicate it wouldn't upset me, at which the players giggle more. While they don't tell me any jokes at this time, they promise to tell me some next week (field notes, Sanford Heights).

On another occasion, I was in a Sanford Heights park with a group of preadolescents who, over a period of about five weeks, had begun to trust me. Suddenly, these boys spotted a group of girls seated at a park bench near a Thermos of water. One boy felt that it would be great sport to bother them (and simultaneously pay attention to them). He and his friends plotted to rush them, steal their Thermos, and pour out the contents—disrupting their gathering. After a short period of insults (mostly obscene) between boys and girls, the plan was put into effect, with the expected screaming and squealing by the girls. At one point several girls turned to me (busily taking notes and appearing, I assume, furtively guilty) and asked me, as the adult presumably in charge, why I didn't do anything to stop them. This reasonable question placed me in a difficult situation as a participant observer. Since no serious harm seemed likely, and I felt from various cues (such as the boys not looking at me) that the behavior was not being done primarily for my benefit, I had decided not to intervene, and I said only that I was not in charge, was only watching them, and had no control over their behavior. The boys were gleeful at hearing this and shortly retreated with their mission completed (and heterosexual contact started). In retrospect, this occasion was a significant step in my acceptance. I indicated to these boys that I could be trusted and that I knew "my place" in the group. While the incident was not specifically staged to test me, in effect it served as a test.

Full acceptance is impossible due to the structure of age roles. After I had become trusted by several boys in Beanville, they would come up to me and inform me that they had just mooned passing traffic.[2] On the first occasion, I was standing with some boys near the field; one of my close contacts sidled up to me and remarked rather conspiratorially that "moons are shining tonight." After a moment of surprise I realized what he was saying and saw a group of boys on the edge of the park near the street. At this time I felt exhilarated that I had been trusted sufficiently to have been told about this example of preadolescent deviance, and yet I was frustrated not to have observed it. After several similar accounts after the fact, I realized that this approach was important to our relationship. I could not witness the mooning so as to protect both parties from embarrassment. Similar events happened in other locations. In Hopewell I heard about egging houses (throwing eggs at homes) but never witnessed this, and in Sanford Heights many pranks and sexual activities were discussed in my presence; I did enquire about going with the boys when they played pranks or attended boy-girl parties, but this never was possible. The anxiety about my observation of sexual matters can be seen in the comment of a Sanford Heights boy who told a player who had invited me to a party, "He wants to see you screw your girlfriend." The only preadolescent party I was invited to was an all-male affair. Trust cannot be stretched beyond certain limits, which differ for every population and observer (see Wax 1979).

Crucial to the establishment of trust is the sponsorship of a key informant. This individual has been cited in sociological literature as the "hero" of the research—the person without whom the research could not have been conducted. During the three years of this research I was assisted by several boys who can properly be termed key informants. These informants expended their time, energy, and prestige to help me, although, of course, they gained prestige among their peers for having access to me. One criterion for the position of *key* informant is that the individual has a central position in the social structure of the group, which implies access to persons and knowledge.

One can distinguish between two components of the key informant role: *sponsor* and *source*. Needless to say, these two roles need not be embodied by the same individual. In this research many coaches and parents sponsored me in gaining access to their charges but were unable, despite their best intentions, to provide much information about the nature of children's culture. Some low-status preadolescents provided much information but little aid in gaining the trust of the group of which they were nominally a part.

The confluence of the abilities to provide the researcher with information and entree is the mark of the key informant. It is difficult to determine why those individuals who became important to the research behaved as they did. One element which seems to characterize these players is a sense of security in their social positions. Like Doc in Whyte's (1955) research, Rich, Justin, Whitney, Tom and Frank in my own research were leaders in their groups and they recognized this. They were all socially self-confident. This self-confidence allowed them to bridge the gap between adult and child and caused them to feel secure in their social competence with a friendly, yet ignorant, adult.

So far I have focused on how my role served players' purposes; now I wish to discuss how the participant observer can facilitate rapport and access. One means is for the adult to adopt the behavior and values of the children being examined—"going native." Another is for the adult to use social rewards and material gifts to promote acceptance.

Access through Adoption of Values and Behavior

While the participant observer who works with children cannot totally "go native," a researcher can adopt some of the behaviors of the children being studied. A thin line exists between being present at quasi-sexual encounters or when preadolescents played pranks, and hearing about them. With subjects of any age, one should not behave in ways which cause one's subjects to feel uncomfortable.

I felt that being approving, sympathetic, and supportive would increase rapport, whereas a false attempt to be "with it" would likely have backfired. Children's slang, like any argot, is difficult for an outsider to acquire and, even when learned correctly, may sound awkward when spoken by an adult. Knowing what one is not and what one cannot be is as important as knowing what one is and legitimately can be.

Access through Rewards and Gifts

Because of the adult's greater access to resources—primarily, though not exclusively, monetary—the participant observer may feel that it is advantageous to employ some of these resources to gain rapport. Although there are dangers in using this approach, it is pragmatically useful. I felt it desirable to perform a wide range of services on occasion, including providing companionship, advice, social support, food, and money (loans). I was trying to be a "friend," so I attempted to provide services that any friend might, although because of my position I had more resources than did most friends. I regularly drove Little League baseball players home, treated them to ice cream, and took some of them to baseball games, movies, miniature golf, and amusement parks. Some of the most interesting data of the study were collected on these occasions; while the settings may not have been totally natural, they allowed me to observe "natural" behaviors in these "unnatural" settings and to ask questions away from other adults.

In terms of monetary resources, Whyte (1955) and Wax (1971) are undoubtedly correct that any serious financial arrangement between researcher and subjects may produce tension, but there may arise some situations in which loaning money is necessary to gain rapport and to fulfill the obligations of friendship. However, it is imperative that loans not be *expected*. I soon recognized the small amounts lent would almost never be repaid—and constituted treats more than loans (I think mostly because the loans were not so salient that players remembered them); it was a pleasant surprise when a boy did reimburse me. On those occasions when I felt that demands for more loans were becoming too frequent, I convincingly fibbed that I was out of money. When I did loan small change (never more than a quarter) I emphasized the loan was for that time only and had justification for refusing to loan money after.

A danger involved in providing services, even those unrelated to money, is that the researchers may be accepted for what they can provide, not for what they are. They may be seen as useful only so long as they provide material rewards. I experienced this problem particularly during the opening weeks of my first year in the field. I brought along sticks of chewing gum, eating them in public view, and when players asked me for some, I was more than happy to oblige. While this tactic aided me in getting to know the players, it eventually produced an insistent demand for gum. This demand was counterproductive to my research goals; after I decided to "forget" to bring gum, the requests stopped. These gifts artificially structured the participant observer's position in the group in a way not conducive to equal-status contact.

Adult Comprehension of Children's Social Meanings

A major difficulty of the adult participant observer in a world of children is to understand their social world. On the surface this task seems simple, but it is deceptively complex. Children share a subculture that is distinct from adult culture and often hidden from adults. Although this situation is somewhat analogous to that of any group that hides its behavior because of possible repercussions, what makes this challenge unique is that all adults have passed through childhood and, as a result, may believe they have a greater knowledge of children's culture than they actually do. The sense of déja vu may be deceptive, presenting an obstacle to successful research in that children's behavior may be interpreted through old frames of reference. For example, the behavioral referents of pre-adolescent male talk about their "sexual conquests" were different (and somewhat more "advanced") than the behavioral referents of similar talk when I was their age. Since this topic is usually handled obliquely, it was difficult to discover precisely what behaviors were being referenced. Only after I had developed considerable trust could I ask candidly about their activities. Because local mores have a considerable impact on quasi-sexual behavior, this investigation had to be carried out separately in each community.

The participant observer who works with middle-class children is working with a group in the "mainstream" of society and may believe that their culture must be similar to middle-class adult culture. Yet, one must not assume that one's social meanings are the social meanings of children. Our spatial proximity to children may lead us to believe that we are closer to them than we really are and, as a result, we may ignore children's reality. Insults are perhaps the clearest example. Insults are spoken frequently by children with a wider range of meanings than adults might guess: to indicate friendship, status, or disdain. An adult who examines these words on the basis of the expectations of adult society, assuming the standard denotative and connotative meanings that adults give these words (e.g., *fag*, *dip*, or *whore*), may overlook their implications when spoken by children (Fine 1981b). To further complicate matters one must not assume that these meanings remain constant over generations (or even between curricular cohorts of one academic year). Meanings also differ between communities. For example, calling someone a *cocksucker* was considered much more hostile in Hopewell than in Sanford Heights.

Assumptions that might seem valid because we believe that we know and understand children, both because we were children once and because we see them so often, present a methodological problem for participant observers who attempt to understand the world from the perspective of children. Essentially this is the problem of ethnocentrism, but it is compounded because often we do not *believe* that it is a problem.

Appendix 3

Research Settings and Data Sources

In the first section of this appendix, I shall present a short description of each of the five communities in which I conducted research. I will describe the community itself and the structure of the Little League in that community. In the second section of this appendix I will briefly describe my data-gathering techniques.

The Communities

Beanville, Massachusetts

When one thinks of a suburb of a large metropolitan area, one is likely to imagine a community much like Beanville: an idyllic upper-middle-class suburb of Boston; perhaps the setting for a situation comedy of the late 1950s—"Leave It to Beaver," "Father Knows Best," or "The Ozzie and Harriet Show." Male residents are upper-middle-class professionals or managers. Beanville is not an exclusive suburb; blue bloods are more likely to reside in a suburb further from the heart of Boston. The suburb is not dominated by Boston Yankees or WASPs but is largely Catholic. While no one ethnic group controls the community, Irish-Americans and Italian-Americans are well represented. The town of Beanville had a total population in the 1980 census of 26,100; fewer than 100 were black. The median age of residents was 36.6 years, and the median family income was $27,700. Because of a skewed income distribution, the mean income is $34,800. However, most of the wealthy families in the community live in the Beanville Vista area—on the opposite side of town from the Little League field—and none of the players on the two teams examined in depth were from this area. Only 2.5 percent of all Beanville families had incomes classified lower than the national poverty level, and fully 86 percent of the adult residents of this community (twenty-five years of age and older) were high school graduates. In terms of basic demographic characteristics, Beanville residents are somewhat wealthier, more educated, and older than those of many Boston suburbs. This was the first suburban home for many residents who had moved from such urban ethnic neighborhoods as the North End (Italian) or Southie (Irish).

245

The Beanville Little League consisted of three leagues, each with four teams. Two of the leagues, the Eastern and Western, drew players from the two opposite sides of town. The Central League, in which the two teams intensively studied played, drew players from both areas of Beanville. The Rangers and the Angels drafted their players from the Eastern League pool, and the White Sox and the Astros drafted with the Western League. Although players were generally similar in their socioeconomic backgrounds, the players on teams in the Eastern and Western leagues knew the players on the other three teams in their league through school; players on the Central League teams only knew players on one other team in the league. This setup may have made the Central League less cohesive than the other two leagues.

Beanville held player tryouts in mid-April and the season began in late April. Three games were played simultaneously at McMaster Avenue Park on Monday through Thursday evenings, beginning at 6:00 P.M., and six games were played on Sunday afternoons (three at 1:00 P.M. and three at 3:00 P.M.). Each team played all others within its league four times and the eight teams in the two other leagues once—a total of twenty games. The Beanville league was the only league of those studied that played games on Sundays. The season was divided into two halves, and the champion from the first half played the champion from the second half. However, this play-off was only within the four-team leagues, and there were no play-offs to determine which team in the entire twelve-team league was the Beanville champion. The closest thing to a play-off was a set of three games held in late June, after the end of the season, that pitted the Central All-Stars against the Eastern All-Stars, the Central All-Stars against the Western All-Stars, and then the Eastern All-Stars against the Western All-Stars. During the first year of observation, the Central League All-Stars triumphed in both games, although they lost the following year.

Generally the Beanville league structure was informal, and a major goal of the league officials was avoiding competition between teams. In my first conversation with Ted Foot, the league president, he suggested that I might wish to examine some other league that was more competitive and therefore, in his mind, more representative. While the Beanville League was one of the two least-competitive leagues examined, players took the game seriously, and on several instances coaches became highly excited.

Of the leagues examined, the quality of baseball play was probably poorest in the Beanville league. Several factors may account for this. First, the Beanville League had no minor league organization in which younger players were trained. There was an informal baseball program for boys aged seven through ten, but it was not comparable in extent or organization with a minor league program. Second, because of the egalitarian ethos of the organizers of the Beanville Little League, a relatively large number of children played Little League baseball—twelve teams with fifteen players each in a community of 26,000. Little League headquarters recommends four teams per 15,000 population. In addition, most leagues limit the number of players per team to thirteen or fourteen. Thus, a fair number of boys who would not be playing Little League baseball in other leagues were playing in Beanville. These policies increased the range of ability between the better players and the poorer players and led to resentment when poorer players were allowed to play in an important game. Further, the most able players had other sports preferences. Beanville, like many Massachusetts towns, was "hockey mad," and several players missed games to participate in a summer hockey league.

Whether this low quality of play is acceptable depends on one's attitude toward competitiveness. At the beginning of the first season, some leaders proposed that the major league be cut to eight teams, with the additional four serving as a minor league. Ted Foot argued forcefully against this proposal, claiming that as many boys as possible should have the opportunity to play in the major leagues. Because of the weight of his opinions, and those of the league's seecretary-treasurer, the proposal was not approved.

Hopewell, Rhode Island

Hopewell is a heterogeneous Rhode Island township located in the southernmost third of the state. Although it is officially outside the Providence metropolitan area, some residents commute to Providence and surrounding industrial towns—twenty to thirty miles distant. Others commute to the small Rhode Island city of Westerly in the southwestern corner of the state, while others work in Newport to the east. Those residents who work within the Hopewell community have a wide range of occupations. Many are associated with the local campus of the state university; others own small businesses in the three small towns in the township: Jamesville and Whisper (combined 1980 population: 6,500), and Asquith (1980 population: 5,500). Still others are employed in local manufacturing plants, and 5 percent of the employed males sixteen years of age and older work in agriculture, forestry, and fisheries. Hopewell also has a long stretch of beachfront land, and while it does not have the popularity of Narragansett or Newport, there is a tourist industry.

The total population of Hopewell according to the 1980 census was 20,000 with a median age of 24.3; however, this figure does not indicate that the community is youthful. Rather, the statistic reflects the presence of university students. Age categories outside the age range fifteen to twenty-four indicate a community slightly younger than Beanville but not dramatically so. Average income figures reveal that Hopewell, while moderately prosperous, is not as wealthy as Beanville; the median family income is $21,300, and the mean family income is $24,200. By comparison the median family income for the entire state of Rhode Island is $19,400, with a mean family income of $22,100. Thus, the residents of Hopewell township have a slightly higher income level than the residents in other parts of the state; economically the township is middle class, though the heterogeneous population includes manual workers as well as professionals. Seven months after the season, questionnaires were mailed to Little League players and their parents. On the questionnaire completed by the parents I asked for parental occupation. Of the ninety-six families who responded, eighty-three provided classifiable data on the father's occupation. An analysis of occupations by means of the Duncan Socio-Economic Index scale suggests that the mean occupational score was considerably higher than that found in national samples, and the standard deviation of occupation scores was also considerably above what one might reasonably expect in a community of 20,000.[1] Actual occupations ranged from bank vice-president, university dean, and oceanographer to fisherman, dairy farmer, house painter, mason, and sheet-metal worker. The sample included eleven professors and fifteen managers and business owners. Thirty-seven percent of the Little League mothers were full-time homemakers. One must recall that the sample of adults for whom occupation is gathered is not a random sample of adults in Hopewell, and while the occupational diversity is great in this sample (particularly compared to other leagues), the high social status may be a result of the fact that Little League parents are somewhat older, more secure, and likely more financially stable than the average in the community. Generally the occupational status of Little League fathers is higher than that which would be predicted from average income of the community. One special feature about Hopewell occupational status is the relatively large number of professors in the sample (13 percent); the fact that relatively many high prestige/moderate income professors live in the community partially accounts for the disparity between Duncan SEI figures and income.

Hopewell's Little League consists of eight major league teams with thirteen players each, five minor league A teams for boys and girls considered not sufficiently proficient to play on a major league team, and four minor league B teams for eight- and nine-year-olds. Each major league team played twice each week (Monday, Tuesday, Thursday, and Friday evenings at six) for seven weeks. Every team played all others twice during the season from May 10 to June 25. At the end of that season a play-off was held among the four best teams in the league, and from all teams an all-star team was chosen to represent the league in the Little League state tournament. The Hopewell all-star team was eliminated in the first round of the tournament.

The Hopewell League was probably the best organized and the most committed to Little League competition of the leagues observed. Although I have no objective comparative evidence, I suspect that the Hopewell League exhibited the highest level of playing excellence—particularly in terms of fundamentals of pitching and fielding. The Hopewell league was one of two leagues that employed an official scorekeeper at games rather than relying upon managerial integrity. The seriousness of the Little League program was also indicated by the amount of time spent in preseason practice. Whereas most leagues began practice two or three weeks before opening day, Hopewell teams started practicing more than six weeks in advance. If Little League is not seen as competitive, and the real season not a "true test" of skill for coaches and players, then it should not matter if the players are not completely ready for the opening day. The length of time necessary to prepare boys for the regular season is an indication of the competitiveness of the league.

The seriousness of the Hopewell league is also seen in disputes between coaches over rule interpretations, and in at least one threat of appealing an umpire's ruling to the league's headquarters in Williamsport. While most games were not characterized by hostility and bad feelings, several games were, and these gave Little League its negative image. On one occasion, a coach was accused of stalling for time so that the game in which his team was behind would be called on account of darkness. In another case, a coach was nearly ejected from a game for refusing to control the aggressive behavior of his players. Although similar activities occurred in all leagues, they seemed more widespread in Hopewell.

Major league players ranged from nine to twelve years old

(twelves: 48 percent; elevens: 34 percent; tens: 14 percent; nines: 4 percent), and they attended eleven different schools, although 77 percent attended four public schools (Green Groves Elementary: 28 percent; Balzac school: 29 percent, Pasquoit school: 10 percent; and Hopewell Junior High: 11 percent; an additional 8 percent attended private and parochial schools outside the township lines). This school-attendance pattern led to cliques when acquaintances played together.

Sanford Heights, Minnesota

Sanford Heights is a bedroom suburb of Minneapolis, located about twenty-five miles from downtown, with a 1980 census population of 35,800. Most of the suburb has been built up since the 1950s, and large areas are developer's tract housing. While Sanford Heights is not a Levittown-type development, the community seems homogeneous—primarily lower-middle-class and middle-class.[2] In terms of occupational status, Sanford Heights is the least prestigious of the five communities. It had a median income of $25,800 and mean income of $27,000, which, while lower than that of Beanville, was higher than Hopewell's. However, the Hopewell figures may be artificially low because of the large number of students in the community. Both communities had approximately equal per capita incomes, and if students are eliminated from the sample, it is clear that Sanford Heights was less prosperous than Hopewell, although also less heterogeneous. Sanford Heights is a typical outer suburb of a large metropolitan area.

For the purpose of Little League (and other sports), Sanford Heights was divided into two districts, and the two Little League organizations had little contact except for playing each other occasionally in preseason games or in tournaments. I studied the Sanford Heights Northern Little League, covering all the territory on the northwest side of Sanford Road, a major thoroughfare. The two halves of Sanford Heights are similar ecologically and demographically.

The major league consisted of seven teams (reduced from eight the previous year) of thirteen players each, with a total of ninety-one players. Tryouts were held during the middle of April, and the games of the regular season were played from May 2 until July 9. Games were scheduled for Monday through Saturday nights at 6:30 and Saturday at 3:30 at Hennepin Heights Park, with each team playing from one to three games each week. Teams played eighteen games during the season (three with every team). Sanford Heights had no all-star games or play-offs; however, the three teams with the best records attended postseason tournaments. The first- and second-place teams attended a small, unofficial tournament in a nearby suburb, the Brooklyn Center American Classic, and the third-place team played in a tournament sponsored by the Little League organization in the Twin Cities metropolitan area, in which teams from twenty-four Minnesota leagues competed. The Brooklyn Center tournament, despite its smaller size, was seen as the more desirable by Sanford Heights players, because Sanford Heights Northern teams had won the tournament three of the past four years; the year I observed, both Sanford Heights teams were eliminated early in the tournament. The third-place team had more success, winning its first three games at the Richfield Invitational Tournament, only to lose to the eventual tournament champions in the semifinal round.

As in Hopewell, the residents of Sanford Heights took Little League seriously, and attendance at games was higher than in any of the other leagues. In addition, the minor league program was extensive and well organized, with five AAA minor league teams, comprised of less-talented ten, eleven, and twelve year olds, and eight AA minor league teams comprised of eight and nine year olds.

Disputes could get quite heated during and after games, and relatively more emphasis was placed on winning in Sanford Heights than in other communities. As in Hopewell, Sanford Heights hired scorekeepers for the games. The Sanford Heights league did not have a rule that required managers to play each child present for a minimum of two innings. The lack of this rule, coupled with the strong desire to win by many managers, made several weaker players dissatisfied, and two players quit during the season because of lack of playing time.

The Sanford Heights major league consisted of fifty boys aged twelve (55 percent), thirty who were eleven-year-olds (33 percent) and eleven ten-year-old boys (12 percent). These players attended eight different schools, with most of the players attending four public schools (Hiawatha School: 43 percent; Cooley School: 19 percent; Buckminster School: 14 percent, and Grove School: 9 percent). An additional group (9 percent) attended the local Catholic school in Sanford Heights, St. Thomas. The Sanford Heights league is somewhat less fragmented than other leagues, primarily because of the effect of the Hiawatha School in channeling intraleague friendships.

Bolton Park, Minnesota

The Arrowhead Little League was open to children from three St. Paul suburbs: the southern half of Bolton Park and the small suburbs of Urban Glen and Wescott. Another league served the remaining section of Bolton Park. The communities of Bolton Park, Wescott, and Urban Glen are similar to Beanville in being upper-middle-class suburbs. Urban Glen had a 1980 census population of 5,300, Wescott of 2,000, and Bolton Park of 35,000, approximately half of whom live within the area of the Arrowhead Little League. Income figures were not available for Wescott, but Urban Glen had a median income of $23,200 and a mean income of $25,700. Bolton Park's median income was $28,100, with a mean of $32,400. Thus, the area was not quite as wealthy as Beanville, but it is substantially wealthier than either Hopewell or Sanford Heights. Only 2.4 percent of Bolton Park families were classified as beneath the poverty level, as were 9.3 percent of the families of Urban Glen. The occupations of Little League fathers revealed that this was a relatively homogeneous, middle-class, professional community: parents were engineers, teachers, insurance agents, probation officers, orthodontists, and personnel officers with a smattering of blue-collar occupations and corporation presidents. The Arrowhead League collected information on fathers' occupations in the registration materials; the Duncan SEI mean score for fathers in this league (seventy of seventy-seven fathers) was 68.8 with a standard deviation of 19.3.[3] Most of the population in this suburban area, as is true for Minnesota generally, is Catholic and Lutheran.

The Little League consisted of six teams with fourteen players each. Each team played an eighteen-game schedule with two games each week from mid-May until mid-July. Games began at 6:30 P.M. Monday through Friday and at 9:30 on Saturday mornings. During a week, a team would play one opponent twice—once as the home team and once as "visitors." This increased team rivalries during those weeks in which the better teams played each other.

The general atmosphere in the league was decidedly less competitive than in either Sanford Heights or Hopewell, with only two of the coaches highly oriented toward victory. While these two men were considered rather extreme by local standards, their behaviors were relatively mild in comparison with that of some other coaches. Their personal rivalry, however, was intense, and neither could pass up an opportunity to needle the other. The fact that the coach with what was considered the best team lost the championship to his archrival produced sparks throughout the season.

Arrowhead had no official scorekeepers, and coaches were expected to be honest and straightforward; generally the league organization was less intrusive than in Hopewell or Sanford Heights. The board of the Arrowhead Little League consisted of a president (Tom Quinn), vice-president (Arne Hanson), and the coaches of the six major league teams.[4] Quinn insisted that the minor league program be given its fair share of funding, and he argued persuasively that any additional equipment that the major league teams received had to come from the profits of the refreshment stand at the major league field. The major league program was deemphasized compared to other leagues. Arrowhead ran what was termed a Farmer's League program for less able boys of ten, eleven, and twelve, and a separate program for eight- and nine-year-olds.

In keeping with the league's deemphasis of competition, play-offs were not held; instead of play-offs and all-star games, the league held a seniors game the week after the end of the season, pitting the twelve-year-olds on the second- and fifth-place teams against the twelve-year-olds on the third- and fourth-place teams, with the twelve-year-olds on the last-place team divided between the other teams. Thus, every twelve-year-old had the opportunity to play in an "all-star game" of sorts.

The boys on the first-place team attended two tournaments: first, the Little League–sponsored Richfield Invitational Tournament, in which Bolton Park, like Sanford Heights, made it into the semifinals, and, second, the White Bear Lake Invitational Tournament, consisting of eight teams, at which the Arrowhead team was defeated in the first round. Bolton Park and Sanford Heights teams seemed approximately equal in their baseball skills.

As in the other leagues in the sample, a large portion of boys playing in Bolton Park were twelve-year-olds (48 percent), with eleven-year-olds and ten-year-olds comprising 33 percent and 19 percent of the league respectively. Players attended nine schools, with 75 percent attending three of them: an Urban Glen elementary school (Urban Glen School: 37 percent); a Bolton Park elementary school (Orkney School: 19 percent); and a Catholic parochial school (Visitation Academy: 19 percent). Two junior high schools, two parochial schools, and two other Bolton Park schools educated the remaining 25 percent.

Maple Bluff, Minnesota

The final research site is Maple Bluff, an upper-middle-class area of St. Paul, Minnesota. Maple Bluff is the home of many wealthier residents of St. Paul and is considered a highly desirable place to live. The tree-lined streets are edged with comfortable family homes which, if they do not have extensive suburban yards, do have urban amenities including stores and restaurants within walking distance. The population of Maple Bluff is split between well-to-do Catholics and well-to-do Jews. While the groups do not differ economically, there is some conflict on social issues such as abortion. The research in Maple Bluff was conducted by my graduate research assistant, Harold Pontiff.

Because the Maple Bluff neighborhood is part of the city of St. Paul, there are no precise population figures for the area from which the Maple Bluff Little League draws its players. Indeed, the league seems not to have clear boundaries either, although de facto boundaries exist. Approximately 85 percent of the players live in five census tracts, with a sprinkling of players in the boundary areas of eight other census tracts. Ignoring these outlying tracts, the 1980 population of the five census tracts primarily served by the league was 23,800 persons, and the pool of potential players from which the league drew is roughly comparable to that of the other communities studied. Median family incomes in these five census tracts were $28,000, $26,000, $25,900, $33,800 and $23,900. The comparable mean figures were $33,100, $33,800, $27,700, $46,300 and $26,900. The grand mean for family income within the five-tract area, weighing the number of families per district, was $32,700. Thus, this community was comparable to Beanville and Bolton Park in income.

Compared to the other leagues, Maple Bluff was least organized, and its rules were most at variance with the official Little League rules. Indeed, Maple Bluff had not renewed its charter and technically was not an official Little League. Part of the difficulty was that for the past several years there had been organizational turmoil. The current president had taken office without a clear understanding of how the league operated, at least according to his critics. In addition, in the previous few years the league had adopted several unusual customs. The president, Randy Lemke, an easygoing man, considered himself an ardent foe of what might be termed "Little Leaguism." Anything that Randy felt would eliminate competitiveness had his endorsement. The problem with this philosophy was that several of the other coaches in the league did not share his feelings, and the issues were never discussed fully at board meetings. Thus, his actions, such as cancelling games because of excessive heat (on the same day that teams in the other Minnesota leagues were playing—and sweating), were resented. Also resented was his decision to eliminate the championship game, which had been played in previous years, and his decision to prevent first-place team from participating in postseason tournaments. At one time during the season a rumor spread that he had submitted his resignation, but this apparently only reflected his sense of frustration over the complaints of the other coaches. While organizational dissension characterized several leagues, nowhere was it more evident than in Maple Bluff.

Unlike other leagues, Maple Bluff ran its major league program for only boys of eleven and twelve; in fact, all eleven and twelve-year-olds who tried out got placed on a major league team, and so the league had no idea of how many teams it would have until tryouts. Ten-year-olds played in a separate league. The Maple Bluff league also had a peculiar manner of drafting; each boy was drafted each year he played in the league. The fact that a boy played on one team one year did not mean that he would play on the same team or with the same coach the following year. Indeed, coaches did not keep the same team name; the coach of the Blue Jays might find himself coaching the Mets the following year. Team names depended on which coach got to the uniform shed first; early coaches obtained the best uniforms for their teams. Teams consisted of twelve or thirteen players, with no attention given to the age of the players. Thus, one team had ten boys aged twelve on its thirteen-player roster, in violation of Little League rules, which specify a maximum of eight twelve-year-old players. The league also instituted a rule to prevent game cancellations. If only seven players showed up (because of vacation plans or lack of interest) the coach could choose players from the ten-year-olds' league to complete his roster. On some occasions even more than two ten-year-old players were recruited, as some teams could not get more than a handful of interested players to their games. This procedure caused ten-year-olds to loiter at the major league field, hoping to be chosen as replacements.

The season itself lasted from opening day in early June until early August: a total of sixteen games—two with every other team in the nine-team league. Games began at 6:30 on weekday evenings.

Because of the method of selecting teams—that is, drafting the entire team each year—and because of the size of the urban area in which players resided, the league was characterized by a loose friendship network. While the league was homogeneous with regard to age, with 71 percent being twelve years old, these 109 preadolescents attended nineteen schools, indicating the educational diversity of an urban social system. Twenty-three percent attended Maple Bluff Catholic; another 13 percent attended the Brentwood School, located in the center of the Maple Bluff area. In total, 49 percent of the players attended parochial schools, with most of the rest attending public schools. The variety of schools combined with the lack of team continuity served to make the Maple Bluff league considerably less cohesive than more traditional leagues.

Data Sources

While conducting this research over a period of three years, I collected data from numerous sources. Since the study was primarily a qualitative analysis of preadolescent behavior and culture, most data are field notes and tape recordings. All quotations cited in field notes are approximations; when I could not recall the basic phraseology of the speaker, I did not use quotation marks. To provide the reader with an indication of the amount of data collected, number of days and hours in the field site are listed in table A.3.1.

In addition to field notes, questionnaires were distributed, and in-depth interviews were conducted with players, parents, and coaches to obtain systematic data not available through observation and informal discussions.

Questionnaires and Interviews

1. At the beginning of the first season in Beanville, questionnaires were distributed to players on four teams and collected from three teams (thirty-five players). One coach was unwilling to aid in the collection of questionnaires. This questionnaire dealt with friendship ties between players, predictions for the season, and ratings of teammates.

2. During the middle of the first season in Beanville, I collected short questionnaires from members of the same three teams (thirty-three players). This is essentially the same questionnaire as the original one, with the evaluative ratings of other players omitted.

3. A questionnaire was distributed to members of the same teams during the final week of the season (thirty-two players). I asked for sociometric ratings of players, satisfaction with the season, and evaluative ratings of teammates.

Table A.3.1   Time Spent in Field Site

	Days in the Field	Hours in the Field
Beanville, 1975	56	182
Beanville, 1976	9	22
Hopewell, 1976	58	163
Sanford Heights, 1977	79	245
Bolton Park, 1977	59	148
Maple Bluff, 1977	43	120

4. In-depth interviews (approximately an hour in length) were conducted, with six members of each of the two teams (the Rangers and the Angels) studied in depth. These interviews focused on attitudes toward Little League baseball and personal attitudes toward parents and peers.

5. A short set of questions was asked of members of the Beanville Rangers and the Beanville Angels during the second week of the second season. A total of thirty players, the entire population of the two teams, responded. These questions focused on friendship ties and predictions for the year.

6. A similar set of questions was asked of members of the Beanville Rangers and the Beanville Angels during the final week of the second season. Questions dealt with sociometric ratings and league evaluations. All thirty boys on the two teams responded.

7. All players in the Hopewell Little League at the first game of the season were given a short written questionnaire that asked about their friendships, their expectations for their teams and themselves, and their satisfaction with the league. Ninety-two of the 104 players responded.

8. During the last week of the season, players in Hopewell received a questionnaire that asked about their friendship patterns, their judgments of their team's performance, and their satisfaction with the Little League baseball experience. Ninety-nine of 103 players completed the questionnaire.

9. During late January following the season, all players in the Hopewell Little League received a short mailed questionnaire asking for sociometric ratings, an open-ended evaluation of the league, and an open-ended discussion of team culture. Ninety-seven players (of 103) responded.

10. During late January, parents of Hopewell Little Leaguers received a questionnaire asking for their reactions to the Little

League program and the number of games they and their spouse attended. Eighty-nine sets of parents responded.

11–13. Players in the Bolton Park, Sanford Heights, and Maple Bluff Little Leagues were asked on the first day of practice (or as shortly thereafter as practical) to complete a brief questionnaire asking them to name their best friends. Players were also asked about their satisfaction with the league. The numbers of players who responded to these questionnaires were all 84 players in Bolton Park, 89 of 91 players from Sanford Heights, and 100 of 112 from Maple Bluff.

14–16. Players in Bolton Park, Sanford Heights, and Maple Bluff completed a second written questionnaire at the last practice (two to three weeks after the first in each league). This duplicated the first questionnaire and, in addition, asked for more detailed sociometric, evaluative, and cultural information. The numbers of players who responded to these questionnaires were eighty-four from Bolton Park, ninety-one from Sanford Heights, and ninety-seven from Maple Bluff.

17–19. I distributed a third wave of questionnaires in all three leagues during the middle of the season, approximately one month after the second questionnaire, focusing on the same issues, with the same high rate of response (Bolton Park: eighty-three; Sanford Heights, ninety; Maple Bluff, ninety-nine).

20. Simultaneously with the midseason questionnaire, I gave players in Sanford Heights (89 of the 90 then in the league) a questionnaire that asked if they had heard rumors about Pop Rocks, a candy then being test-marketed in Minnesota. In addition, 114 children not in the league were given the same questionnaire. These data have been reported elsewhere (Fine 1979a).

21–23. I distributed and collected the final wave of questionnaires during the last week of the season. These questionnaires dealt with personal relationships, evaluations of the Little League experience, and preadolescent culture (stamp collecting, dating patterns, nicknames). Again, the response rate for these short, personally distributed questionnaires was high (Bolton Park, 83; Sanford Heights, 90; Maple Bluff, 107).

24–25. In both Bolton Park and Sanford Heights, I randomly selected a sample of the twelve year olds in the league for an in-depth interview lasting approximately forty-five minutes. Four twelve-year-old players were chosen from each team, for a total of twenty-four players in Bolton Park and twenty-seven in Sanford Heights (the parents of one boy refused to allow him to be interviewed). Questions dealt with the player's evaluation of, and attitudes toward, Little League baseball, his attitudes toward preadolescence, and his knowledge of preadolescent culture.

26. In Sanford Heights I contacted all twelve year olds in the major league for a thirty-minute questionnaire-interview testing the diffusion patterns of preadolescent culture. Of the fifty twelve-year-olds in the league, forty-eight were interviewed. This interview occurred at the same time as the in-depth interview described above.

27–28. Twelve-year-old players in Sanford Heights (forty-eight players) and Bolton Park (twenty-four players) were asked to complete a time budget schedule describing their activities on the previous Saturday. This survey permits inferences about preadolescent activity patterns.

29–30. Fourteen parents of twelve-year-olds in Sanford Heights and twelve parents in Bolton Park were interviewed, using both open-ended and closed-ended questions. The forty-five-minute interview asked for their evaluation of the Little League program and their knowledge of children's culture.

31–33. I asked all coaches in Bolton Park, Sanford Heights, and Maple Bluff at the beginning of the season to predict how well their team would do, and who were the best players and the team leaders. Eleven coaches completed the one page questionnaire in Bolton Park; ten in Sanford Heights, and twelve in Maple Bluff.

34–36. Parallel questionnaires were handed out during the final week of the season, asking for ability ratings of players, team leaders, and whether the team played up to the coach's expectations. Questionnaires were completed by eleven Bolton Park coaches, eight in Sanford Heights, and twelve in Maple Bluff.

37–38. All six head coaches in Bolton Park and all seven head coaches in Sanford Heights participated in a one-hour open-ended interview about their league, their team's performance, and their attitudes toward Little League baseball, sports, and children. This interview was conducted from two weeks to a month after the end of the season.

A large amount of data was collected during the three years of this research. Each year the questionnaire measures evolved, both becoming more sophisticated and changing focus as my interests changed. I do not see this as detrimental to the research, although there are some instances in which data are only available from a single league or available in different forms in different leagues. This research is "grounded" research in that research hypotheses emerged from observations. While each year the field research began with certain hypotheses, often by the middle of the year these had become reformulated, altered, or discarded, and new ones were considered. This book is the result of internal and external debates, endless changes, forgetfulness, mistakes in data collection and perhaps most of all my own education.

Notes

Introduction

1. One of these leagues was studied by a research assistant, Harold Pontiff.

2. Research has indicated that males and females may differ considerably in their leisure patterns (Lever 1976, 1978; Garvey 1977), although Sutton-Smith and Rosenberg (1961) have presented evidence that these differences may be narrowing. Still, few girls have taken the opportunity the Little League organization has grudgingly given them and played in the same league with the boys (five in the leagues studied; none on the ten focal teams). Girls' sports activities deserve a separate study. Boys, it is said, will be boys; what girls are is an issue for others.

3. For a detailed economic critique of the Little League baseball industry, see Ralbovsky (1973). He claims: "Little League is a big business with two heads: (1) earning money, and (2) promoting America. Boys and baseball are merely the fronts." The Little League is, needless to say, not in agreement with this critique—its leaders argue that the organization is a leadership program for youth.

4. The main details of this account, when not directly cited, derive from Watson 1973; Turkin 1954; Paxton 1949; and Original League, Inc. n.d.

5. *Myth* is not the acceptable folkloristic term for this account, since it is not a sacred narrative set in nonhistorical time; rather, it would be better to refer to this as an "organizational legend" (Fine 1984).

6. It is not clear whether Stotz resigned (Stotz Asks Jury Trial in U.S. Court, 1955) or was fired (Little League Asks Support against Stotz, 1955).

7. Most generally accepted definitions of preadolescence focus on the ages nine to twelve or thirteen (Thornburg 1974; Kohen-Raz 1971), and this age division is adequate. It is particularly convenient for this research because of the structural consideration that Little League baseball is limited to children aged nine through twelve. The fact that Little League Baseball, Incorporated, sets these age limits for competitive play indicates there is some social reality for limiting the period of preadolescence to these four years. For a general discussion of the biological, social, and cognitive aspects of preadolescence, see Kohen-Raz (1971).

Chapter 1

1. The arrangement of grandstands appears to affect parental activity. In leagues in which grandstands were relatively close to the playing field, the parents' presence was felt more intensely. Where the grandstands were distant from the playing area (as in Beanville, where they were located beyond first base) the spectators were not only less audible but cheered and yelled less. Leagues with grandstands on opposite sides of the field seemed to have more parental cheering than those with single grandstands where parents from the opposing teams sat together. The proximity of the two sets of fans, in many cases personal friends, reminded parents that Little League was, after all, only a game.

2. In four of the five leagues, umpires were paid a nominal fee for their time (not in Sanford Heights). Although organizations supply "professional Little League umpires," none of these five leagues used them. Most umpires were athletic young men in their late teens or twenties who desired to earn a little pocket money for a few hours' work; several claimed that working for the league was altruistic community service. Each league faced the problem of umpire recruitment, as in each league there were days on which umpires did not show up, and "umpires" had to be recruited from the spectators—coaches from the teams playing were sometimes used, as were fathers, brothers, and even on a few occasions recently graduated Little League players. Because being a Little League umpire is a low-status position filled (as umpires see it) with hassles from players, coaches, and parents, the ranks of potential umpires are always thin, and temporary recruitment of umpires who are not always well versed in the Little League rules is common. Often these umpires are friends of the coaches or are themselves interested in the outcome of the games they work. As a result, their judgments may be the subject of acrimonious and bitter disputes if coaches or parents conclude an umpire is out to get their team: "In the second game of the season Sharpstone is playing Furniture Mart. Sharpstone is ahead 10–0 in the top of the fourth inning when Ted Lundy, the chief umpire in Hopewell, who is umpiring, suddenly cancels the game because of fog, meaning that the game doesn't count and will have to be replayed. Peter Chadbourne, the Sharpstone coach, is furious and claims that 'the umpires are out to get Sharpstone' and that Lundy, a friend of the coach of Furniture Mart, is showing favoritism in cancelling the game" (field notes, Hopewell).

3. The timing of a game poses logistical problems for interested parents. As one mother told me: "We don't have too many good meals during Little League season" (field notes, Sanford Heights).

4. Maple Bluff is not included in this analysis because only one game was observed between two teams with losing records.

5. The extent of side involvements varies as a function of each sport and also as a function of level of competition. Thus, basketball and soccer, with

their emphasis on continuous action, seems to allow for fewer side involvements than does baseball or golf, both of which have relatively long intervals between each short sequence of action.

Chapter 3

1. Attribution theory suggests that people may be relatively willing to attribute dispositional, rather than situational, causes to the actions of others (Nisbett et al. 1973), at least when that public attribution is congruent with their own desired presentation of self.

2. One difference between the socialization of boys and girls is male involvement in sport which, until recently, had little counterpart in the upbringing of females. Males learn early how to win and, perhaps more significantly, how not to take defeat as a blow to self-esteem—to see tomorrow as another game in a lifetime season. This may have ramifications on ability to cope in a competitive corporate environment.

Chapter 5

1. Best (1983) discusses these issues among younger children—ages six to nine.

2. In the postseason interviews with twelve-year-old Little Leaguers in Bolton Park and Sanford Heights, players were asked: "What do kids talk about when they are together?" Twenty-nine percent spontaneously named girls or "making out" as regular topics of conversation—second only to sports (50 percent).

3. The bases are the sexual "bases" of which preadolescent males often speak. While there are variations in what each base implies, in Sanford Heights the accepted meaning is that first base is kissing, second base is petting above the waist (fondling a girl's breasts), third base is petting below the waist (hand-genital contact, or "finger-fucking"), a home run is sexual intercourse or "going all the way." This imagery is by no means unique to Little Leaguers as, for example, the song "Paradise by the Dashboard Light" by Meat Loaf.

4. This learning is evident in one conversation in which Rich Toland asked John-John Danville how one is supposed to go up a girl's shirt while kissing her. Rich said that his current girlfriend wanted him to go up her shirt—that all five of her previous boyfriends had done it.

5. The escalation of insults can also be seen in the black adolescent insult ritual "The Dozens" (Abrahams 1970; Dollard 1939) as well as in insult contests in other societies (Elliott 1960).

6. These include such activities as urinating in another boy's locker (field notes Bolton Park).

7. In Sanford Heights this prank also goes by the racist name of "Nigger Knocking" (a symptomatic example of racial projection), and in Bolton Park

it is also known as Ring and Run (a term the Opies found in Liverpool). The Opies (1959, 378–82) in their national study of Great Britain, present sixty-eight terms used to describe this simple activity. It is significant that in the context of Britain in the 1950s, most of these terms referred to knocking on doors, while the American versions are based on the existence of doorbells.

8. The prank of setting a bag of dog manure on fire is certainly not original, being mentioned in Sanford Heights as well as in a sketch in a Minneapolis comedy review, Dudley Riggs's Brave New Workshop's production of "If Only We'd Left It to Beaver" (1978).

9. I do not mean that children do not develop at different rates or that this development does not affect their social learning. Within the school system, friends are stratified in part by age, even within the age-graded classroom (Challman 1932; Furfey 1926) which correlates with physiological maturity.

Chapter 6

1. The use of neologisms is to be avoided. However, I felt it necessary to coin a new term because the most logical phrase, *group culture*, has been used previously with several different meanings. I hope confusion will be avoided by a new term. *Idio* derives from *idios*, the Greek root for "own" (not *ideo*).

2. Ethnologists have noticed that groups of animals, notably primates, learn behaviors that are particular to local groups, are known throughout these groups, and do not appear to have a significant genetic component. Examples of local dialects among birds (Marler and Hamilton 1966; Lemon 1971; Thielcke 1969) and seals (LeBoeuf and Peterson 1969) indicate the effects of the group upon learning—even when there is no conscious acquisition. Of more direct relevance to human culture are observations of primate "protoculture." Primate groups have been shown to differ in sexual symbolism (D'Aquili 1972) and food preference (Poirier 1969). Spontaneous cultural creation and spread have been described for tool use (Goodall 1972), food washing (Kawai 1965), and snowball making (Eaton 1972).

3. Kelley (1967) notes that distinctiveness or uniqueness creates attributions focusing on the characteristics or properties of the distinctive other. In the case of persons, these attributions generally refer to the person's disposition. Kelley also notes that consistency of behavior over time or modality (as in the case of recurring triggering events) produces attribution based on the characteristics of the other.

4. Age (in years) and the percentage of the total number of sociometric choices received (with each boy naming three team members as friends) correlated $+.48$ ($p<.05$) at the beginning of the season, $+.59$ ($p<.02$) in the middle of the season, and $+.61$ ($p = .01$) at the end of the season.

5. Sharpstone players were asked, in the end-of-season questionnaire, how happy they were on their team. The average rating was 4.8 on a 5-point scale.

6. Once Frank struck out, angrily returning to the dugout, muttering "Jesus Christ." Fred commented drily, "Well, at least you're learning to swear."

7. I asked players to name their three best friends in the world and three best friends in the Little League at the end of the season. Sharpstone players received ten and twenty-three within-team choices respectively, while TI players received six and nineteen—suggesting that ties within Sharpstone were closer. While these differences are not large, they correspond with my observations. Both teams had three boys who were close personal friends. On Sharpstone these were the leaders, whereas on TI these were three eleven year olds with marginal athletic abilities (Jay, Jeff, and Sandy).

8. Similar attitudes are evident in the orientation to pitching. Justin and his teammates (particularly Harry) talked about throwing at opposing batters to scare them. Once when the coaches told Harry that he would be pitching the next inning, Justin suggested that he hit the first batter, and Harry did. I don't know if this was intentional.

9. Some intriguing, though speculative, quantitative data support the connection between the presence of an elite clique and emotion during actual or expected defeat. In order for the test to be relatively free of my bias, only Maple Bluff teams were analyzed. Shortly after the season, I asked my research assistant—who was unaware of the hypothesis—to examine his field notes and rank the nine teams on how emotional they were when losing. Without seeing his ratings or the team sociometric diagrams, I devised a scale to measure the presence of an elite clique. Fifteen questions were used to judge whether an elite clique was present, including extent of mutual ties, percent of the team with two or fewer choices, whether the two most popular boys had an asymmetric tie or a mutual tie (questions available from the author). From these questions, the sociometric diagrams from the end of the season were analyzed to determine the presence of an elite clique. Teams were then ranked according to the extent to which they could be said to be characterized by the presence of an elite clique. The teams could have a maximum clique score of eighteen or a minimum of zero. In fact, the teams in Maple Bluff ranged from fourteen to one, suggesting that the measure did differentiate teams. Using Spearman's rho, the rank-order correlation between emotionality and presence of an elite clique was calculated at $r = +.62$ ($n = 9$, $p < .05$). Although this finding is hardly definitive because of the small sample, idiosyncratic operationalization of the presence of an elite clique, and the uncertainty of causation, the finding provides a basis for additional research.

10. These marginally significant figures (based upon self-reports from parents) do not present the entire difference between the teams. From observation it appeared that TI parents from Jamesville would leave the game early and only return in the last few innings, whereas Sharpstone parents were likely to stay for the entire game. When Sharpstone was to play, the stands were often filled, whereas they were relatively empty when TI

played. When Sharpstone played, there were many cars at the field; there were relatively few when TI played.

Chapter 7

1. Although the folk speech of regions and occupations has been collected, age-based slang has largely been overlooked. Some glossaries include the speech of adolescents, particularly college students (Dundes and Schonhorn 1963; Kratz 1964; Poston 1964) but prepubertal children have been ignored. The only studies that hint at the existence of a vocabulary of childhood deal with marble games (Harder 1955; Combs 1955; Cassidy 1958; Sackett 1962). Berkovits (1970) described the extensive secret languages of children, but in most cases secret languages do not depend upon a new vocabulary but on a systematic transformational process that allows the preadolescent to translate English words to Pig Latin, Op, or whatever. This talk has more characteristics of a code than of a language—despite the presence of oddly vocalized lexemes. With the exception of material from this research (Fine 1979–81), there has been no published study of American children's slang; however, two glossaries have chronicled the slang of legions of British "public school" children (Farmer 1968, orig. 1900; Marples 1940).

2. Slang is a socially defined set of words, with social meanings provided through interaction. Partridge (1960:1) cites the *Encyclopaedia Britannica:* "at one moment a word or locution may be felt definitely as slang, but in another set of circumstances the same word or locution may not produce this impression at all." Further, the boundary between slang and correct speech is by no means impermeable—words migrate back and forth across this border, perhaps being considered slang in one group and acceptable speech in another. Is *cool* a slang expression or standard English? One's reading will depend upon one's linguistic reference group and the occasion and context in which such a word is uttered.

3. Banchero and Flinn (1967) suggest that college slang consists of slang learned on campus. If we extend this definition to preadolescence, one might suggest that preadolescent slang consists of words learned in informal preadolescent communication. This reading, however, includes general American slang terms as preadolescent slang, for they are for the most part learned from peers (or near peers). I shall use group exclusivity as a means to determine which words qualify as preadolescent slang.

4. This list excludes some of the most common American slang expressions (*shit, fuck, bitch,* etc.) on the assumption that they are virtually a part of our standard vocabulary.

5. Some Sanford Heights preadolescents used a devastatingly effective telephone prank. One boy would telephone his adult victim, pretending to be a three year old. He would claim he was left alone and was very scared. Typically the victim would become very concerned and would do everything possible to comfort the lost child, who appeared unable to understand the instructions and would begin to whimper (very convincingly). When the

preadolescent tired of this charade, he would say to his victim, "there's one more thing, FUCK YOU!" This prank was both cruel and immensely satisfying to the preadolescents (see Jorgenson 1984:107). Boys also used traditional telephone pranks.

6. Census data (U.S. Bureau of the Census 1977) indicate that 13.6 percent of all twelve-year-old boys (266,000 individuals) had changed residence in the twelve-month period between March 1975 and March 1976. Of these, 2.3 percent had moved from a different county in the same state, 2.6 percent had moved from another state, and 0.4 percent had moved from abroad. Thus, national figures indicate migration at this age is sufficient, despite small percentages, for cultural diffusion.

7. The origin of this word is interesting as cultural change. *Zoid* developed as a transformation of *zap*, a common insult to indicate that someone has been "put down" or beaten, as in "I *zapped* him" (Wentworth and Flexner 1975: 757–58). In this peer group, *zap* was transformed from a verb to a noun, indicating the person who was "zapped." Thus, a *zap* was a loser (or a "sap"). This word was embroidered to zapazoid, with the same meaning (rhyming with trapazoid, derived from their mathematical education), and finally was shortened to *zoid*. This cultural change occurred over a school year.

8. In this analysis, I do not examine the extent to which the ties reported are mutual. Each dyadic relationship is coded from each boy's perspective.

Appendix 1

1. Two of these boys claimed their parents made them nervous. One said he felt he played better when they were not present, and the fourth boy liked his mother to watch but not his father.

2. One defeated team in a state tournament vented frustration by destroying the lobby of the hotel at which they were staying (Bucher 1954). At tournaments some children lose sleep and appetite, have upset stomachs, and suffer from homesickness.

3. On one Sanford Heights team, only three boys aged twelve were interviewed.

4. A student of mine who had spent time on a Zuni reservation commented on the frustrations of Anglo adults in teaching the noncompetitive Zuni youngsters the nuances of baseball. These boys would lose interest in the game at points that seemed exciting to their coaches, leading the Anglos to assume that the Zuni children really didn't understand the game.

5. These data come from parental reports on the league registration forms, and the occupational labels were generally vaguer than those collected specifically in Hopewell.

6. Dickie (1966:37) presents data from a Little League in Fayetteville, Arkansas, which suggest that coaches have a higher occupational status than do parents. However, Dickie treats the major occupational groups listed by the *Dictionary of Occupational Titles* as an interval scale, whereas

it is actually a nominal scale. He also determines parental occupation through preadolescent reports.

7. Three years was the median length of time coaches in Bolton Park and Sanford Heights had been involved in the program. There is a significant correlation between the number of years that a man has coached and his success. The number of years coached correlates with the number of games won in the season under study ($r = .616$, $n = 13$, $p = .012$) and position in the final league standing ($r = .547$, $n = 13$, $p = .027$). The number of years that a man has coached also correlates positively with the importance that he gives to winning when rank-ordering the importance of winning, teaching baseball skills, building character, and having fun ($r = .802$, $n = 13$, $p = .001$). This finding suggests that veteran coaches are more traditional in their orientation to sports, although this difference may be a function of the selective retention of coaches.

8. Bolton Park and Sanford Heights players are not the same in this respect. Combining mixed and negative comments into a single category, we find a significant difference between the two leagues ($\chi^2 = 6.37$, $df = 1$, $p < .025$). This finding is curious in that one does not find similar differences among parents. It can perhaps be attributed to the fact that most of the criticism of coaches in Sanford Heights centers around their lack of strictness and their not holding sufficient practices—features that some parents might consider virtues. As Paxton (1949) points out, players want their coaches to act like major league managers.

9. The differences between the two leagues are statistically significant ($\chi^2 = 11.55$, $df = 1$, $p < .005$). This result could indicate a higher level of satisfaction among parents and players in Bolton Park or could possibly be attributed to the greater park space available in Sanford Heights. There appeared to be more informal baseball games played in Sanford Heights.

10. The Scheffé Test indicates that there are no significant differences between groups at the .05 level of significance for team satisfaction; however, in terms of league satisfaction, Maple Bluff does differ significantly from the results from the second year of research in Beanville.

11. All three measures of ability correlate highly with each other. "Objective" batting average correlates $+.68$ ($n = 169$, $p = .001$), with players' "subjective" batting average and correlates $+.61$ ($n = 147$, $p = .001$) with coach's rating of ability. Coach's rating correlates $+.44$ ($n = 143$, $p = .001$) with player's "subjective" batting average.

Appendix 2

1. For example, one boy in Sanford Heights was grounded for a week when his mother learned from his babysitter that he told a peer (in a phrase that psychoanalysts would find deliciously symptomatic) that "my cock has teeth."

2. In this prank, preadolescents quickly pull down their trousers and un-

derpants while facing away from passing traffic. See Licht (1974) for a more extensive description.

Appendix 3

1. The Duncan SEI mean score for the sample of adult males is 59.4 with a standard deviation of 22.8. This sample included thirty-two professional, technical, and kindred workers (39 percent), twenty-four managers and administrators (29 percent), four sales workers and clerical workers (5 percent), eighteen craftsmen (22 percent), one operative (1 percent), one laborer (1 percent), one farmer (1 percent), and two service workers (2 percent). A chi-square analysis between our sample of adult males and the adult males listed in the 1970 census for Hopewell revealed a highly significant difference between the sample and the population. Adult males were classified into five categories: (1) professionals, (2) managers, (3) sales and clerical, (4) craftsmen, and (5) other workers (operatives, laborers, farm, service workers). In our Little League sample, professionals and managers were substantially overrepresented, and sales and clerical workers and other workers (generally the less prestigious occupations) were underrepresented ($\chi^2 = 61$, $df = 4$, $p = .001$). Thus, the parental sample was not representative of the local population in terms of socioeconomic status.

2. No systematic occupational survey was conducted in any league aside from Hopewell and Bolton Park.

3. This sample included thirty-five professional, technical, and kindred workers (50 percent), seventeen managers and administrators (24 percent), eight sales and clerical workers (11 percent), six craftsmen (9 percent), two operatives (3 percent), one service worker (1 percent), and no laborers or farmers. As in Hopewell, the higher-status occupations seem overrepresented, but because the Arrowhead Little League does not correspond to political boundaries, a systematic comparison cannot be made.

4. Perhaps as a result of the active involvement of the league head coaches, all six head coaches said that the league was run well; this contrasts to Sanford Heights, where only two of seven coaches said the league was run well (Fisher's Exact Test, $p = .03$).

References

Abrahams, Roger D. 1970. *Deep down in the jungle.* 2d ed. Chicago: Aldine.

———. 1978. Toward a sociological theory of folklore: Performing services. In *Working Americans: Contemporary approaches to occupational folklore*, edited by Robert H. Byington. Washington, D.C.: Smithsonian Folklore Studies.

Adams, J. E. 1965. Injury to the throwing arm: A study of traumatic changes in the elbow joints of boy baseball players. *California Medicine* 102:127–32.

Adler, Peter. 1984. The sociologist as celebrity: The role of media in field research. *Qualitative Sociology* 7:310–26.

Adler, Peter, and Patricia Adler. 1978. The role of momentum in sport. *Urban Life* 7 (July): 153–176.

Allen, Harold B. 1973. *The linguistic atlas of the upper midwest.* Minneapolis: University of Minnesota Press.

Allison, Maria T. 1981. Sportsmanship: Socialization, game structure, and the ethical system of sport. Paper presented to the North American Society for the Sociology of Sport, Fort Worth, Texas.

Allport, Gordon W. 1954. *The nature of prejudice.* New York: Doubleday, Anchor Books.

American Academy of Pediatrics. 1956. What about organized competitive sports for children? *Safety Education* 36(Oct.): 35–37.

American Sociological Association. 1968. Toward a code of ethics for sociologists. *American Sociologist* 3:316–18.

Anderson, Alan Ross and Omar Khayyam Moore. 1960. Autotelic folkmodels. *Sociological Quarterly* 1(Oct.): 203–16.

Anderson, George F. 1953. What's the score in athletics—in elementary education. *National Education Association Journal* 42(Jan.): 16–17.

Angell, Roger. 1972. *The summer game.* New York: Popular Library.

Askins, Roy L., Timothy J. Carter, and Michael Wood. 1981. Rule enforcement in a public setting: The case of basketball officiating. *Qualitative Sociology* 4:87–101.

Athletic competition for children. 1954. *Athletic Journal* 34(Jan.): 18–20, 55.

Ayoub, Millicent. 1966. The family reunion. *Ethnology* 5:415–33.

Baby bonus babies. 1958. *Time*, June 17, 58.

Bales, Robert Freed. 1970. *Personality and interpersonal relations*. New York: Holt, Rinehart and Winston.

Ball, Donald. 1976. Failure in sport. *American Sociological Review* 41: 726–39.

Banchero, Lawrence, and William L. Flinn. 1967. The application of sociological techniques to the study of college slang. *American Speech* 42:51–57.

Barker, Roger G., and Herbert F. Wright. 1951. *One boy's day: A specimen record of behavior*. New York: Harper.

Barnes, J. A. 1967. Some ethical problems of modern field work. *British Journal of Sociology* 14:118–34.

———. 1969. Networks and political process. In *Social networks in urban situations*, edited by J. Clyde Mitchell. Manchester, England: Manchester University Press.

Becker, Howard S., and Blanche Geer. 1960. Latent culture: A note on the theory of latent social roles. *Administrative Science Quarterly* 5:304–13.

Beleaguered Little Leaguers. 1964. *New England Journal of Medicine* 270:1015.

Bennett, David J., and Judith D. Bennett. 1970. Making the scene. In *Social psychology through symbolic interaction*, edited by Gregory P. Stone and Harvey A. Farberman. Waltham, Mass.: Xerox.

Berkovits, Rochelle. 1970. Secret languages of school children. *New York Folklore Quarterly* 26:127–52.

Berryman, Jack W. 1975. From the cradle to the playing field: America's emphasis on highly organized competitive sports for preadolescent boys. *Journal of Sport History* 2:112–31.

Best, Raphaela. 1983. *We've all got scars*. Bloomington: Indiana University Press.

Biddulph, Lowell G. 1954. Athletic achievement and the personal and social adjustment of high school boys. *Research Quarterly* 25:1–7.

Bion, W. F. 1961. *Experiences in groups*. New York: Basic.

Birksted, Ian K. 1976. School performance viewed from the boys. *Sociological Review* 24:63–78.

Blumer, Herbert. 1969. *Symbolic interactionism*. Englewood Cliffs, N.J.: Prentice Hall.

Bogdan, Robert, and Steven Taylor. 1975. *Introduction to qualitative research methods*. New York: Wiley.

Borgatta, Edgar G., and Robert Freed Bales. 1953. Task and accumulation of experience as factors in the interaction of small groups. *Sociometry* 16:239–52.

Bossard, James H. S., and Eleanor S. Boll. 1950. *Ritual in family living*. Philadelphia: University of Pennsylvania Press.

Bouton, Jim. 1970. *Ball four*. New York: Dell.

———. 1971. *I'm glad you didn't take it personally*. New York: Dell.

A Boy with a Bat and a Ball. 1969. *Sports Illustrated*, May 26, 9.

Bradney, Pamela. 1957. The joking relationship in industry. *Human Relations* 10:179–87.

Brittain, Clay V. 1963. Adolescent choices and parent-peer cross-pressures. *American Sociological Review* 28:385–91.

Broadus, Catherine, and Loren Broadus. 1972. *Laughing and Crying with Little League*. New York: Harper and Row.

Broderick, Carlfred B. 1966. Socio-sexual development in a suburban community. *Journal of Sex Research* 2:1–24.

Bronner, Simon J. 1978a. A re-examination of dozens among white American adolescents. *Western Folklore* 37:118–28.

———. 1978b. Who says?: A further investigation of ritual insults among white American adolescents. *Midwestern Journal of Language and Folklore* 4:53–69.

Brosnan, Jim. 1963. Little leaguers have big problems—their parents. *Atlantic* 211(March): 117–20.

Brugel, Barbara A. 1972. The self-concept of eight and nine year old boys participating in a competitive baseball league. Master's thesis, Pennsylvania State University.

Brunvand, Jan. 1978. *The study of American folklore*. 2d ed. New York: W. W. Norton.

Buchanan, H., J. Blankenbaker, and D. Cotton. 1976. Academic and athletic ability as popularity factors in elementary school children. *Research Quarterly* 47:320–25.

Bucher, Charles A. 1954. Athletic competition for children. *Athletic Journal* 35:18.

Cahill, B. R., H. S. Tullos, and R. H. Fain. 1974. Little league shoulder: Lesions of the proximal humeral epiphyseal plate. *Journal of Sports Medicine* 2:150–52.

Caldwell, Frances. 1977. Adults play big role in children's sports. *The Physician and Sportsmedicine* (April): 103–08.

Cartwright, Dorwin, and Alvin Zander, eds. 1953. *Group dynamics*. Evanston, Ill.: Row, Peterson.

The case for Little League. 1976. *The Christian Athlete*, n.v., n.p.

Cassidy, Frederic G. 1958. Report on a research project of collecting. *Publications of the American Dialect Society* 29:19–41.

Caughey, John. 1984. *Imaginary social worlds*. Lincoln: University of Nebraska Press.

Challman, R. C. 1932. Factors influencing friendships among preschool children. *Child Development* 3:146–58.

Chambliss, William J. 1973. The saints and the roughnecks. *Society* 11 (Nov.): 24–31.

Clark, Burton R. 1970. *The distinctive college*. Chicago: Aldine.

Clark, Mark W. 1981. Strategic rule breaking: Existence, function, and outcome in American sport. Paper presented at the North American Society for the Sociology of Sport, Fort Worth, Texas.

Coakley, Jay J. 1980. Play, games, and sport: Develpomental implications for young people. *Journal of Sport Behavior* 33:99–118.

Coffin, Tristram P. 1971. *The old ball game: Baseball in folklore and fiction.* New York: Herder and Herder.

Cohane, Tim. 1961. Juvenile parents hurt Little League baseball. *Look,* August 1, 57–59.

Cohen, Albert K. 1955. *Delinquent boys.* Glencoe, Ill.: Free Press.

Coles, Robert. 1967. *Children of crisis.* Boston: Little, Brown.

Combs, Josiah H. 1955. More marble words. *Publications of the American Dialect Society* 23:33–34.

Conger, John J. 1972. A world they never knew: The family and social change. In *Twelve to sixteen: Early adolescence,* edited by Jerome Kagan and Robert Coles. New York: W. W. Norton.

Cooley, Charles Horton. 1964 [1902]. *Human nature and the social order.* New York: Schocken.

Coover, Robert. 1968. *The Universal Baseball Association, Inc., J. Henry Waugh, Prop.* New York: New American Library.

Cottle, Thomas J. 1973. The life study: On mutual recognition and the subjective inquiry. *Urban Life and Culture* 2:344–60.

Cowell, Charles C., and A. H. Ismail. 1962. Relationships between selected social and physical factors. *Research Quarterly* 33:40–43.

Crane, A. R. 1942. Preadolescent gangs: A topological interpretation. *Journal of Genetic Psychology* 81:113–23.

Csikszentmihalyi, Mihalyi. 1975. *Beyond boredom and anxiety.* San Francisco: Jossey-Bass.

Cutting-Baker, Holly; Sandra Gross; Amy Kotkin; and Steve Zeitlin. 1976. *Family folklore.* Washington, D.C.: Smithsonian Institution.

D'Aquili, Eugene G. 1972. *The biopsychological determinants of culture.* (McCaleb Module in anthropology.) Reading, Mass.: Addison-Wesley.

Davies, Bronwyn. 1982. *Life in the classroom and playground.* London: Routledge and Kegan Paul.

Davis, Murray S. 1973. *Intimate Relations.* New York: Free Press.

Dégh, Linda, and Andrew Vázsonyi. 1975. The hypothesis of multi-conduit transmission in folklore. In *Folklore performance and communication,* edited by Dan Ben-Amos and Kenneth S. Goldstein. The Hague: Mouton.

DeHaven, Kenneth E. 1976. Symposium: Throwing injuries to the adolescent elbow. *Contemporary Surgery* 9:65–80.

Denzin, Norman E. 1977. *Childhood socialization.* San Francisco: Jossey-Bass.

DeSantis, Al. 1953. Slap on kid sports unfair. *Youth Leaders Digest* 15:189–90.

Devereux, Edward C. 1976. Backyard versus Little League baseball: The impoverishment of children's games. In *Social problems in athletics,* edited by Daniel M. Landers. Urbana: University of Illinois Press.

Dickie, Billy Albert. 1966. Little league baseball and its effect on social and personal adjustment. Ed.D. diss., University of Arkansas.

Dollard, John. 1939. The dozens: The dialect of insult. *American Imago* 1:3–24.

Dorson, Richard. 1972. *Folklore and folklife.* Chicago: University of Chicago Press.

Douglas, Jack. 1976. *Investigative social research.* Beverly Hills, Calif.: Sage.

Dreitzel, Hans Peter. 1973. Introduction: Childhood and socialization. In *Recent sociology #5: Childhood and socialization,* edited by Hans Peter Dreitzel. New York: Macmillan.

Dresser, Norine. 1973. Telephone pranks. *New York Folklore Quarterly* 29:121–30.

Dundes, Alan. 1971. Folk ideas as units of worldview. In *Toward new perspectives in folklore,* edited by Americo Paredes and Richard Bauman. Austin: University of Texas Press.

———. 1977. Who are the folk? In *Frontiers of folklore,* edited by William R. Bascom. Boulder, Colo.: Westview.

Dundes, Alan, and Manuel R. Schonhorn. 1963. Kansas University slang: A new generation. *American Speech* 38:163–77.

Dunphy, Dexter. 1969. *Cliques, crowds and gangs.* Melbourne, Australia: Cheshire.

DuWors, Richard E. 1952. Persistence and change in local values of two New England communities. *Rural Sociology* 17:207–17.

Eaton, Gray. 1972. Snowball construction by a feral troop of Japanese macaques (*Macaca fuscata*) living under seminatural conditions. *Primates* 13:411–14.

Edwards, Harry. 1973. *Sociology of sport.* Homewood, Ill.: Dorsey.

Eitzen, D. Stanley, and George Sage. 1978. *Sociology of American sport.* Dubuque: W. C. Brown.

Elkins, Deborah. 1958. Some factors related to the choice-status of ninety eighth-grade children in a social setting. *Genetic Psychology Monographs* 58:207–72.

Elliott, Robert C. 1960. *The power of satire.* Princeton: Princeton University Press.

Erikson, Erik H. 1963. *Children and society.* 2d ed. New York: W. W. Norton.

Farmer, John S. 1968 [1900]. *The public school word-book.* Detroit: Gale.

Father's day. 1964. *Nation,* May 25, 520.

Feller, Bob, with Hal Lebovitz. 1956. Don't knock Little Leagues. *Collier's,* Aug. 3, 78–80.

Fine, Gary Alan. 1979–81. Preadolescent male-slang (I–VIII). *Children's Folklore Newsletter* 2–4: various pages.

———. 1979a. Folklore diffusion through interactive social networks: Conduits in a preadolescent community. *New York Folklore* 5:87–126.

————. 1979b. Small groups and culture creation: The idioculture of Little League baseball teams. *American Sociological Review* 44:733–45.

————. 1980a. Cracking diamonds: Observer role in Little League baseball settings and the acquisition of social competence. In *The social experience of field-work*, edited by William Shaffir, Allen Turowetz, and Robert Stebbins. New York: St. Martins.

————. 1980b. Multi-conduit transmission and social structure: Expanding a folklore classic. In *Folklore on two continents: Essays in honor of Linda Dégh*, edited by Nikolai Burlakoff and Carl Lindahl. Bloomington: Trickster Press.

————. 1980c. The natural history of preadolescent male friendship groups. In *Friendship and Social Relations in Children*, edited by Hugh Foot, Anthony J. Chapman, and Jean Smith, Chichester, England: Wiley.

————. 1981a. Friends, impression management, and preadolescent behavior. In *The development of children's friendships*, edited by Steven R. Asher and John M. Gottman. Cambridge: Cambridge University Press.

————. 1981b. Rude words: Insults and narration in preadolescent obscene talk. *Maledicta* 5:51–68.

————. 1982. The Manson family: The folklore traditions of a small group. *Journal of the Folklore Institute* 19:47–60.

————. 1983. *Shared fantasy*. Chicago: University of Chicago Press.

————. 1984. Negotiated orders and organizational cultures. *Annual Review of Sociology* 10:239–62.

————. 1986. Friendships in the work place. In *Friendship and social interaction*, edited by Valerian J. Derlega and Barbara A. Winstead. New York: Springer-Verlag.

Fine, Gary Alan, and Barry Glassner. 1979. Participant observation with children: Promises and problems. *Urban Life* 8:153–74.

Fine, Gary Alan, and Sherryl Kleinman. 1979. Rethinking subculture: An interactionist analysis. *American Journal of Sociology* 85:1–20.

Fine, Gary Alan, and C. Steven West. 1979. Do Little Leagues work? Player satisfaction with organized preadolescent baseball programs. *Minnesota Journal for Health, Physical Education and Recreation* 7 (Winter): 4–6.

Fischer, John L. 1968. Microethnology: Small-scale comparative studies. In *Introduction to cultural anthropology*, edited by J. A. Clifton. Boston: Houghton Mifflin.

Flowtow, Ernest A. 1946. Charting social relationships of school children. *Elementary School Journal* 46:498–504.

Fontana, Andrea. 1978. Over the edge: A return to primative sensations in play and games. *Urban Life* 7:213–29.

Furfey, Paul H. 1926. Some factors influencing the selection of boys' chums. *Journal of Applied Psychology* 11:47–51.

————. 1927. *The gang age*. New York: Macmillan.

Garfinkel, Harold. 1967. *Studies in ethnomethodology*. Englewood Cliffs, N.J.: Prentice-Hall.

Garvey, Catherine. 1977. *Play*. Cambridge: Harvard University Press.

Geer, Blanche. 1970. Studying a college. In *Pathways to data*, edited by Robert W. Habenstein. Chicago: Aldine.

Giallombardo, Rosa. 1974. *The social world of imprisoned girls*. New York: Wiley.

Glassner, Barry. 1976. Kid society. *Urban Education* 11:5–22.

Gmelch, George J. 1971. Baseball magic. *Trans-action* 8 (June): 39–41, 54.

Goffman, Erving. 1959. *Presentation of self in everyday life*. New York: Doubleday, Anchor Books.

———. 1961. *Encounters*. Indianapolis: Bobbs-Merrill.

———. 1971. *Relations in public*. New York: Basic Books.

———. 1974. *Frame analysis*. Cambridge: Harvard University Press.

Gold, Raymond L. 1958. Roles in sociological field observations. *Social Forces* 36:217–23.

Goldstein, Kenneth. 1970. Strategy in counting out: An ethnographic folklore field study. In *The study of games*, edited by Elliott M. Avedon and Brian Sutton-Smith. New York: Wiley.

Goodall, Jane. 1972. *In the shadow of man*. New York: Dell.

Gordon, Wayne. 1957. *The social system of the high school*. Glencoe, Ill.: Free Press.

Granovetter, Mark S. 1973. The strength of weak ties. *American Journal of Sociology* 78:1360–80.

———. 1974. *Getting a job*. Cambridge: Harvard University Press.

Greeley, Andrew, and James Casey. 1963. An upper middle class deviant gang. *American Catholic Sociological Review* 24:33–41.

Guegner, Charles. 1955. Baseball for big city kids. *Sports Review: Baseball* 15:90–92.

Guttmann, Allen. 1978. *From ritual to record*. New York: Columbia University Press.

Hale, Creighton J. 1959. Athletics for pre–high school age children. *The Journal of Health, Physical Education and Recreation* 30 (Dec.): 19–21, 43.

———. 1967. Injuries in Little League. Paper presented to the American Academy of Orthopedic Surgeons.

Hanson, Dale L. 1967. Cardiac response to participation in Little League baseball competition as determined by telemetry. *Research Quarterly* 38:384–88.

Hantover, Jeffrey P. 1978. The Boy Scouts and the validation of masculinity. *Journal of Social Issues* 34:184–95.

Harder, Kelsie B. 1955. The vocabulary of marble playing. *Publications of the American Dialect Society* 23:3–33.

Hardy, Martha C. 1937. Social recognition at the elementary school age. *Journal of Social Psychology* 8:365–84.

Harris, Donald S., and D. Stanley Eitzen. 1978. The consequences of failure in sport. *Urban Life* 7:177–88.

Harris, Trudier. 1978. Telephone pranks: A thriving pastime. *Journal of Popular Culture* 12:138–45.

Hartup, Willard W. 1970. Peer interaction and social organization. In *Car michael's manual of child psychology*, edited by P. Mussen. New York: Wiley.

Hartup, Willard W., J. A. Glazer, and R. Charlesworth. 1967. Peer reinforcement and sociometric status. *Child Development* 38:1017–24.

Hastorf, A. H., and Hadley Cantril. 1954. They saw a game: A case study. *Journal of Abnormal and Social Psychology* 44:129–34.

Hebb, Donald O. 1974. What psychology is about. *American Psychologist* 29:71–87.

Herskovits, Melville. 1948. *Man and his works*. New York: Random House.

Hilbert, Richard A. 1981. Toward an improved understanding of "role." *Theory and Society* 10:207–26.

Hochschild, Arlie R. 1983. *The managed heart*. Berkeley: University of California Press.

Hollander, Edwin P. 1958. Conformity, status, and idiosyncrasy credit. *Psychological Review* 65:117–27.

Hollingshead, August B. 1939. Behavior systems as a field for research. *American Sociological Review* 4:816–22.

Hughes, Everett C., Howard S. Becker, and Blance Geer. 1968. Student culture and academic effort. In *The sociology of education*, edited by R. R. Bell and H. R. Stub. Rev. ed. Homewood, Ill.: Dorsey Press.

Irace, Charles. 1960. That winning attitude. *Scholastic Coach* 29 (March): 18–20.

Iso-Ahola, S. 1976. Evaluation of self and team performance and feelings of satisfaction after success and failure. *International Review of Sport Sociology* 11:33–46.

———. 1977a. Effects of team outcome on children's self-perception: Little League baseball. *Scandinavian Journal of Psychology* 18:38–42.

———. 1977b. Immediate attributional effects of success and failure in the field: Testing some laboratory hypotheses. *European Journal of Social Psychology* 7:11–32.

Jackson, C. O. 1949. What about sportsmanship? *Physical Educator* 6: 12–15.

Jacobs, Joseph. 1893. The folk. *Folk-Lore* 4:233–38.

Janes, Robert W. 1961. A note on phases of the community role of the participant observer. *American Sociological Review* 26:446–50.

Johnson, John M. 1975. *Doing social research*. New York: Free Press.

Johnson, Thomas P. 1973. . . . *happiness is Little League baseball*. U.S.A.: CNA/insurance.

Jones, Michael Owen. 1980. A feeling for form, as illustrated by people at work. In *Folklore on two continents: Essays in honor of Linda Dégh*, edited by Nicholas Burlakoff and Carl Lindahl. Bloomington, Ind.: Trickster Press.

Jones, W. T. 1972. World views: Their nature and their function. *Current Anthropology* 13:79–91.

Jorgenson, Marilyn. 1984. A social-interactional analysis of phone pranks. *Western Folklore* 43:104–16.

Kahn, Robert L., and Floyd Mann. 1952. Developing research partnerships. *Journal of Social Issues* 8:4–10.

Katz, Elihu, and Paul Lazarsfeld. 1955. *Personal influence.* New York: Free Press.

Kawai, Masao. 1965. Newly acquired pre-cultural behavior on the natural troop of Japanese monkeys on Koshima Islet. *Primates* 6:1–30.

Kelley, Harold H. 1967. Attribution theory in social psychology. In *Nebraska symposium on motivation,* edited by David Levine. Vol. 15. Lincoln: University of Nebraska Press.

Kleiber, Douglas A. 1978. Games and sport in children's personality and social development. Unpublished manuscript.

———. 1981. Searching for enjoyment in children's sports. *The Physical Educator* 38:77–84.

Kleinman, Sherryl. 1984. *Equals before God.* Chicago: University of Chicago Press.

Knapp, Mary, and Herbert Knapp. 1976. *One potato, two potato. . . : The secret education of American children.* New York: W. W. Norton.

Kohen-Raz, Rachel. 1971. *The child from 9 to 13.* Chicago: Aldine-Atherton.

Kratz, Henry. 1964. What is college slang? *American Speech* 39:188–95.

Kurath, Hans. 1970. *A word geography of the Eastern United States.* Ann Arbor: University of Michigan Press.

Landers, Daniel M., and Donna M. Landers. 1978. Socialization via interscholastic athletics: Its effects on delinquency and educational attainment. *Sociology of Education* 51:299–303.

Larson, Karen. 1980. "Keep up the chatter": Ritual communication in American summer softball. Paper presented at the annual meeting of the American Anthropological Association, Washington, D.C.

Larson, R. L., K. M. Singer, and R. Bergstrom. 1976. Little League survey: The Eugene study. *American Journal of Sports Medicine* 4:201–9.

LeBoeuf, B. J., and R. S. Peterson. 1969. Dialects in elephant seals. *Science* 166 (Dec. 26): 1654–56.

LeMasters, E. E. 1975. *Blue collar aristocrats.* Madison: University of Wisconsin Press.

Lemon, Robert E. 1971. Differentiation of song dialects in cardinals. *Ibis* 113:373–77.

Lever, Janet. 1976. Sex differences in the games children play. *Social Problems* 23:478–87.

———. 1978. Sex differences in the complexity of children's play and games. *American Sociological Review* 43:471–83.

Levin, Martin. 1969. Tell it like it was. *Saturday Review,* June 21, 4, 6.

Licht, Michael. 1975. Some automotive play activities of suburban teenagers. *New York Folklore Quarterly* 30:44–65.

Little League asks support against Stotz. 1955. New York Herald Tribune, Nov. 29, n.p.

Little League Baseball, Inc. 1984. *Official regulations and playing rules.* Williamsport, Pa.: Little League Baseball, Inc.

Little League Baseball produces rhubarb. 1959. *Christian Century,* June 29, 870.

Lofland, John. 1970. The youth ghetto. In *The logic of social hierarchies,* edited by Edward O. Laumann, Paul M. Siegel, and Robert W. Hodge. Chicago: Markham.

Luciano, Ron, and David Fisher. 1982. *The Umpire Strikes Back.* New York: Bantam.

Ma, it's only a game! 1961. *Life* 51:71–72.

McConnell, Mickey. 1960. *How to play Little League baseball.* New York: Ronald.

McCraw, Lynn W. 1955. Athletics and elementary school children. *The Texas Outlook* 39 (June): 12–14, 29.

McFeat,Tom. 1974. *Small-group cultures.* New York: Pergamon Press.

Macleod, David I. 1983. *Building character in the American boy.* Madison: University of Wisconsin Press.

McNeil, Donald R. 1961. Leave your little leaguer alone. *Parents' Magazine* 36:40, 78–80.

Mannheim, Karl. 1952. *Essays on the sociology of knowledge.* London: Routledge & Kegan Paul.

Marler, Peter, and William J. Hamilton III. 1966. *Mechanisms of animal behavior.* New York: Wiley.

Marples, Morris. 1940. *Public school slang.* London: Constable.

Martens, Rainer. 1978. The emergence of children's sports. In *Joy and sadness in children's sports,* edited by Rainer Martens. Champaign, Ill.: Human Kinetics.

Martinson, Floyd M. 1973. Infant and Child Sexuality: A Sociological Perspective. Unpublished manuscript.

Martinson, Floyd M. 1981. Preadolescent sexuality: Latent or manifest? In *Children and sex,* edited by Larry L. Constantine and Floyd M. Martinson. Boston: Little, Brown.

Mead, George Herbert. 1934. *Mind, self and society.* Chicago: University of Chicago Press.

Mechling, Jay. 1984. Patois and paradox in a Boy Scout treasure hunt. *Journal of American Folklore* 97:24–42.

Meyer, John W., and Brian Rowan. 1977. Institution organizations: Formal structures as myth and ceremony. *American Journal of Sociology* 83: 340–63.

Michener, James. 1976. *Sports in America.* New York: Random House.

Milgram, Stanley. 1967. The small-world problem. *Psychology Today* 1(May): 62–67.

Miller, Walter B. 1958. Lower class culture as a generating milieu of gang delinquency. *Journal of Social Issues* 14:5–19.

Mitchell, M. G. 1954. Athletic competition for children. *Athletic Journal* 35:18.

Mitchell, Richard G. 1983. *Mountain Experience.* Chicago: University of Chicago Press.

Moore, Robert A. 1966. *Sports and mental health.* Springfield, Ill.: Charles C. Thomas.

Morgan, Jane, Christopher O'Neill, and Rom Harré. 1978. *Nicknames: Their origins and consequences.* London: Routledge & Kegan Paul.

Mungham, Geoff. 1976. Youth in pursuit of itself. In *Working class youth culture,* edited by Geoff Mungham and Geoff Pearson. London: Routledge & Kegan Paul.

Nash, Dennison, J., and Alvin W. Wolfe. 1957. The stranger in laboratory culture. *American Sociological Review* 22:400–405.

Nisbett, R. E., C. Caputo, P. Legant, and J. Marecek. 1973. Behavior as seen by the actor and as seen by the observer. *Journal of Personality and Social Psychology* 27:154–164.

Novak, Michael. 1976. *The joy of sports.* New York: Basic Books.

Nusbaum, Phillip. 1978. A conversational approach to occupational folklore: Conversation, work, play and the workplace. *Folklore Forum* 11:18–28.

Ogilvie, B. C., and Thomas A. Tutko. 1971. Sport: If you want to build character try something else. *Psychology Today* 5(Oct.): 61.

Olesen, Virginia L., and Elvi Whittaker. 1968. *The silent dialogue: A study in the social psychology of professional socialization.* San Francisco: Jossey-Bass.

Olweus, Dan. 1978. *Aggression in the schools: Bullies and whipping boys.* Washington, D.C.: Halstead.

Opie, Peter, and Iona Opie. 1959. *The lore and language of schoolchildren.* New York: Oxford University Press.

Original League, Inc. n.d. *The founding of Little League baseball.* No publisher, 8 pp.

Oring, Elliott. 1984. Dyadic traditions. *Journal of Folklore Research* 21: 19–28.

Partridge, Eric. 1960. *Slang: To-day and yesterday.* New York: Macmillan.

Patterson, Norris A. 1959. Are Little Leagues too big for their britches? *Childhood Education* 35:359–61.

Paxton, Harry T. 1949. Small boy's dream comes true. *Saturday Evening Post,* May 14, 137–40.

Pellegrin, Roland J. 1953. The achievement of high status and leadership in the small group. *Social Forces* 32:10–16.

Petty, Richard. 1967. Baseball. In *Motivations in play, games, and sports,* edited by Ralph Slovenko and James A. Knight. Springfield, Ill. Charles C. Thomas.

Piaget, Jean. 1962 [1932]. *The moral judgement of the child.* New York: Collier.

Poirier, F. E. 1969. Behavioral flexibility and intertroop variation among

Nilgiri langurs (Presbytis Johnii) of South India. *Folia Primatologica* 11:119–33.

Polansky, Norman; Willa Freeman; Murray Horowitz; Lucietta Irwin; Ned Papania; Dorothy Rapaport; and Francis Whaley. 1949. Problems of interpersonal relations in groups. *Human Relations* 2:281–91.

Polsky, Howard W. 1962. *Cottage six.* New York: Wiley.

Polsky, Ned. 1967. *Hustlers, Beats and Others.* New York: Anchor.

Posen, I. Sheldon. 1974. Pranks and practical jokes at children's summer camps. *Southern Folklore Quarterly* 38:299–309.

Poston, Lawrence, III. 1964. Some problems in the study of campus slang. *American Speech* 39:114–23.

Powers, Eugene. 1955. A study of the effects of interschool athletics on the physical well-being, mental health and social acceptance of boys in grade 4, 5, and 6. *Dissertation Abstracts* 14:2456.

Puffer, Joseph A. 1912. *The boy and his gang.* Boston: Houghton Mifflin.

Ralbovsky, Martin. 1973. Little League: It's more than just baseball for kids. *Los Angeles Times*, Aug. 24, III, 1, 10.

————. 1974. *Lords of the locker room.* New York: Wyden.

Rarick, G. Lawrence. 1978. Competitive sports in childhood and early adolescence. In *Children in sport: a contemporary anthology*, edited by Richard A. Magill, Michael J. Ash and Frank L. Smoll. Champaign, Ill.: Human Kinetics.

Read, Allen Walker. 1962. Family words in English. *American Speech* 37:5–12.

Reany, M. Jane. 1914. The correlation between general intelligence and play ability as shown in organized group games. *British Journal of Psychology* 7:226–52.

Redl, Fritz. 1966. *When we deal with children.* New York: Free Press.

Redmond, Donald E. 1954. It happened in Harlingen. *Christian Century*, Feb. 10, 175–76.

Riemer, Jeffrey. 1981. Deviance as fun. *Adolescence* 16:39–43.

Robbins, June. 1969. The case against Little League mothers. *McCall's*, July, 130.

Roberts, Glyn C. 1978. Children's assignment of responsibility for winning and losing. In *Psychological perspectives in youth sports*, edited by Frank L. Smoll and Ronald E. Smith. Washington, D.C.: Hemisphere.

Roberts, John M. 1951. Three Navaho households: A comparative study in small group culture. *Peabody Museum of Harvard University Papers* 40(3).

Roberts, Robin. 1975. Strike out Little League. *Newsweek*, July 21, 11.

Rogers, William B., and R. E. Gardner. 1969. Linked changes in values and behavior in the out island Bahamas. *American Anthropologist* 71:21–35.

Rossel, Robert Denton. 1976. Micro-history: Studying social change in the laboratory. *History of Childhood Quarterly* 3:373–400.

Roth, Julius. 1962. Comments on "secret observation." *Social Problems* 9:283–84.

Roy, Donald F. 1959–60. "Banana time": Job satisfaction and informal inter-action. *Human Organization* 18:158–68.

Sackett, S. J. 1962. Marble words from Hays, Kansas. *Publications of the American Dialect Society* 37:1–3.

Salz, Arthur E. 1957. Comparative study of personality of Little League champions, other players in Little League, and non-playing peers. Master's thesis, Pennsylvania State University.

Schafer, Walter E. 1969. Participation in interscholastic athletics and delinquency: A preliminary study. *Social Problems* 17:40–47.

Schulian, John. 1981. The statistician is the poet of baseball. *St. Paul Sunday Pioneer Press*, Aug. 9, 3.

Schwartz, Gary, and Don Merten. 1967. The language of adolescence: An anthropological approach to the youth culture. *American Journal of Sociology* 72:453–68.

Schwertley, Donald F. 1970. You may not agree but . . . Little League can hurt kids. *Today's Education*, May, 40–41.

Scott, Phoebe. 1953. Attitudes toward athletic competition in the elementary school. *Research Quarterly* 24:352–61.

Seymour, Emery W. 1956. Comparative study of certain behavior characteristics of participant and non-participant boys in Little League baseball. *Research Quarterly* 27:338–46.

Sherif, Carolyn W. 1976. The social context of competition. In *Social problems in athletics*, edited by Daniel M. Landers. Urbana: University of Illinois Press.

Sherif, Muzafer; O. J. Harvey: B. J. White; W. R. Hood, and Carolyn Sherif. 1961. *Intergroup conflict and cooperation: The robbers cave experiment.* Norman, Okla.: Oklahoma Book Exchange.

Sherif, Muzafer, and Carolyn Sherif. 1953. *Groups in harmony and tension.* New York: Harper.

———. 1964. *Reference groups.* Chicago: Regnery.

Shibutani, Tamotsu. 1955. Reference groups as perspectives. *American Journal of Sociology* 60 (May): 562–69.

———. 1966. *Improvised news: A sociological study of rumor.* Indianapolis: Bobbs-Merrill.

———. 1978. *The derelicts of Company K.* Berkeley: University of California Press.

Short, James F., Jr., and Fred L. Strodtbeck. 1965. *Group process and gang delinquency.* Chicago: University of Chicago Press.

Simmel, Georg. 1950. *The sociology of Georg Simmel.* New York: Free Press.

Skubic, Elvera. 1955. Emotional responses of boys to Little League and Middle League competitive baseball. *Research Quarterly* 26:342–52.

———. 1956. Studies of Little League and Middle League baseball. *Research Quarterly* 27:97–110.

Smelser, Neil J. 1962. *Theory of collective behavior.* New York: Free Press.

Smith, Michael D. 1978. Social learning of violence in minor league hockey.

In *Psychological perspectives in youth sports*, edited by Frank L. Smoll and Ronald E. Smith. Washington, D.C.: Hemisphere.

Smith, Ronald E., Frank L. Smoll, and Bill Curtis. 1979. Coach effectiveness training: A cognitive-behavioral approach to enhancing relationship skills in youth sport coaches. *Journal of Sport Psychology* 1:59–75.

Smoll, Frank L., and Ronald E. Smith. 1981. Preparation of youth sport coaches: An educational application of sport psychology. *The Physical Educator* 38:85–94.

Snyder, Eldon E. 1972. Athletic dressing room slogans as folklore: A means of socialization. *International Review of Sport Sociology* 7:89–102.

Solomon, Ben. 1953. Little League—menace or blessing? *Youth Leaders Digest* 15 (Feb.): 161–213.

Spector, Malcolm. 1973. Secrecy in job seeking among government attorneys: Two contingencies in the theory of subcultures. *Urban Life and Culture* 2:211–29.

Speier, Matthew. 1973. *How to observe face-to-face communication.* Pacific Palisades, Calif.: Goodyear.

Stevenson, Christopher L. 1975. Socialization effects of participation in sports: A critical review of the research. *Research Quarterly* 46:287–301.

Stone, Gregory P. 1955. American sports: Play and display. *Chicago Review* 9:83–100.

———. 1962. Appearance and the self. *Human behavior and social processes*, edited by Arnold Rose. Boston: Houghton Mifflin.

———. 1978. Sport and community. Unpublished manuscript.

———. 1981. Sport as a community representation. In *Handbook of social science of sport*, edited by Gunther R. F. Lüschen and George H. Sage. Champaign, Ill.: Stipes.

Stone, L. Joseph, and Joseph Church. 1968. *Childhood and adolescence.* 2d ed. New York: Random House.

Stotz asks jury trial in U.S. court. 1955. *New York Herald Tribune*, Nov. 30, n.p.

Sullivan, Harry Stack. 1953. *The interpersonal theory of psychiatry.* New York: W. W. Norton.

Sumner, William. 1978. Strike out Little League parents. *Saint Paul Dispatch*, August 24, 10.

Sutton-Smith, Brian. 1959. The kissing games of adolescents in Ohio. *Midwestern Folklore* 9:189–211.

Sutton-Smith, Brian, and B. G. Rosenberg. 1961. Sixty years of historical change in the game preferences of American children. *Journal of American Folklore* 74:17–46.

Swanson, Catherine. 1978. Joking at the office: Coffee-break humor. *Folklore Forum* 11:42–47.

Sykes, Gresham M. 1958. *The society of captives.* Princeton: Princeton University Press.

Thelen, Herbert H. 1954. *Dynamics of groups at work.* Chicago: University of Chicago Press.

Thielcke, Gerhard. 1969. Geographical variation in bird vocalization. In *Bird vocalizations*, edited by R. A. Hinde. Cambridge: Cambridge University Press.

Thornburg, Hershel D. 1974. General introduction. In *Preadolescent development*, edited by Hershel D. Thornburg. Tucson: University of Arizona Press.

Thrasher, Frederick. 1927. *The gang.* Chicago: University of Chicago Press.

Travers, Jeffrey, and Stanley Milgram. 1969. An experimental study of the "small world problem." *Sociometry* 32:425–43.

Trice, Harrison M. 1956. The outsider's role in field study. *Sociology and Social Research* 41:27–32.

Tryon, Caroline C. 1939. Evaluation of adolescent personality by adolescents. *Monograph of the Society for Research in Child Development* 4:4 (serial no. 23).

Turkin, Hy. 1954. *Official encyclopedia of Little League baseball.* New York: A. S. Barnes.

Turner, Ralph. 1978. The role and the person. *American Journal of Sociology* 84:1–23.

Underwood, Gary N. 1975. Razorback slang. *American Speech* 50:50–69.

U.S. Bureau of the Census. 1977. *Current population reports*, ser. P-20, no. 305, Geographical Mobility: March 1975 to March 1976. Washington, D.C.: GPO.

Vaz, Edmund W. 1982. *The professionalization of young hockey players.* Lincoln: University of Nebraska Press.

Vogt, Evon Z., and Thomas O'Dea. 1953. Cultural differences in two ecologically similar communities. *American Sociological Review* 18:645–54.

Voigt, David Q. 1974a. *A Little League journal.* Bowling Green, Ohio: Popular Press.

———. 1974b. Reflections on diamonds: American baseball and American culture. *Journal of Sport History* 1:3–25.

Wake up, wake up. 1960. *Newsweek*, Sept. 5, 69.

Waller, Willard. 1937. The rating and dating complex. *American Sociological Review* 2:727–34.

Watson, Geoffrey G. 1973. Game interaction in Little League baseball and family organization. Ph.D. diss., University of Illinois.

———. 1974. Family organization and Little League baseball. *International Review of Sport Sociology* 9:5–32.

———. 1977. Games, socialization and parental values: Social class differences in parental evaluation of Little League baseball. *International Review of Sport Sociology* 12:17–47.

Wax, Rosalie H. 1971. *Doing fieldwork.* Chicago: University of Chicago Press.

———. 1979. Gender and age in fieldwork and fieldwork education: No good thing is done by any man alone. *Social Problems* 26:509–22.

Weick, Karl, and D. P. Gilfillan. 1971. Fate of arbitrary traditions in a laboratory microculture. *Journal of Personality and Social Psychology* 17: 179–91.

Weinstein, Eugene A. 1969. The development of interpersonal competence. In *Handbook of socialization theory and research*, edited by D. A. Goslin. Chicago: Rand McNally.

Weinstein, Eugene A., and Paul Deutschberger. 1963. Some dimensions of altercasting. *Sociometry* 4:454–66.

Wentworth, Harold, and Stuart B. Flexner. 1975. *Dictionary of American slang*. Rev. ed. New York: Thomas Y. Crowell.

Whiting, Bernice B., and John W. M. Whiting. 1975. *Children of six cultures*. Cambridge: Harvard University Press.

Whyte, William Foote. 1955. *Street corner society*. Chicago: University of Chicago Press.

Wittgenstein, Ludwig. 1968. *Philosophical investigations*. Translated by G. E. M. Anscombe. New York: Macmillan.

Wolman, B. 1951. Spontaneous groups of children and adolescents in Israel. *Journal of Social Psychology* 34:171–82.

Woodley, Richard. 1976. *The bad news bears*. New York: Dell.

Yablonsky, Lewis. 1962. *The violent gang*. New York: Macmillan.

Yablonsky, Lewis; and Jonathan J. Brower. 1979. *The Little League game*. New York: Times Books.

Yerkovich, Sally. 1976. Gossiping; or, the creation of fictional lives. Ph.D. diss., University of Pennsylvania.

Yohe, Charles. 1950. Observations on an adolescent folkway. *Psychoanalytic Review* 37:79–81.

Zimmerman, Carle C. 1938. *The changing community*. New York: Harper & Brothers.

Zinser, Ben. 1979. Baseball accidents worry doctors. *St. Paul Dispatch*, March 5, 11.

Zucher, Louis A. 1982. The staging of emotion: A dramaturgical analysis. *Symbolic Interaction* 5:1–22.

Index